'Tis Sixty Years Since

Other books Edited by Eberhard Bort

BORNE ON THE CARRYING STREAM
The Legacy of Hamish Henderson

Front cover: Alan Lomax (with microphone) and Hamish Henderson (with tape machine) recording the student revels at the University of Edinburgh, 1951. Photographer unknown. Courtesy of the Alan Lomax Archive.

'Tis Sixty Years Since

The 1951 Edinburgh People's Festival Ceilidh
and the Scottish Folk Revival

Editor
Eberhard Bort
University of Edinburgh

'Tis Sixty Years Since
The 1951 Edinburgh People's Festival Ceilidh
and the Scottish Folk Revival
Edited by Eberhard Bort

First published 2011 by Grace Note Publications
in collaboration with the Carrying Stream Festival
Grange of Locherlour, Ochtertyre, PH7 4JS, Scotland

ISBN 978-1-907676-10-9

Front cover: Alan Lomax (with microphone) and Hamish Henderson
(with tape machine) recording the student revels
at the University of Edinburgh, 1951. Photographer unknown.
Courtesy of the Alan Lomax Archive.

Back cover: Painting by Michael McVeigh for the cover of the Rounder Records
release of The 1951 Edinburgh People's Festival Ceilidh.
Reproduced with the artist's kind permission.

Contents

Photos and Illustrations

Acknowledgements

This book is published on the occasion of the tenth Carrying Stream Festival in November 2011, celebrating the sixtieth anniversary of both the 1951 Edinburgh People's Festival Ceilidh and the foundation of he School of Scottish Studies, both closely connected with the work of Hamish Henderson (1919-2002).

The contributions gathered in this volume deal with the history of the People's Festivals, focusing particularly on the 1951 event, and give personal perspectives, reminiscences and recollections of participants and observers of the Scottish Folk Revival which received a jolt from these momentous stirrings in the early 1950s.

The Carrying Stream Festival 2011 is organised by Edinburgh Folk Club, in association with the School of Scottish Studies and the Royal Conservatoire of Scotland. Particular thanks are due to Talitha MacKenzie of the Royal Conservatoire, Cathlin Macaulay and Gary West of the School of Scottish Studies, and my colleagues at Edinburgh Folk Club, Allan McMillan, John Jessiman, Kathleen Smith and Jack Foster.

This book would not have been possible without the amazing commitment and enthusiasm of Gonzalo Mazzei of Grace Note Publications.

We also gratefully acknowledge the financial support from Enterprise Music Scotland for the anniversary concert in Oddfellows' Hall – now occupied by Malones Irish Bar.

Nathan Salsburg of the Alan Lomax Archive has given us permission to use the cover photograph of Hamish Henderson and Alan Lomax at work in Old College, Edinburgh; and Edinburgh artist Michael McVeigh was so kind to let us use his painting for he cover of the Rounder Records release of *The 1951 Edinburgh People's Ceilidh* on our back cover.

I would like to thank all contributors who have worked to a very tight deadline and have made this volume possible. Hamish Henderson's chapter is reproduced with the kind permission of Pluto Press; Peter Urpeth's with the kind permission of Pete Heywood, the editor of *Living Tradition*; Maurice Fleming's contribution appeared first in *The Scots Magazine*, which he edited – it is reproduced with his kind permission; David Stenhouse kindly allowed us to reprint his 'Scotland's Internationale', which was first published in the *Sunday Herald*; the contributions by Tessa Ransford and Tom Hubbard are based on their joint 2011 Hamish Henderson Lecture at this year's People's Festival, convened by Colin Fox who has enthusiastically agreed to their publication in this form.

Eberhard 'Paddy' Bort
Edinburgh
October 2011

1951 and all that...

Eberhard Bort

*"The national consciousness is stirring; if we act promptly and boldly, we can make
the folk-song revival a powerful component part of the Scottish Renaissance."*
Hamish Henderson[1]

The above is a quote from 1955, four years after the First People's
Festival Ceilidh at Oddfellows' Hall had galvanised the modern
Scottish Folk Revival. As Hamish Henderson and other contributors to
this volume describe, the impact of that seminal concert can hardly be
overestimated. It introduced an urban, Lowland Scots audience to a
treasure of songs – preserved in the rural parts of Scotland, mainly by
the Travellers – that contrasted in their earthiness and raw beauty with
the prettified, 'salonified' way folk songs, and in particular the songs of
Robert Burns, had been interpreted hitherto, if at all. Here, at the end
of August 1951, Hamish Henderson presided over a Ceilidh that brought
together some of the finest source singers and tradition bearers he had
encountered in his travels. And the effect must have been electrifying.

In the same year, the School of Scottish Studies was founded at the
University of Edinburgh, and the collecting of Alan Lomax, Calum Maclean
and Hamish Henderson formed the corner stone of the School's ever-
enlarging archive of ballads, songs and stories. Sixty years later, most of
the archive has gone online as part of Tobar an Dualchais / Kist o Riches
project. This project, part-funded by the Heritage Lottery Fund, has seen
11,500 hours of recordings digitised, from the School of Scottish Studies,
but also from the BBC and from the Canna Collection. The range is amazing
– going back to a time over hundred years ago, when wax cylinders were
the latest in recording technology, there are among the more than 15,000
recordings "bothy ballads, love songs, children's rhymes, laments and
songs composed by village poets along with fairy stories and tales of
ghosts and kelpies."[2]

[1] Hamish Henderson , *Alias MacAlias: Writings on Songs, Folk and Literature*
(edited by Alec Finlay), Edinburgh: Polygon, second edition, 2004, p.50.
[2] 'Oral archives opened by £3 million project', *The Living Tradition*, Issue 87
(January/February 2011), p.5.

Last Leaves to Carrying Stream

Having met Ewan McColl at the BBC earlier in that year, Alan Lomax came to Edinburgh in June 1951. He had "blagged his way to a contract with Columbia to produce a 40-disc anthology of world music," as Peter Cox described it, and "it had the useful by-product of getting him out of McCarthy's firing line – anyone with anything to do with folk music was a prime target for his committee."[3] There are two ironies in the Lomax connection – that Senator Joe McCarthy should become at least partly responsible for the British and Scottish folk revival, and that the Edinburgh People's Festivals should come to a premature end when, as Hamish Henderson put it, "not long after the 1953 Festival there was an outbreak of ludicrous McCarthyism in the Labour Party itself, and the People's Festival was banned."[4]

All this already indicates that, while there is no doubt about 1951 having been a pivotal year for folk music and folklore studies in Scotland, not everything started in 1951. There were tradition bearers and collectors before Jeannie Robertson and Hamish Henderson. In the 1930s, John Lorne Campbell (1906-1996) and Margaret Fay Shaw (1903-2004) carried their Ediphone around the Outer Hebrides, moving on to the Presto Disc recorder and Webster wire equipment, later to the Grundig Tape Recorder and a Phillips Portable Recorder, collecting way over 1500 songs and 350 folk tales from the people of the Southern Isles – the collection is still stored at Canna House.

> Canna House contains a collection of literature, recordings, photos and film images which is invaluable. Campbell has published 15 books on Gaelic language, history and culture; he has recordings of singers in Barra in the 1930s and the Gaels of Nova Scotia...[5]

Some of the collection has been published, for example the 135 waulking songs in the three volumes of *Hebridean Folksongs*, edited in a collaborative effort with Francis Collinson from 1966 until 1981. Working "outside the conventional institutional framework of the universities," Hugh Cheape argued on the occasion of Campbell's death in 1996, gave "his work a freshness of approach in the study of Gaelic literature and history."[6] Margaret Fay Shaw's *Folksongs and Folklore of South Uist*, first

---

[3] Peter Cox, *Set into Song: Ewan McColl, Charles Parker, Peggy Seeger and the Radio Ballads*, Cambridge: Labatie Books, 2008, p.44.

[4] Hamish Henderson, *Alias MacAlias*, p.17.

[5] Torcuil Crichton, 'Enduring passion of the Canna collector', *The Scotsman*, 30 March 1995.

[6] Hugh Cheape 'Obituary: John Lorne Campbell', *The Independent*, 2 May 1996.

published in 1955, is a modern classic of folklore studies by "one of the most notable collectors of authentic Scottish Gaelic song and traditions in the 20th century."[7]

Before them came Marjorie Kennedy Fraser (1857-1930) from Perth. Her father was a noted singer, and she became a musical teacher in Edinburgh, when she was widowed aged 33. She discovered Gaelic song on a visit to Eriskay in 1905. Fearing that these traditional songs were on the verge of disappearing, she made it her mission to record (on a wax cylinder phonograph) and transcribe the music of the Hebrides. She arranged the songs for piano and clàrsach, making them fit for parlour consumption in the tradition of the Schubert and Silcher *Lieder* (or 'art song'), and published the three-volume *Songs of the Hebrides* (1909-1921), and a fourth volume a few years later. In 1930, she presented her song archive to Edinburgh University Library, including her original wax cylinders of recordings, and from there they found their way into the archive of the School of Scottish Studies – and Tobar an Dualchais / Kist o Riches.

More than 3000 songs and tunes are contained in the magnificent *Greig-Duncan Collection* (8 vols, 1981-2002),[8] remarkable for its "sheer breadth and range; the quality of content; the thoroughness and 'modernity' of the collecting techniques employed; the relationship of the collectors to their informants; the revolutionary nature of the songs (especially as far as Scotland is concerned)."[9] Songs from the North-East of Scotland are at the core of the collecting of schoolmaster Gavin Greig (1856-1914) and Reverend James Duncan (1848-1917), a minister of the Kirk. Ian Olson puts the collectors and their collection into their historical context. It was, he writes:

> an era of rapid change and social instability, with people throughout
> Europe afraid that their 'traditional' cultures might soon be lost
> forever. There were plenty throughout the industrialised world
> who were driven to 'rescue' and 'glean' as many 'last leaves' as
> possible in the short time they feared was left. It's best to see
> Greig and Duncan's efforts as part of a universal interest and
> activity, appearing in newspaper columns, popular and scholarly

---

[7] Brian Wilson, 'Obituary: Margaret Fay Shaw', *The Guardian*, 17 December 2004.

[8] Pat Shuldham-Shaw and Emily B Lyle (eds.), *The Greig-Duncan Folk Song Collection*, 8 vols, Edinburgh: Mercat Press (for the University of Aberdeen in association with the School of Scottish Studies, University of Edinburgh), 1981-2002.

[9] Ian A Olson, 'The Greig-Duncan Folk Song Collection', *Musical Traditions Web Services* (2003), www.mustrad.org.uk/reviews/gregdun2.htm

writings and lectures, and by the formation of 'rescue' groups such as the British *Folk-Lore Society* in 1878 or the *Folk-Song Society* in 1898.[10]

On their deaths in 1914 and 1917, respectively, the collected manuscripts got deposited at Aberdeen University. Only the 'proper' folk songs made it into a publication,[11] while all the material recorded under the Gavin-Greig definition of folk song ('songs which people sing') and their motto 'Give exactly what you get' (i.e. no bowdlerisation, no 'improvement') had to wait more than a half-century before it appeared in print, under the editorship of Pat Shuldham-Shaw and Emily B Lyle (with Peter Hall, Andy Hunter, Elaine Petrie, Adam McNaughtan, Sheila Douglas and Katherine Campbell), showing its glorious diversity, from music hall ditties to street ballads.

Gavin Greig had also edited, in 1904, *The Harp & Claymore Collection*, the music of the fiddle maestro James Scott Skinner, also known as the 'Strathspey King', who had made his first cylinder recordings in 1899. Tunes like 'Hector the Hero' (1903) made him the first international Celtic music star.

As *Last Leaves* indicates, many of these collections – and that includes previous, eighteenth- and nineteenth-century efforts – had this ring about decline and preservation about them. David Herd's *Ancient and Modern Scottish Songs, Heroic Ballads, etc.: collected from memory, tradition and ancient authors* (1776) were incorporated into *The Scots Musical Museum* which was published in six volumes between 1787 and 1803 by James Johnson and Robert Burns, and the *Select Scottish Airs*, collected by George Thomson (1799-1818), included contributions from Burns and Walter Scott.

In the early 1950s, to get back to our pivotal date, there was also a sense that the onslaught of gramophone and radio and, just about to happen, television, would sound the death knell for traditional song and music. It was now mainly the travellers and a few stubborn tradition bearers who upheld the oral tradition. Not only in the North-East and in the Hebrides. Willie Scott, the Borders shepherd, was a unique figure whose significant presence at the time of the folk song revival bridged the old world and the new. He was a masterly, veteran tradition-bearer and ambassador of the songs and lore of the Borders:

> Willie Scott's legacy cannot be overestimated. A son of the Borders, his song collection portrays a long tradition that has expressed

---

[10] *Ibid.*

[11] Alexander Keith (ed.) *Last Leaves of Traditional Ballads and Ballad Airs, collected in Aberdeenshire by the late Gavin Greig*, Aberdeen: University of Aberdeen, 1925.

people's hardships and love stories; their humour and sadness; their sense of history and connection with the land.[12]

The People's Festival Ceilidh of 1951 was as much a wake-up call, or call-to-arms, as it was in itself a manifestation of a 'living tradition', of the fact that the carrying stream had not run dry yet, despite the fact that a way of life was vanishing. And Hamish Henderson's belief in that carrying stream became firmer as the Folk Revival took its course.

From the 'Stane' to 'Ding Dong Dollar'

The year before the first People's Festival Ceilidh had seen the Christmas caper of repatriating the 'Stone of Destiny' from Westminster Abbey, itself a reaction to the frustration of two million signatures on John McCormick's Scottish Covenant (demanding Home Rule for Scotland) having no effect on the body politic. "Half the best poets of Scotland wrote songs to praise the act,"[13] with the Bo'ness Rebels taking the lead – among them Norman MacCaig, Tom Law, Sydney Goodsir Smith and Morris Blythman (Thurso Berwick).

If the 'Sangs of the Stane' were the first wave of political songwriting, two years later, the coronation of Queen Elizabeth (II of England, I of Scotland) triggered the next wave, with Morris Blythman's 'Nae Liz the Twa, Nae Lillibet the Wan' and 'Coronation Coronach' – songs reasserting Scottish nationality and standing up to (British) authority seemed ubiquitous, and the *Bo'ness Rebels Ceilidh Songbook* became the essential carrier for them.

Ten years after the 'stane', it was the "unholy doings at the holy loch"[14] that inspired a new wave of protests, when American nuclear submarines with their Polaris missiles arrived to be stationed north of Glasgow. This produced a body of 'agit prop' song – the most famous among them were 'Ding Dong Dollar' by the Glasgow Song Guild and 'The Glasgow Eskimo' by T S Law and Jim McLean. But the most enduring and lyrically far superior song of that period is Hamish Henderson's 'The Freedom Come-All-Ye' – a veritable alternative anthem for an internationalist Scotland.[15]

The next wave came with the S.N.P. campaign which, eventually in 1967, led to the victory in the Hamilton by-election. "The S.N.P. were coinciding with a major movement of the people," wrote Morris Blythman at the time,

---

[12] Alison McMorland, 'Herd Laddie o the Glen': Songs of a Border Shepherd, St Boswells: Scottish Borders Council, revised and expanded edition, 2006.
[13] Ewan McVicar, The Eskimo Republic: Scots Political Song in Action, 1951-1999, Linlithgow: Gallus Publishing, 2010, p.17.
[14] Ibid,, pp.95-113.
[15] See David Stenhouse's chapter in this volume.

and we were happy to work with them. The Party had nothing really to do with this changing climate of opinion but they were there to reap the benefit of this movement of mind. Our obvious decision was, therefore, to back them up as the movement most likely to bring Scottish independence. They had become the popular movement in the same way as the C.N.D. had been the popular movement some years before.[16]

Again, popular tunes like 'Michael Row the Boat Ashore' or 'I Shall not be Moved' were given new words in songs named 'Swing to the S.N.P.' or 'I'm Going o Change my Vote' – agit-prop for immediate use in demonstrations, rallies and marches. Many of these songs were indebted to Woody Guthrie and Pete Seeger, and the songs of the American civil rights movement of the 1960s, but also to Glasgow street songs and ballads.

The Ballad Boom

From the early 1950s, American Blues musicians had been touring in Britain, and Big Bill Broonzy played the Usher Hall in 1952.[17] Between 1954 and 1964, there were repeated visits to these shores by Sonny Terry & Brownie McGhee, Muddy Waters, Sister Rosetta Tharpe and Memphis Slim.[18] Their influence can be seen in the ensuing skiffle boom, led by the Glaswegian Lonnie Donegan and taking its cue from the likes of Leadbelly, Woody Guthrie and Cisco Houston. They also exercised a huge influence on a new generation of guitar players like Davy Graham, John Renbourn and Bert Jansch. In 2007, Jansch described to Mike Barnes how he first listened to Big Bill Broonzy when he was an Edinburgh boy of 15:

> I found a little EP in an Edinburgh store and for the next year that's all I listened to. It was a complete mystery to me at the time, because I was trying to learn guitar, but couldn't understand how you could pick out more than one melody at the same time. I was really intrigued by that. And to this day I wear a thumb pick like he did.[19]

[16] Morris Blythman, 'Rebel Songs of Scotland', Special Feature in *Chapbook*, vol.4, no.6 [1968].

[17] Released as a double CD – Big Bill Broonzy, *On Tour in Britain, 1952: Live in England and Scotland*, Jasmine Records, 2002. Unfortunately, Broonzy had an off night in the Usher Hall, recorded in good sound quality; his brilliant performance south of the Border, by contrast, is poorly recorded.

[18] Colin Harper, *Dazzling Stranger: Bert Jansch and the British Folk and Blues Revival*, London: Bloomsbury, second revised edition, 2006, p.17.

[19] Mike Barnes, 'Invisible Jukebox with Bert Jansch' in *The Wire*, 276 (February 2007).

Blues and American roots music – the American folk revival – had a huge influence on Irish music, giving rise to The Clancy Brothers and Tommy Makem in Greenwich Village, and to the ballad boom in 1960s Ireland, culminating in the formation of The Dubliners in O'Donoghue's of Merrion Row in Dublin. The American and the Irish influence also influenced the Scottish ballad revival. In 1956, the Clarion Skiffle Group was formed in Birmingham by Aberdonian Ian Campbell; it would morph into the Ian Campbell Folk Group, boasting in its long career until 1978 players like Dave Swarbrick and Dave Pegg, and performing at the Newport Folk Festival in 1964, showing that the transatlantic link was a two-way street.

Jean Redpath went to the US in 1961 and made her name as a Scottish singer there, as Ed Miller would do a few years later. Ayrshire-born David Francey found a new home in Ontario, Canada, and Peebles-lad Eric Bogle made a name for himself from Australia with 'The Band Played Waltzing Mathilda' and 'No Man's Land'.

Ewan McColl, Alex Campbell and Hamish Imlach became the arch balladeers of the 1960s and 1970s, soon to be joined by Iain MacKintosh, extending their popularity across the European continent. Tradition bearers, singers and songwriters became a strong feature of the folk revival: Lizzie Higgins, Elizabeth Stewart, Robin Hall & Jimmie MacGregor, Dolina McLellan, Arthur Argo, The Gaugers, Ray and Archie Fisher, Alastair McDonald, Danny Couper, Mike Whellans, Rab Noakes, Gerry Rafferty (in the 'Humblebums' with Billy Connolly), Bob Bertram, Matt McGinn, Liz & Maggie Cruickshank, Barbara Dickson, John Watt, Adam McNaughtan, Sheena Wellington, Arthur Johnstone, Enoch Kent, Owen Hand, The Laggan, Aileen Carr, The McCalmans, Danny Kyle, Alistair Russell, Chorda, Elspeth Cowie (of Seannachie and Chantan), Gaberlunzie, Bill Barclay, Tich Frier, Dougie MacLean, Bobby Eaglesham, Janet Russell, Christine Kydd, Barbara Dymock, Rankin File, Davy Steele, Drinker's Drouth, Mick West, Haggerdash, Isla St Clair, Jim Reid, Ivan Drever, Dick Gaughan, Brian McNeill, Eileen Penman, Nancy Nicolson, Stramash, Palaver, Maureen Jelks, Anne Neilson, North Sea Gas, Chris Miles, George Duff, The Linties, Calluna, Sinsheen, Peter Nardini, Ian Walker, Kinrick, Heather Heywood, Jimmy Hutchinson, Jack Beck, Robin Laing, Fraser and Ian Bruce, Alistair Hulett, Gill Bowman, Dave Gibb, Jim King, Ken Campbell, Back of the Moon, Rallion, Real Time, Other Roads, Ragged Glory, Chris Rogers, Martin Boland, Mark Barnett, Tom Fairnie, Tom Clelland, Jim Malcolm... an impressive list, but by no means an exhaustive one!

The Clutha were formed at Norman Buchan's Ballads Club in 1964, and soon recruited the singer Gordeanna McCulloch to their line-up. The

Corries, founded in 1962, became the dominant folk group, for a time featuring the Irish singer Paddie Bell. They became the resident group in the BBC's *Hoot'nanny* Show on TV, and impressing not just with their balladry, but also through their instrumental sets.

In Ireland, the composer Seán Ó Riada (1931-1971) had set up Ceoltóiri Chualann in 1961, out of which The Chieftains evolved. Their emphasis on Celtic tunes found an echo in Scotland in the Corries, but particularly in The Whistlebinkies, formed in 1967 in Glasgow, and their composer and flute player Eddie McGuire. They led the revival in the use of the bellows-blown bagpipes in Scotland and were the first to combine the three national instruments: the fiddle, bagpipes and clàrsach (Scottish harp) in regular performance. And performances have taken them across the globe, from the Celtic countries through Europe and, as the first Scottish group ever, to the People's Republic of China.

One of the most exciting and influential bands to come out of the Scottish folk Revival was Silly Wizard in the early 1970s, with youngster Johnny Cunningham on fiddle and, a few years later, his younger brother Phil on accordion. In Andy M Stewart they also had a great singer and songwriter. Their untamed inventiveness was to influence coming generations of bands, from Shoogienifty to the Peat Bog Faeries.

The Battlefield Band came together in 1969 in Glasgow on the initiative of Brian McNeill and Alan Reid, who were joined by Jenny Clark and piper Duncan McGillivray. They have since clocked up more than 30 albums and travelled the world with their music. But by 2010, with Alan Reid's departure, there was no longer any founder member involved in the band. Like the Batties, The Tannahill Weavers, named after the poet and songwriter Robert Tannahill (1774-1810) and formed in 1976 in Tannahill's home town of Paisley, successfully incorporated the Highland Pipes into their sound, and they, too, are still on the go, albeit with many personnel changes – only Roy Gullane and Phil Smillie have been with them right from the start.

In the late 1970s, when Planxty and the Bothy Band had set the standards, and Irish music ruled OK, Jock Tamson's Bairns – Rod Paterson, John Croall, Derek Hoy and Norman Chalmers – set a distinctly Scottish accent. Disbanded between 1983 and 1995, the original members have now been together for another one-and-half decade or so, delighting audiences with their fine arrangements. Scotland's most original songwriter, Dundee's Michael Marra, saw them worthy of a wee paen:

> Jock Tamson's Bairns are Rare
> And Rare is the new Cool
> Bold and Bountiful on Grand Scales
> These Oatmeal Brothers

Fed on Scones of Destiny
And Tunes of Glory
Neither lightly cooked nor underdone
Through Real Time and Strathspace
An International Adventure
True Romance and Universal Riches
In the Big Picture of the Handing Over
Jock Tamson's Bairns' Fingerprints are Ubiquitous
Ubiquitous and Rare[20]

Members of the short-lived Contraband formed Ossian in 1976. Singing in Scots, Gaelic and English, with each member being a multi-instrumentalist, Billy Ross (later replaced by the remarkable guitar player and singer Tony Cuffe), Billy Jackson, John Martin and George Jackson impressed with their filigrane arrangements.

From within the traditional framework, Glasgow duo Findask (Willie Lindsay and Stuart Campbell) made an impression in the 1980s with heir original material. The music of the North-East of Scotland lies at the core of the Old Blind Dogs, with Johnny Hardie on fiddle and Ex-Craobh Rua frontman Aaron Jones on vocals. Deaf Shepherd, a six-piece based in Edinburgh, encompassed pipes, fiddles, bouzouki and the magnificent voice of John Morran, to make them one of he favourites of the 1990s folk circuit. The Shee is a cross-border enterprise involving six young female musicians with an astonishing level of instrumental prowess, and boasting no less than three powerful vocalists. Bodega is the product of The National Centre for Excellence in Traditional Music at Plockton High School, from which all five group members graduated. And the latest band to make waves from Glasgow is the Paul McKenna Band.

The Rise of the Folk Clubs... and Sandy Bell's

The late 1950s and early 1960s were the time when folk clubs began to materialise. The very first one was the Edinburgh University Folk Society, founded by the writer Stuart McGregor.[21] It celebrated its sixtieth anniversary at the 2008 Carrying Stream Festival. Ewan McColl, born in 1915 as Jimmy Miller in Perthshire, founded the first British folk club. Norman and Janey Buchan in Glasgow followed, Roy Guest ran Edinburgh's Howff, and then there are the survivers: Dunfermline Folk Club (which just celebrated its fiftieth anniversary), or Aberdeen Folk Club (which will celebrate its fiftieth anniversary in 2012). Scotland's clubs

---

[20] www.jtbairns.com/
[21] See Hamish Henderson, *Alias MacAlias*, p.2.

were fairly open-minded, as Alastair McDonald recalls in his contribution to this volume. Britta Sweers had this to say:

> The early 1960s ... witnessed a mushrooming folk club culture. With the background of the thriving living tradition, however, Scottish clubs were never as dogmatic as in England and always presented a mixture of American, Irish, Scottish, and English music.[22]

This eclecticism is well reflected in an obituary of Owen Hand, who was a very fine singer based in Edinburgh and embodied this typically Scottish "maverick" approach:

> Musically, he was an unreconstructed eclectic maverick of the folk revival to his dying day, the last of the seriously wild rovers, interested in anything that made traditional sense, whether it be a Woody Guthrie song from the Dust Bowl, a low-down, gonna-miss-ya-if-it-kills-me-baby John Lee Hooker blues, a palpitatingly poignant Aly Bain slow air, a Gaelic congregation moaning in straggly unison to the precentor's call, a rasping gaggle of Breton pipers. He taught the burgeoning British folk-club scene of the Sixties a lesson that it eventually learned: there is not ONE traditional music – there are LOTS of traditional musics. And some of them, believe it or not, come from America.[23]

Folk Clubs were the place to be. Licensing hours were restricted – most clubs were dry. And after-club parties were all the rave. Here is how Maggie Cruickshank remembers it:

> We had such a busy life ... there was a continual round of socialising. It was hectic but it was also very relaxed – you wafted in and out of things and weave in and around each other. You saw people like Archie and Hamish and Josh McRea as being high up in the hierarchy and us down below. But we didn't stay there for long – everybody was so encouraging to each other.[24]

As to pubs, yes, we need to mention the Scotia and Clutha bars in Glasgow and, more recently, Laurie's; and in Edinburgh The Royal Oak has kept music alive, on a daily basis, week in, week out, for nigh-on 30 years; there

---

[22] Britta Sweers, *Electric Folk: The Changing Face of English Traditional Music*, New York: Oxford University Press, 2005, p.257.

[23] Obituary of Owen Hand, *The Scotsman*, 24 February 2003.

[24] Colin Harper, *Dazzling Stranger: Bert Jansch and the British Folk and Blues Revival*, p.77.

is the Taybank Bar in Dunkeld, the Ceilidh House in Ullapool, Hootananny's in Inverness and the Waverley Bar back in Edinburgh – the birth place of The McCalmans. But the undoubted doyen of traditional music howffs in Scotland is the capital's Sandy Bell's Bar – the "oldest unofficial folk club in Scotland," as Hamish Henderson put it in 1965:

> The oldest unofficial folk club in Scotland is undoubtedly the Forrest Hill Bar, better known as Sandy Bell's. This was our local during all the early Festival ceilidhs, and is still the local of the School of Scottish Studies. Dozens of songs which are now the common currency of the folk clubs had their 'revival première' at Sandy Bell's. In April 1952, old Willie Mathieson, source-singer of 'I'm a Rover and Seldom Sober', gave spirited renderings of this and other songs for an audience which included Johnny McEvoy (author of 'The Wee Magic Stane') and two professors of the 'Toon's College'.
>
> Sandy's first theme-song was my own version of the 'D-Day Dodgers', but it soon acquired songs of its own – for example, 'Old Bell's Bar' and 'I've been wronged by a Sandy Bell's man', written by Stuart McGregor (...). [25]

Greentrax has re-released *Sandy Bell's Ceilidh*,[26] which features a host of the Sandy Bell's Bar regulars of the 1970s, including Aly Bain, Dick Gaughan, The McCalmans, Chorda, Liz and Maggie Cruickshank, plus The Bell's Big Ceilidh Band – local musicians (like Jimmy Elliot, Jimmy Greenan, Jock Brown and Adam Jack) who regularly played music in the Bar – and The Bell's Chorus, made up of regulars who were known to join into song at the drop of Hamish's hat.

Whither the Folk Revival?

But the 1960s were also a decade of controversies. As the opening quotation from Hamish Henderson indicates, the plan was to have the folk song revival complement the Scottish (Literary) Renaissance. But as it gathered pace, the 'custodian' of that renaissance, Hugh MacDiarmid, distanced himself from what he called, in one of his more flowery phrases in the letters pages of the *Scotsman* in 1960, "unlettered ballad-singers

---

[25] Hamish Henderson, *Alias MacAlias*, p.12. By far the best description of the conviviality of a Sandy Bell's gathering under the aegis of Hamish was penned by the late Angus Calder – it is quoted in Christopher Harvie's piece for this collection.
[26] Various Artists, *Sandy Bell's Ceilidh*, originally recorded and released in the 1970s, Greentrax (Celtic Collections vol.10), CDGMP8010 (2006).

yowling like so many cats on the tiles in moonlight".[27] Four years later, when the flyting reached its climax, he claimed:

> At the present stage in human history, there are far more important things to do than bawl out folksongs, which, whatever function they may have had in the past, have little or no relevance to most people in advanced highly industrialized countries today.[28]

In his polemical swerve, he went so far as to state: "I ... have been bored to death listening to more of it [folksong], including the renderings of Jeannie Robertson, Jimmy MacBeath, and others ... and I certainly never want to hear any more of it."[29]

Hamish Henderson begged to disagree. He had "no doubt that in the long run it is the folksong revival which offers the best hope for a genuine popular poetry, a poetry which, when it gathers strength, will make many of the raucous booths of Tin Pan Alley shut up shop."[30] He cites the Italian Marxist Antonio Gramsci, for whom folk song is "a separate and distinct way of perceiving life and the world, as opposed to that of 'official' society."[31] Back in 1956, he had made the point that

> Scottish folk-song is part of the submerged resistance movement which reacted against the tyranny of John Knox's Kirk at a time when the Kirk was making a bid for absolute rule in Scotland. This explains why, in the whole range of our folk-song, there is hardly a reference to ministers or to religion – apart from the most formal – which is not hostile or satiric.[32]

When, in 1967, The Dubliners climbed to No.7 in the British Pop Charts with 'Seven Drunken Nights', another controversy came to the boil – the agonising over the commercialisation of folk music, its reduction to mere 'entertainment'. When the Beatles manager Brian Epstein had predicted folk would be the main trend of popular music in 1965, purists feared

---

[27] Hamish Henderson, *The Armstrong Nose: Selected Letters* (edited by Alec Finlay), Edinburgh: Polygon, 1996, p.98.
[28] *Ibid.*, p.134.
[29] *Ibid.*, p.118.
[30] *Ibid.*, p.96. See also Corey Gibson, 'Hamish Henderson's Conception of the Scottish Folk-Song Revival and its Place in Literary Scotland', *The Drouth*, no.32 (2009), pp.49-58.
[31] Gramsci, quoted by Hamish Henderson, "'It was in You that it a' Began'", in Edward J Cowan, *The People's Past: Scottish Folk – Scottish History*, Edinburgh: Edinburgh University Students Publication Board, 1980, p.14.
[32] Hamish Henderson, *Alias MacAlias*, p.28.

what they knew as folk-song might be "devoured in the same manner as the Skiffle craze."[33] And Hamish Imlach was slightly chided for having produced "a happy night with an audience rather than ... presenting a serious folk-song production."[34] Countering the 'folk police', the record producer Nathan Joseph warned:

> When you hear the cry "commercialism", be careful to ask yourself before you swallow it whole whether it isn't just a bait to get you to condemn 'in toto' all that is new, experimental, professional and exciting in folk music in favour of all that is old, static, amateurish and dull. Because it often is.[35]

That folk singers could make a (meagre) living out of their music caused some people to accuse them of selling out, of becoming 'professional'. Colin Wilkie and Shirley Hart vented their anger at this idiocy, shortly before they emigrated to Germany (where Colin to this day is a folk icon, having influenced a whole generation of German guitarists and singers):

> We are sick, sick, sick of a small minority (whose knowledge of the English language is apparently non-existent) using the word professional as if it was a dirty word. For our part we are proud to be professionals.[36]

Hamish Henderson foresaw that "a certain stream of the folk-song revival may well go commercial, and become a new type of pop song," and he adds, "in which case it will probably do the pop-song world a lot of good." He was firmly convinced that "new generations of Bob Bertrams and Matt McGinns will come forward, to make new songs, and adapt old ones, whether they are invited to go commercial, or not."[37]

Folk Fusion and Folk Rock

Towards the end of the 1960s, new trends were appearing. In 1966, The Incredible String Band was formed in Clive Palmer's Incredible Folk Club in Glasgow, playing psychedelic folk and winning the *Melody Maker*'s 'Folk Album of the Year' award with their first, eponymous LP.

---

[33] Peter A. Hall, 'Pop goes the ethnic?', *Chapbook*, Vol.2, No.1 (1965), p.6.

[34] *Chapbook*, Vol.4, No.3 (1967), p.23.

[35] Nathan Joseph, 'Revival or Standstill?', *Folk Scene*, No.9, July 1965, p.29.

[36] Colin Wilkie & Shirley Hart, 'Proud to be Professional', *Folk Scene*, No.4, January 1965, p.30.

[37] Hamish Henderson, talk given to the 125th meeting of the British Association of the Advancement of Science, Aberdeen, 1963, first published in Folklore, Vol.75, Spring 1964, reprinted in *Alias MacAlias*, p.42.

But their best year was undoubtedly 1968, when they released their most durable and most celebrated albums *Wee Tam and The Big Huge* and *The Hangman's Beautiful Daughter*. The following year the band, led by Robin Williamson and Mike Heron, appeared at the legendary Woodstock festival.

A dose of Dylan, and a smidgen of psychedelic flower-power, and you have Donovan, from Maryhill in Glasgow. That is perhaps a slightly unfair categorisation for the man who had a huge hit with Buffy Sainte-Mairie's 'Universal Soldier', and whose other hit singles included the folk anthem 'Catch the Wind' and songs like 'Sunshine Superman', 'Mellow Yellow', 'Jennifer Juniper' and 'Atlantis'. "The press were fond of calling Donovan a 'Dylan Clone'," his friend and guitar-mentor Mac McLeod remarked in a US radio interview in 2004, "as they had both been influenced by the same sources: Ramblin' Jack Elliott, Jesse Fuller, Woody Guthrie, and many more."[38]

In 1967, Bert Jansch got involved with Pentangle, fusing folk, rock and jazz, and they were signed up for Transatlantic Records by Nathan Joseph. Pentangle disbanded 1973, but reformed in 2008 – and Bert Jansch's last public appearance was with the band on 1 August 2011 in the Royal Festival Hall in London.

In 1969, Jim Divers, Sean O'Rourke and Des Coffield founded The JSD Band, soon to be joined by the irrepressible fiddler Chuck Fleming and Colin Finn. They were the first truly electric folk band in Scotland. Dick Gaughan and Bobby Eaglesham were the frontmen of Scotland's most successful 'Celtic Rock' band, Five Hand Reel, formed in 1974. On their second album, *For A' That* (1977), they cut the first Gaelic folk-rock song – 'Bratach Bana'. Thus, in a way, they paved the path for two of Scotland's most famous bands of all time, Runrig and Capercaillie. Seelyhoo, with Gaelic singer Fiona MacKenzie and the Orcadian twins Jennifer and Hazel Wrigley, plus the formidable talents of 'out of his box' Sandy Brechin, have sometimes been compared to Capercaillie. Dàimh, a band based on the West Coast of Scotland, boast members from Ireland, Scotland, Cape Breton and California. Their Gaelic music is high octane, with a live energy matched by few contemporary outfits in Scotland. In a different kind of fusion, traditional, swing and blues influences can be heard in the music of Saltfishforty from Orkney. Bluegrass is also the *forte* of Blueflint, of Home Made Jam, of Kathy Stewart & the Frequent Flyers and of the Edinburgh-based Southern Tenant Folk Union. Every July, the Scottish Bluegrass Association brings the finest of that musical genre 'home' to Guildtown in Perthshire.[39]

---

[38] http://en.wikipedia.org/wiki/Donovan
[39] www.scottishbluegrass.com/

Bagpipes had, by the 1980s, been integrated into the folk band sound, with the Tannahill Weavers and the Battlefield Band. Now, Wolfestone used them to good effect in their Highland folk-rock approach. In the 1990s, Big Country, a rock band with folk leanings, used the ebow guitar to create a bagpipe effect. One of the most exciting outfits to come out of the 1980s was The Easy Club, playing a kind of folk-swing which was well ahead of its time. Jack Evans and Jock Tamson's Bairn Norman Chalmers were among the personnel of the Cauld Blast Orchestra, which started as a project for Glasgow's stint as European City of Culture in 1990, with writer Liz Lochhead involved, as well as musicians from all walks of musical life.

Legend has it how Ian Green discovered Shooglenifty in the Central Bar in Leith, where they played in session. Their music combines traditional tunes with contemporary dance rhythms, loops and beats. Around the same time, the Tartan Amoebas were mixing up the ceilidh dance scene, and a little later the Peatbog Faeries from Skye would unleash their fusion of electronica with a fiery concoction of bagpipes, fiddles, and whistles onto the dance floors of Scotland and beyond – twice winning the 'Life Act of the Year' title at he Scots Trad Awards.

Jazzy themes were taken up by Bachué Café in the 1990s, with Harpist Corinna Hewat and pianist Dave Milligan. The latter worked also with concertina-wizard Simon Thoumire who, in turn, kept it up with…. Keep It Up, featuring guitarist Kevin McKenzie, who is equally at home in jazz and folk settings (Trio AAB). From a slightly different angle comes Salsa Celtica, an 11 piece world music fusion band, based in Edinburgh, whose synthesis of Scottish and Irish traditional music with Latin American salsa elements makes them feel equally at home (or different) at celtic, jazz, world music and salsa festivals.

Twins Charlie and Craig Reid formed The Proclaimers in 1983. With their rockabilly meets Buddy Holly meets Scots anthems like 'Letter from America' or 'I'm Gonna Be (500 Miles)', with 'Sunshine on Leith' adopted by Hibernian FC as their theme song – and their own story told in a successful musical, named after that hit – they have been called "national treasures" and "arguably the most popular Scottish band on home turf."[40] Mike Whellans, who started out with Aly Bain and the Boys of the Lough as a traditional musician, turned himself into Scotland's only one-man blues sensation, just as if Lauder in the Borders had a 42nd Street.

A new generation of Scottish singer/songwriters were inspired by the likes of (Bennie) Gallagher & (Graham) Lyle and John Martyn, leading to Jackie Leven, Alasdair Roberts and the Fence Collective of Anstruther, most prominent among them James Yorkston and King Creosote (aka Kenny Anderson). The greatest among the singer/songwriters is Michael

---

[40] *The Scotsman*, 31 August 2007.

Marra – Scotland's own Randy Newman, with a highly idiosyncratic leftfield view of the world, as spotted from the vantage perspective of Dundee.

New York-born Talitha MacKenzie, working solo and with Mouth Music, first joined Jamie MacDonald Reid's Scottish folk ensemble Drumalban, then worked with Martin Swan in Mouth Music and subsequently became a star on the world music scene. Also in Drumalban was the boldest experimentalist of them all, the piper and violin virtuoso Martyn Bennett. Particularly his last two albums *Bothy Culture* (1998) and *Grit* (2003) – Martyn died aged 33 of cancer in 2005 – pushed out the frontiers of traditional music, as he increasingly relied on samples and synthesizers to create his music.

The trio presently credited as being the cutting edge of Scottish folk music is Lau, comprising the prodigious talents of Orcadian singer and guitarist extraordinaire Kris Drever, award-winning fiddler and composer Aidan O'Rourke from Oban, and maverick accordionist Martin Green from East Anglia. They quote the Bothy Bnd as their musical heroes and have recently recorded with the legendary Jack Bruce of Cream fame.

The Gaels

There was a strong Gaelic element in the People's Festival Ceilidhs – with the Barra singers Flora MacNeil and Calum Johnston, who "presented Hebridean folksong, stripped of its Kennedy Fraser mummy-wrappings."[41] A more comprehensive impression of Gaelic singing at that time can be gleaned from *Gaelic Songs of Scotland: Women at Work in the Western Isles*, also recorded by Alan Lomax on his 1951 collecting trip and issued by Rounder in 2006, curated by Margaret Bennett. Here, we have spinning and milking songs and waulking songs – twenty-six songs by seventeen women from the Outer Hebridean islands of South Uist, Benbecula, Barra, and Lewis, as well as the mainland area of Moidart – interspersed with snippets from Lomax's interviews with the singers. A more detailed insight into Lomax's interview technique is given in Margaret Bennett's piece for this collection. Margaret Bennett, originally from Skye and now based in Perthshire, is Scotland's greatest living folklorist, and sings in both Gaelic and Scots.

Like Flora MacNeil and Calum Johnston, Catherine-Ann McPhee was born in Barra. Other notable Gaelic singers are Maggie Macinnes (the daughter of Flora MacNeil) and Màiri Macinnes (no relative), the Glasgow-born harpist and radio and TV presenter Mary-Ann Kennedy, Lewis-born Margaret Stewart, and the late Ishbel MacAskill, who was born in the Isle

---

[41] Hamish Henderson, *Alias MacAlias*, p.9.

of Lewis. Alyth McCormack also grew up on Lewis and has toured with the Chieftains and Deaf Shepherd.

Blair Douglas, a founder member of Scotland's most successful Celtic folk-rock outfit Runrig, is not only a renowned accordion player, but also an accomplished all-round musician, arranger and composer. In 2009, he received an award from the Highland Branch of the Saltire Society for his composition *The Gaelic Mass, An Aifreann Ghàidhlig*.

The best example for the resurgence of Gaelic culture, part of a new-found confidence in place, language and culture, is the 'Highland supergroup' Cliar, a six-piece band with some of the finest singers and instrumentalists – the Mod Gold Medal winner of 1992, Arthur Cormack, piano and clàrsach player Ingrid Henderson, the aforementioned Mary Ann Kennedy, Maggie MacDonald from Skye, a master of the *puirt-a-beul* or mouth music, Hector Henderson on bagpipes and whistles, and the ubiquitous, dazzling guitarist Ross Martin (Harem Scarem and Dàimh also employ his nimble fretwork). For *FolkWorld*, on the other hand, "Mackenzie is the most beautiful act of Gaelic song to be found on the folk music scene. Eilidh, Fiona and Gillian Mackenzie are three sisters with bittersweet voices, creating a heavenlike soundsphere – absolutely stunning!"[42]

Huge international popularity for Gaelic song and music has been achieved by Runrig and Capercaillie. Is Karen Matheson or Julie Fowlis the most famous Gaelic singer at present? Born and brought up in North Uist, Julie became a member of the Gaelic group Dòchas, and went on to win the 2008 BBC Radio 2 Folk Singer of the Year (the first ever Scottish Gaelic singer to win this prestigious award). In he same year, the Scottish Parliament bestowed on her the inaugural title of Scotland's Gaelic Ambassador – *Tosgaire na Gàidhlig*.

The Celtic Neighbour

There are many similarities between Irish and Scottish traditional music, but also notable differences – the Scottish piping tradition is very different from the Irish, the musical styles seem to reflect the landscape: the Scottish Highlands, more dramatic than the more gentle, lilting hills of Ireland. The Scots and the Irish share a lot of songs, and many tunes are known in both areas. As mentioned already, the influence of the Clancys and Dubliners, of the Chieftains, Planxty and the Bothy Band, of the Horslips in folk rock, and of Christy Moore, Paul Brady, Mary Black and Dolores Keane as singers and songwriters has been immense. Moreover, Irish musicians have settled in Scotland and collaborated with Scottish musicians since the early days of the folk revival.

[42] *FolkWorld*, 29 March 2000.

Finbar and Eddie Furey lived in Edinburgh in the 1960s, Paddie Bell sang with the Corries. Cathal McConnell, Irish Traditional Singer of the Year in 2010, was a founder member of the Boys of the Lough, together with Robin Morton, who now runs Temple Records. In latter years, Brendan Begley also joined the band. These days, Cathal, who has just published a collection of 123 of his songs,[43] can most often be heard in a fine duo with Highland fiddler Duncan Wood; the two of them recorded a masterful album, *Auld Springs*, and are occasionally working with Fairport's legendary fiddler Dave Swarbrick.

Five Hand Reel had Tony Hickland and Sam Bracken in their midst. Kieran Halpin moved to Edinburgh in the early 1990s, and then made his home in Stow in the Borders. Corner House was very much a project involving the accordion playing of Leo McCann. And Kevin MacLeod used to tour with De Dannan and has recorded with Alec Finn. Tomás Lynch, the piper and guitarist from Dublin with a knack of giving old songs a new lease of life, formerly part of Afterhours, is another Irishman settled in Scotland.

More recently, Malinky, founded by Karine Polwart and Steve Byrne, had Mark Dunlop from Co Antrim in their line-up. Aaron Jones, with a Belfast background, is now the voice of the Old Blind Dogs, one of Scotlands premier touring bands. Ciaran Dorris is a fine singer/songwriter from the North of Ireland who has settled in Glasgow. Glasgow fiddler Jamie Smith moved on from Beneche to not one, but two 'Irish' bands, The Long Notes (featuring the Bumblebees' Colette O'Leary on accordion and the Shane MacGowan-experienced banjo and mandolin dervish Brian Kelly) and SBO (Smith, singer and guitarist Steve Byrnes and Liam O'Sullivan, one of the finest button accordion players on the London-Irish scene). The current incarnation of the Battlefield Band has harnessed the talents of guitarist and singer Seán O'Donnell.

Originally from Dundalk in Co Louth, the flautist and singer Nuala Kennedy first came to prominence here in Scotland through Fine Friday, a band that emerged from the Friday session at Sandy Bell's (with Anna-Wendy Stevenson and Kris Drever). She has worked with her own band, The New Shoes, and with an impressive list of international artists, including Will Oldham, Norman Blake, Cathal McConnell, Caoimhin O'Raghaillaigh, Filippo Gambetta and the late great Canadian composer and fiddler Oliver Schroer, with whom she recorded *Enthralled*, a duo album of original compositions.

---

[43] Cathal McConnell, *I have Travelled This Country: The Songs of Cathal McConnell*, compiled and edited by Gerry O'Connor and Síle Boylan, with audio recording, Dundalk: Lughnasa Music, 2011.

The Canadian Connection

We have already encountered the impact of American roots music on the Folk Revival, the flirting with pop, rock and jazz from the late 1960s, perhaps as a defence against being crowded out of 'popular music'. And these influences continue, through the likes of Steve Earle, Bruce Molsky, and the music 'Down from the Mountain', given a jolt in the arm by the success of the Coens' *Oh Brother, Where Art Though?* In the 1990s, the Scottish diaspora was 'discovered'. Was it not interesting that in Nova Scotia, particularly in Cape Breton Island and Prince Edward Island, Scots Gaelic was still spoken? Mairi Campbell brought back set dances which had emigrated across the Atlantic, and could now be reintroduced to Scotland where they had been forgotten in the meantime.

The Barra MacNeils from Sydney Mines in Nova Scotia, whose ancestral home was the island of Barra in the Outer Hebrides, made frequent forays into Scotland, particularly after they won an Album of the Year award in 1992 for *Time Frame*.

Artists like the Juno Award-winning fiddler Natalie MacMaster (a niece of Cape Breton fiddler Buddy MacMaster and cousin of fiddler Ashley MacIsaac) came to play at the Edinburgh Folk Festival and at Celtic Connections. Since 1997, this link with maritime Canada has most definitely become a two-way traffic, as the Celtic Colours Festival attracts a host of Scottish musicians to Cape Breton Island every October.

Of course, the great Canadian songwriters, from Neil Young (with whom Bert Jansch toured in 2010) to Joni Mitchell, Buffy Sainte-Marie, Leonard Cohen, Stan Rogers, Gordon Lightfoot, Loudon Wainright III, Bruce Cockburn, Jimmy Rankin (of the Rankin Family), James Keelaghan, Leslie Feist, Joel Plaskett, Ron Hynes, Dan McKinnon, Ron Sexsmith, Catherine MacLellan – they all have been popular in Scotland and have had an influence on Scottish songwriters.

Northern Streams

Over the past decade, the music of the Nordic countries has made astonishing inroads into Scottish music. There has long been a very fond connection between Scotland and Denmark – Tønder Festival at the end of August has been a popular destination for Scottish folkies since the days of Alex Campbell, Hamish Imlach and Iain MacKintosh. Five Hand Reel even recorded an album, *Ebbe, Dagmar, Svend og Alan*, with Danish folk singer and radio presenter Alan Kiltgaard. Alex Campbell lived in Denmark for the last years of his life, Mike Whellans lived there for years, and others found love, not just for the country, but for, in Nick Keir's words, 'Denmark's Girls'.

One of those, Bente Kure, was a regular visitor to these shores throughout the 1980s and '90s. These days, bands and soloists like Faerd, Habbadam from Bornholm, Väsen from Sweden, Ale Möller from Norway, who introduced Aly Bain to the Hardanger fiddle, and the Finnish accordionist Maria Kalaniemi, are frequent and welcome guests in Scotland. The Swedish Nyckelharpa has, thanks to visits by Väsen, become the instrument of the moment in Scotland – Ruth Morris of Bellevue Rendezvous and Gavin Pennycook (with his Celtic Nyckelhapa Project) are excellent exponents of this bowed string instrument.[44] When Fiddlers' Bid met Väsen at a Festival in Stockholm, the idea of *Foogy* was born, an album on which harpist Catriona McKay and Nyckelharpa world champion Olov Johansson collaborated in 2009. Fribo is the product of a Scottish-Norwegian musical encounter.

From Blairgowrie to Celtic Connections

In 1966, the newly-founded Traditional Song and Music Association of Scotland (TMSA) organised the first Folk Festival in Scotland in Blairgowrie. That small Perthshire town was chosen, Hamish Henderson explains,

> ... because it already hosted a huge informal get-together in the berryfields at the height of summer, when pickers from all over Scotland came to pick raspberries and to have a good time. Also, it was the home of the 'Stewarts of Blair' – Alec and Belle Stewart and their daughters Sheila and Cathie – one of Scotland's foremost folk-singing families. Last but not least, Blair was in berry-time the temporary home of hundreds of gifted traveller musicians and singers from as far away as the northern Highlands and Ireland. Collecting in the berryfields – songs as well as berries – often seemed like holding a tin can under the Niagara Falls.[45]

'Blairgowrie' moved to Kinross, and then to Kirriemuir, and other festivals were set up – Keith in the bothy ballad-singing North-East, and Newcastleton in the Borders. "To these festivals," Hamish continues, "the revival singers came as apprentices; the invited guests were mainly authentic traditional singers such as Jane Turriff, Stanley Robertson,

---

[44] Gavin Pennycook, 'Celtic Nyckelharpa: a cross between a fiddle and a battleship', *Living Tradition*, issue 87 (January/February 2011), pp.30-32.
[45] Hamish Henderson, *Alias MacAlias*, p.2

Betsy Whyte and the veteran Border shepherd Willie Scott."[46] Adam McNaughtan wrote 'Yellow on the Broom' as a tribute to Betsy and Scotland's travelling people – a fine example of Adam's apprenticeship.

In the meantime, festivals have mushroomed. Some have come and gone, like the Highland Traditional Music Festival, reflected on in this volume by Rob Gibson and Rita Hunter, some are recent additions. Hardly an area of Scotland is without its folk festival, from Girvan in the South-West to the Mull of Kintyre and the Isle of Bute Festivals, the Hebridean Celtic Festival in Stornaway, the Blàs Festival across the Highlands, Blazin' in Beauly, the 'First Hairst' near Banchory on the river Dee, the phenomenal Orkney and Shetland Folk Festivals, and down again to Auchtermuchty and the Lomond Folk Festival, or the Denham and Innerleithen music festivals in the Borders. Towards the end of October, Dougie MacLean's Perthshire Amber weekend attracts visitors to the 'Celtic Colours' of one of Scotland's most picturesque counties. And in November, the Fiddle Festival beckons in Edinburgh – and in between Edinburgh Folk Club has, over the past decade, established the Carrying Stream Festival.

Edinburgh used to have an international folk festival over the two Easter weekends, but it foundered after two decades in 1999, when the Council refused to bail it out. For the past ten years we have had Ceilidh Culture, not quite a folk festival, but a promotion of the traditional arts in Edinburgh, supported by Edinburgh City Council. Across in the West, Glasgow's Celtic Connections has developed into one of the biggest Celtic Music festivals on the globe – also paying copious homage to the West of Scotland fancy for Country & Western and Bluegrass music, with a healthy dose of Americana on the January agenda.

Fiddles, Pipes and Harps

The Folk Revival, initially dominated by unaccompanied singing, then by guitars and banjos, increasingly became more diversified in its instrumentation. Via Ireland (Johnny Moynihan and Andy Irvine), the bouzouki was introduced – and in Aaron Jones, the Scottish folk scene has one of the finest bouzouki accompanist imaginable, while Kevin MacLeod has a whole collection of the Greek beasts, alongside vintage resonator guitars.

Apart from Tony McManus, the finest Celtic guitarist of his generation, and the late Tony Cuffe – and, of course, Bert Jansch, Dick Gaughan and Brian McNeill – other notable Scottish guitar players include Malcolm Jones of Runrig and Kris Drever of Lau, Kevin MacKenzie, Anna Massie, Jenn Butterworth, Frank McLaughlin, Stevie Lawrence, Sandy Stanage, Edinburgh's guitar teacher Tony Mitchell, Ewan MacPherson, John Carnie

---

[46] *Ibid.*

and the hugely talented Matheu Watson. There is also the Albanach Guitar Duo (Russell Ballantine and Paul Devery) and Wingin' It (the guitar and mandolin duo of Adam Bulley and Chas Mackenzie). Seylan Baxter and Wendy Weatherby are noted cello players (as well as singers), and Claire Mann and Calum Stewart excell on flute. The concertina has become rarer since the days of Hamish Bayne in the Macs, but Norman Chalmers' and Simon Thoumire's inventiveness on the instrument makes up for it. Even the piano has attracted some fine folk players recently, from Mhairi Hall and Mary McCarthy to Andy Thorburn, Hamish Napier and James Ross.

In the course of the Revival, regional fiddle styles have been rediscovered. In 1968, Arthur Argo met the Shetland fiddler Aly Bain and persuaded him to take part in the Irvine Folk Festival.

> It was there that a remarkable musical career was launched. It was there that Aly Bain found, as he puts it, a niche in life. And it was there that a kind of one-man crusade began. The task: to put traditional music, especially fiddle music, back into its rightful place in the public domain., where it could be heard, enjoyed and played. (...) The folk fans at Irvine that summer could hardly have been aware that Aly Bain was a messenger heralding a new era which would ultimately see the singers toppled from their bill-topping perches by a swarm of predominantly instrumental, rather than vocal, groups.[47]

Thus, the fiddle broke away, as it were, from the confines of the Accordion and Fiddle Clubs, which are still a force in the country. The accordion is easily one of the most popular instruments in Scottish music – from the venerable Jimmy Shand to Will Starr and, in the modern folk scene, Phil Cunningham, Freeland Barbour, Emily Smith, Mairearad Green and Sandy Brechin. Come the 1990s, fiddle mania breaks out. Fiddlers' Bid from Shetland, led by Chris Stout, pioneer the quadruple fiddle frontline – and they set a trend soon to be taken up by bands like Blazin' Fiddles and Session A9. There is no shortage of great and talented fiddle players, from Kevin Henderson to Jennifer Wrigley, from Aidan O'Rourke to Alasdair Fraser, Bruce MacGregor, John Martin, Pete Clark, Lauren McColl, Rua Macmillan, Eilidh Shaw, Shona Mooney, Mike Vass, Jenna Reid and Paul Anderson. Also fiddle-driven are The Chair from Orkney, even if they feature 'only' two of them.

Since 1996, the Scots Fiddle Festival in Edinburgh has put the focus firmly on the instrument, presenting some of the greatest players, from said Aly Bain to Aladair Fraser and Duncan Chisholm and Ireland's Martin Hayes. But the most heart-warming feature is the Youth Gaitherin for

[47] Alastair Clark, *Aly Bain: Fiddler on the Loose*, Edinburgh: Mainstream, 1993, p.8.

9-18 year olds over the festival weekend – watching dozens and dozens of youngsters emerging with their fiddle cases from tuition classes and workshops, you never again fear for the future of the music.

Scottish dance music, dominated by fiddles and accordions, is popular, both in the country dance format and in the wilder form of the ceilidh. Robbie Shepherd's *Take the Floor* on BBC Radio Scotland features all the great dance bands Scotland has produced, from Sir Jimmy Shand to Tom Orr's Scottish Dance Band. Some of the great contemporary ceilidh bands are The Occasionals, The Robert Fish Band, Alasdair MacCuish & The Black Rose Ceilidh Band, Skipinish, Skelpaig, Sandy Brechin's The Jimi Shandrix Experience and – an even finer name – Gavin Marwick's Ceilidh Minogue.

As Gary West, himself an exquisite piper, points out in his contribution to this volume, John D Burgess's piping performance at he first Edinburgh People's Festival Ceilidh signalled the incorporation of the Highland Pipes into the folk revival. Bands like the Tannahill weavers and the Battlefield Band integrated the Highland Pipes into their sound, as, in their footsteps, did Deaf Shepherd, Breabach and Rura. The Whistlebinkies have championed the use of the small or Border pipes, as has pipe maker Hamish Moore, while Allan Macdonald from Glenuig plays them all - Highland, Lowland and Irish!

Every August, Piping Live! in Glasgow highlights how innovative the piping scene in Scotland has become, with the likes of Fred Morrison, Finlay MacDonald and the late Gordon Duncan. I remember when Tony McManus joined me for a late pint in the Royal Oak, coming directly from the studio where he was producing Gordon's *Thunderstruck* album, marvelling at the inventiveness of his pipe playing.

Alan Stivell and Derek Bell were early champions of he Celtic harp. The Edinburgh International Harp Festival can by now look back on a thirty-year history. All the great clàrsach players, from Alison Kinnaird and Savourna Stevenson, Patsy Seddon and Mary Macmaster to Phamie Gow, Rachel Hair, and Ailie Robertson of The Outside Track, have performed at he festival, which takes place during Easter Week.

Poetry, Folksong and Politics

Throughout Scottish history," wrote Hamish Henderson in the foreword to the programme of the second People's Festival Ceilidh in 1952,

> there has been a constant interplay between the folk tradition and the learned literary tradition – an interplay more constant and more fruitful with us than in the literatures of most other European countries.[48]

---

[48] Quoted in Timothy Neat, *Hamish Henderson: A Biography, Vol.1, The Making of*

In 1965, In McDaid's in Dublin, he jotted in his note book, that "the folk revival in Scotland exists within a particular milieu. It is a unique mixture of poetry, folksong and politics."[49] That was just after his very public flytings with Hugh MacDiarmid about the very relationship between 'high' literature and the folk idiom.

There has always been a strand of politics, satirical comment and protest in the revival, from Burns to the 'Wee Magic Stane', from 'Ding Dong Dollar' to Alistair Hulett's songs for the campaign to save the Glasgow Southside baths. Scottish folk singers were part of the artists' movement that helped the Campaign for a Scottish Parliament to eventually succeed. Thus, Chris Harvie wrote: "It is perhaps apt that the world's first purpose-built poetry library preceded the parliament building at Edinburgh's Holyrood."[50]

I remember a spirited performance by Jim Malcolm on the eve of the 1997 general election of his little ditty 'Vote a Tory Out'; likewise at the Tron Folk Club, run by Elspeth Cowie and Rob Stokes, Davy Steele helped us while away the waiting time for he result of the 1997 devolution referendum. He had written a new song for the occasion:

Scotland Yet

Gie noo a thocht to what we hae in this land o' the leal
The Highland glen, the Doric stream the fertile Lowland field
They seem tae offer different views when looked at from within
Can strangers be the only eyes to see it a' as yin

Chorus

The choice will be upon us soon tae set oor destiny
I'll drink a toast tae Scotland yet whatever yet may be

Oor mither tongue spoke different weys that past tae present ties
Each separate and yet entwined that's where oor real strength lies
For should one strand unwind itself the others tae forsake
Then a' would be forever lost fur a' the strands would break

While we still seek to blame oor woes and pains on someone else
We'll never have the strength tae solve oor problems for ourselves
In truth we fought each other mair learn this from oor past
Then together we can choose fur oorsells at last[51]

the Poet (1919-1953), Edinburgh: Birlinn, 2007, p.307.
[49] Ibid., p.312.
[50] Christopher Harvie, 'Ballads of a Nation', History Today, vol.49, no.9 (1999).
[51] Steele The Show: The Songs of Davy Steele, Greentrax CDTRAX358, 2011.

It is to be welcomed that folk and traditional song has been honoured by the new Parliament – Martyn Bennett's composition, 'Mackay's Memoirs', played by the band of Broughton High School, and Sheena Wellington's rendering of 'A Man's A Man For A' That' at the opening of the Parliament in 1999, Eddie Reader's 'Wild Mountain Side' at the opening ceremony of the new Parliament building in 2004, Brian McNeill's gig at the Festival of Politics, and Karine Polwart's participation in this year's opening celebration have established a fine new tradition. And Dougie MacLean's 'Caledonia' was not just the song used in a beer commercial, it was also picked by the Scottish Government as the theme song of Scotland's Homecoming Festival in 2009.

Back in the early 1970s, John McGrath assembled his Scottish 7:84 theatre company for perhaps the most momentous theatrical event in twentieth-century Scottish drama – *The Cheviot, the Stag and the Black Black Oil* (1973), a musical drama in Gaelic, Scots and English telling the Highland story from the Clearances to the oil boom, making the point in dialogue, poetry and song that the Highland Scots have largely been dispossessed, disinherited and disenfranchised; that they do not own their own land and have precious little genuine say in its use. Hamish Henderson was consulted by McGrath on the play, and he was enthusiastic about it, attesting it "satire and song galore."[52]

Folk singers like Dolina McLellan and Nick Keir were involved in 7:84. Nick was also working with the poet Norman MacCaig. At the Edinburgh International Festival of 1992, the long friendship between MacCaig and Aly Bain resulted in a two-man show at the Traverse Theatre. It was "built on the delightfully simple foundation of a few tunes, some conversation, and poems."[53]

Dr Fred Freeman, a literary scholar, has produced a ream of CDs of literary and musical import, including: *The Complete Songs of Robert Burns* (Linn Records, 1996-2003); *A' Adam's Bairns – a tribute to Hamish Henderson* (Greentrax, 2004); *The Complete Songs of Robert Tannahill* (Brechin-All Records, 2006). And Jock Tamson's Bairns have collaborated with the writer Billy Kay in *Fergusson's Old Reekie*, a show about the 'elder in the muse' of Robert Burns, the Edinburgh poet Robert Fergusson (1750-1774).

Adam McNaughtan is exploring the poetic connections to the folk revival in this volume, so one more example may here suffice. In 2007, *Ballads of the Book* was released,[54] an album of collaborations of Scots

---

[52] Quoted in Timothy Neat, *Hamish Henderson: A Biography, Vol.2, Poetry Becomes People (1952-2002)*, Edinburgh: Birlinn, 2009, p.254

[53] Alastair Clark, *Aly Bain: Fiddler on the Loose*, p.13.

[54] Chemikal Underground Records (CHEM098DD, 2007).

musicians and Scots writers, curated by Roddy Woomble of Idlewild. On the musical side, there were 'old' and 'new folkies' like Mike Heron, Karine Polwart and Emma Pollock – the writers included Alasdair Gray, John Burnside, Edwin Morgan, A L Kennedy, Louise Welsh and Ian Rankin, with cover art by Alasdair Gray, bearing the adapted motto 'Sing as if you live in the early days of a better nation.'

Revival?

So, how can we sum up this conundrum – a folk revival when folk music was not actually dead? In her piece for this collection, Jean Bechhofer suggests that 'survival' may be he more appropriate term.

There was certainly a watershed in the 1950s. The aftermath of the Second World War, which had impacted on even the remotest parts of Europe, the arrival of television – an older way of life was clearly slipping away.

> It was largely the middle classes who enjoyed their Scottish country dances in the privacy of their own parlours. The rest of the nation was either at the pictures, in the pub, or on the couch listening to Henry Hall.[55]

Folk song collecting had been seen primarily as an antiquarian undertaking, while the concept of folk-song got mixed with parlour and music hall. The Alexander Brothers, Moira Anderson and Kenneth McKellar, and Andy Stewart, featured on TV in the BBC's *White Heather Club'* (1958-1968):

> These singers were in a long and vibrant tradition predating music hall, but have tended to suffer critical neglect... They were also somewhat anomalous for post-war folk revivalists searching out the 'pure' tradition and its bearers. Ironically, many 'tradition' bearers often had a good smattering of Harry Lauder and parlour ballads in their repertoires...[56]

That is why Alastair McDonald was welcomed at the Dundee Folk Festival with open arms by the Stewarts of Blair – they knew that there were many traditions in Scottish music.

---

[55] Michael Brocken, *The British Folk Revival, 1944-2002*, Aldershot: Ashgate, 2003, p.18. Henry Hall (1898-1989) was the leader of the BBC Dance Orchestra.
[56] Frank Bruce, *Scottish Showbusiness: Music Hall, Variety and Pantomime*, Edinburgh: National Museums of Scotland, 2000, p.80.

One thing is clear, the manner in which this folk survival unfolded, surprised even its instigator, Hamish Henderson. In 1973, in an interview with the *Melody Maker*, he said:

> I certainly couldn't dream (....) that it would become so vast. I did certainly foresee that something was going to happen. But I don't think honestly that anyone could have foreseen the tremendous, exuberant success of the revival.[57]

He also tried to contextualise the Folk Revival, which he called one of the "most interesting psycho-cultural phenomena of the mid-twentieth century":

> It sprang out of the period of the civil war in Spain in my opinion, and out of World War Two, out of the realization to what terrible extent of horror and inhumanity technological progress could lead. It could lead to Auschwitz on the one hand and to Hiroshima on the other. I think personally that this folk revival is part of this human defence against a gross assault on humanity.[58]

And he asserted that, for him, this particular folk revival started in America:

> There's no coincidence in the fact, it seems to me, that it was in the United States, which was itself growing into this tremendous capitalist society, this bloodstained goliath.... that you got the beginnings of the present folksong revival.[59]

Closer to home, the folk revival helped to break the grip of what he called the "old Kirk":

> The folk revival has been a tremendous catalyst..., releasing new energies, giving place for new feelings and creative imagination and everything. In breaking this terrible, hard coarse mould of the old Kirk thing which lays so heavily on Scotland you can't believe it.[60]

---

[57] Andrew Means, 'Scottish Studies', *Melody Maker*, 17 March 1973.
[58] *Ibid.*
[59] *Ibid.*
[60] *Ibid.*

He reiterates his Gramscian view that "folk music in Scotland right from the time of the Reformation onwards and even before has been a kind of protest movement."[61] With the fading power of the Kirk, that has certainly changed. Protest, the 'underground', the alternative world view, is still an integral part of the folk music scene but, overall, the scene has become more diverse and pluralistic. Whether that has weakened the core is debatable. What seems sure is that the Revival is locked in, has become permanent, a process rather than an event.

The Future

Linda Fabiani, then Minister for Culture, Europe and External Affairs, announced at the Scots Trad Awards in 2008 the setting up of a Ministerial Working Group on the Traditional Arts. That group, convened by David Francis, comprised Fiona Dalgetty, Ruth Kirkpatrick, Mary Ann Kennedy, Mats Melin and Stuart Eydmann. They produced their Report in January 2010, and found that over the past years progress had been made, manifested in many successful projects and schemes, but also that "recognition and respect for the traditional arts, and those working in them, is still patchy." [62] Among the many suggestions the Report makes, there is one that rings with Steve Byrne's progress report in this volume on the efforts to secure Hamish Henderson's papers for the nation:

> [T]aking a cue from the Irish Traditional Music Archive housed in Georgian Dublin, there might be possibilities for some kind of national traditional arts centre or archive finding a home in an iconic Scottish building, the better to encourage a sense of national ownership of the traditions represented.[63]

Anyway, it is encouraging that the Scottish Government commissioned such a Report. And it can only be hoped that its findings will lead to greater esteem and improved support for the traditional arts. As John Barrow points out in his contribution, there are also positive messages from Creative Scotland.

Scottish traditional music is now anchored better than ever in education, from the efforts of the New Makars' Trust to put singers and instrumentalists in schools for workshops to the Plockton High School National Centre for Excellence in Traditional Music – which was threatened with closure in 2010 but seems to have weathered the storm (for the time being, at least) – and the School of Scottish Studies and the Scottish Music

---

[61] *ibid.*
[62] www.scotland.gov.uk/Publications/2010/01/28100441/0
[63] *Ibid.*

degree course at the Royal Conservatoire. The *fèisean* movement is going from strength to strength, and even the Mod seems to enjoy rude health, reporting improvement in the quality of the Gaelic performances,[64] perhaps due to benefits brought by the Scottish parliament's 2005 Gaelic Act. The Scots Music Group, set up by the Adult Learning Project (ALP) in Edinburgh, has become an internationally renowned community project, with workshops in singing and instrument playing.[65]

The Scots Trad Awards, masterminded by Simon Thoumire and his team and handed out in a glitzy ceremony in December (broadcast on BBC Alba), have doubtlessly raised the public awareness of folk and traditional music in Scotland, as do BBC Scotland's Young Traditional Musician of the Year competition and, to a more limited degree, the BBC Radio 2 Folk Awards.

Greentrax Records have just celebrated their twenty-fifth anniversary,[66] and there are a number of other, smaller labels serving folk music in Scotland, from Robin Morton's Temple Records to Pete Shepheard's Springthyme and Pete Heywood's Tradition Bearers Records, as well as Footstompin' Records and, for Gaelic music, Arthur Cormack's Macmeanmna label. Unfortunately, the small magazines have all but vanished, but *The Living Tradition* has survived, and we have, of course, the nigh unlimited resourcefulness of the internet at our fingertips, with forums like Footstompin' or Mudcat Café.[67]

Folkies – musicians, fans and organisers – will always be disappointed that the media do not take enough notice of them. What – our gig is yet again not listed on the events pages? Again, no review in the papers? And where is folk music on radio and telly? Well, there are programmes like *Travelling Folk*, there are stations like Celtic Music Radio, and since BBC Alba has become available on Freeview, the amount of traditional music offered on TV has increased significantly. And, in terms of our press, Rob Adams for *The Herald*, and Sue Wilson and Jim Gilchrist for *The Scotsman*, as well as Norman Chalmers for *The List*, and others, do their best to cover the traditional music scene in Scotland at a difficult time for newspapers.

The session scene is thriving, the festival circuit ever widening, and there is plenty of new talent. Undoubtedly, the instrumental side of the music is flourishing. Every now and then, though, somebody anxiously asks: where are the young singers? Well, how about these, for a start:

---

[64] Neil MacPhail, 'Stornoway Mod is blow-away success', *The Press and Journal*, 22 October 2011.

[65] See Gerri Kirkwood and Colin Kirkwood, *Living Adult Education: Freire in Scotland*, Rotterdam:Sense Publishers, second edition, 2011.

[66] The Greentrax story is told by founder Ian Green in his autobiography, *Fuzz to Folk: Trax of My Life*, Edinburgh: Luath Press, 2011.

[67] www.footstompin.com/public/forum/; www.mudcat.org/

Karine Polwart, Steve Byrne, Mark Dunlop, Fiona Hunter, Emily Smith, Julie Fowlis, Lucy Pringle, Chris Wright, Scott Gardiner, Ewan Henderson, Darcy Da Silva, Alistair Ogilvy, Ewan McLennan, Kris Drever, Siobhan Miller, Ewan Wilkinson, James Graham, Wendy Arrowsmith, Eilidh Grant, Maeve McKinnon, David Ferrard, Kim Edgar, Heidi Talbot, Caroline Scott, Stevie Palmer, Wendy Taylor, Chloe Matharu.... On top of that, young bands are constantly emerging – Corran Raa, Whirlypit, Lurach, Tattie Jam, Rura, Horizontal Sunday...

Yes, folk clubs have seen ups and downs in their fortunes. And the present economic climate is not conducive to healthy turnouts, especially for weekly clubs. Also, the very vibrant session scene means, particularly for urban clubs, lots of free competition. Still run by volunteers, the club scene has seen a degree of professionalisation over the years. Clubs had to invest in state of the art sound equipment. Gone are the days when the proceedings would be dominated by floor singers (except for clubs that have only occasional guests and otherwise meet as an informal singaround). What would have been anathema to the purists of he 1960s has happened – folk clubs do present concerts, albeit that they still have a chance of doing that in a more convivial, club-like atmosphere than that of a concert hall. And, of course, there's always the raffle....

Even the People's Festival itself has seen a revival – thanks to the commendable efforts of Colin Fox and his team, it made a comeback in 2002, offering an alternative to the established August fare.

There are concerns, about the levelling intrusion of 'celtic' and world music, of too much emphasis on technique, perhaps neglecting context and soul, too much 'folk celebrity'. But, on the whole, I think we can agree with Hamish Henderson's optimistic outlook, which he expressed at a conference a decade after the first Edinburgh People's Festival Ceilidh:

> ... the manifest vitality of Scots folk-song emboldens me to say with confidence that we will survive the boom – and the doom – and come through singing on the other side. I know that it would be over-sanguine for me to expect every folklorist and musicologist present to take the same optimistic view, but I can assure you that many young Scots folk-singers of today, who have respect for their art, and have taken the trouble to learn something about it, do share this view with ardent enthusiasm. And that, I submit, is what will count in the long run.[68]

If that was true in 1963, it surely rings true nearly half a century later.

[68] Hamish Henderson, talk given to the 125th meeting of the British Association of the Advancement of Science, Aberdeen, 1963, first published in *Folklore*, Vol.75, Spring 1964, reprinted in *Alias MacAlias*, p.43.

Reflecting on the first Edinburgh People's Festival Ceilidh, Hamish wrote:

> Later that night – or was it that morning – Jimmy MacBeath
> stopped in York Place, shook himself loose from the friends who
> were supporting him home, and lifting his mottled face to the
> moon, sang *The Bleacher Lassie o' Kelvinhaugh*.
> All over Auld Reekie the ceilidh was continuing. In a sense, it is
> continuing still.[69]

Indeed, it is. So, here's to sixty years of the Scottish Folk Revival – a bit like devolution, not an event, important as the People's Festival Ceilidhs were, but a process, constantly renewing and reinventing itself – or, in the term coined by Hamish Henderson, Scotland's carrying stream.[70]

---

[69] Hamish Henderson, *Alias MacAlias*, p.9.
[70] I am grateful to Moira Burns who has given me a bundle of copies of folk publications from her late husband Alex Burns's collection, including *Folk Scene*, *Folk's On*, *Chapbook*, *Club Folk*, *Folk News*, and cuttings from the *Melody* Maker, covering the 1960s, '70s and '80s.

The People's Festival

The Edinburgh People's Festival, 1951-1954

Hamish Henderson[1]

When the political decision was made in 1946, under Clem Attlee's government, to inaugurate an International Festival of the Arts in an attempt to counterbalance the effects of world war weariness, the likeliest venue seemed to be not Edinburgh, but Bath. Indeed, the latter appears to have been that most favoured by the Festival's guiding spirit, Rudolf Bing. The rival claims of these two handsome cities were by no means based on their respective cultural qualifications or backgrounds; the context was purely a matter of the number of undamaged buildings which would be at the hands of the organisers. It was a close run thing, but Edinburgh came out on top.

There was a club on the go in Princes Street at the time, International House, which had been founded during the war by the British Council to cater for the off duty needs of officers of the Polish Forces, and the 'arty' sections of the Edinbourgeoisie were encouraged to join it. After the war it widened its appeal somewhat, and for practical reasons – I used it for years as a *poste restante*, when I was 'in the field' collecting songs and stories up north – I eventually applied for membership myself. Not long after the end of the war, while I was still 'sounding the joint out', I overheard a priceless conversation between H Harvey Wood, who was an official of the British council, and an ex-army colonel who had been co-opted to join the organisation. They were discussing the opportunities that this new projected International

[1] This chapter was first published in Andy Croft (ed.), *A Weapon in the Struggle: The Cultural History of the Communist Party in Britain*, London: Pluto Press, 1998, pp.163-70; it is here reproduced with the kind permission of Pluto Press (www. plutobooks.com).

Festival of the Arts offered the local branch of the British Council and they were talking entirely in terms of which celebrated foreign orchestras, opera companies, ballet light-footers and suchlike they might be able to attract to Auld Reekie. Right enough, it was to be an *International* Festival but the idea that the host nation, Scotland, might be considered as one of the participant nations seemed not to enter into it.

Inevitably, news of this and similar discussions reached the ears of the great Hugh McDiarmid, Scotland's leading poet, and one of the outstanding poets writing in Europe at that time. His reaction was not difficult to forecast. He regarded the entire International Festival project as a sort of English / cosmopolitan plot to subvert our native Scottish culture and thus to put paid to the Scottish Renaissance in literature which he had inaugurated – almost single-handedly – way back in the 1920s. In 1949 he wrote a virulent article for an Edinburgh-based magazine called *The Galliard*, the implicit tenor of which was that all nationally committed Scottish poets and cultural figures should unite to oppose the International Festival and try to ensure its eventual failure.

This appeared to me and to several other left-wing individuals an entirely self-defeating attitude. The Communist Party had welcomed the festival, which had been covered in the *Daily Worker* since 1947 (when Sir Hugh Robertson, conductor of the Glasgow Orpheus choir, had reported on the first festival for the paper.)

And, for all its faults, the Festival did bring to Edinburgh, in its first five years, a great many films from the Soviet Union and the 'new democracies'. The Party's support was not unqualified, however. The announcement, during the second Edinburgh Festival, that the Arts Council of Great Britain was to withdraw funding from Glasgow Unity Theatre, confirmed our feelings of a widening gap between what the festival was and what it could have been. So long as the festival relied on 'big names' (mainly non-Scots) it isolated itself (by high admission prices) from the Scottish people and therefore from new cultural developments in Scotland. The Communist Party was greatly interested at the time in helping to develop a national cultural identity for Scotland. I was asked to review books by and about Scottish writers (Sorley McLean, Burns, McDiarmid, Boswell, Stevenson) for the *Daily Worker*, which also gave generous space to a number of literary controversies among Scottish readers at this time (notably regarding Burns, Lallans and Gaelic).[2]

Shortly before Christmas 1950, a meeting was convened by Martin Milligan, a Communist Party member and a man of great brilliance. He had just returned a short time before from Oxford, where he had studied

---

[2] The correspondence columns of the *Daily Worker* were once filled for several weeks with letters taking sides for and against an article of mine on the poet Sorley MacLean (30 March, 4 April, 12 April, 17 April, 18 April 1950).

philosophy, although his philosophy was hardly the establishment kind. The meeting took place at the Scottish Miners' HQ in Rothesay Place, Edinburgh.[3] The central idea behind the discussion was that, far from opposing the 'big' festival, the left should welcome its existence, take advantage of the presence of so many five-star foreign actors, singers, etc. on Scottish soil, and try to present an Edinburgh People's Festival which would complement its senior brother, and in some select zones of cultural enterprise, actually outdo it. And this in fact is what actually happened.

The Edinburgh Labour Festival committee soon comprised 40 people, representing 17 trade union branches, five Labour Party organisations, the WMA, the Musicians' Union, the local Labour League of Youth and the Edinburgh Trades Council. There were various poets, artists and story writers belonging to the Cultural committee of the Scottish District of the Communist Party – Norman and Janey Buchan, Hugh Paterson, Simon and Ella Ward, Bill Maclellan; several left-inclined Labour Party members (and indeed one or two who turned out to be right-wingers) and last, but not least, one or two non- attached cultural figures such as John MacDonald, a Highland psychologist who originally hailed from Sutherlandshire and who spoke up vigorously for a Gaelic component in any future People's Festival. He it was who, in the event, with his wife, did a great deal of donkey work of organisation when the People's Festival got going. The organiser was Martin Milligan. Under the slogan 'By Working People for Working People' we wanted to show the International Festival what it still could be.

> To initiate action designed to bring the Edinburgh International Festival closer to the people as a whole and to make it serve more fully the cause of international understanding and good will; and also to initiate action such as will more generally make what is best in the cultural life of our country more accessible to working people, and will secure fuller facilities for the development of the cultural activities of working people.[4]

Attracting people who felt excluded by the International Festival, keeping the admission prices low and including children – it was Gramsci in action! One of the things that attracted me to Gramsci was his great interest in popular culture. He was a Sardinian, and the Sardinian folk song is rich

---

[3] For other accounts of the People's Festival, see Antaire MacAnair, 'Democracy, Intellect and the Muse', *Cencrastus*, no.57, Summer 1997; Hamish Henderson, 'Folk Champions', *The Carrying Stream*, vol.1, no.2, 1991; and Hamish Henderson, *AliasMacAlias: Writings on Songs, Folk and Literature*, Edinburgh: Polygon, 1992.
[4] *People's Festival Week*, 1951, programme, p.12.

and bountiful and vigorous to the nth degree. When he was in prison, he wrote to his mother and sisters asking for details about their folk festivals. Gramsci in action *was* the People's Festival.

The committee set its sights high. The festival ran for a full week, from 26 August to 1 September 1951. Glasgow Unity Theatre performed Joe Corrie's *In Time of Strife*, and there was a Theatre Workshop production of Ewan MacColl's brilliant historical gallimaufry, *Uranium 235*, which, when first produced in London, had been accorded great praise by both Bernard Shaw and Sean O'Casey. There were performances by Barrhead Co-Op Junior Choir, the Tranent Fa'side Players (winners that year of the NCB drama festival), the Lesmahagow Male Voice Choir, and a production by the Ferranti Drama Group of Ena Lamont Stewart's *Starched Aprons*. There were 'film-strip lectures', coffee-time lectures and tea-time lectures (given by Ralph Bond, Tom Driberg, Ewan MacColl, Helen Cruickshank, Hugh MacDiarmid and myself, among others) designed to show how all forms of cultural activity, at their best, depend on ordinary working people, and also how much the happiness of the people as a whole depends on the condition of science and the arts.[5] There was a festival club and a day conference, 'Towards a People's Culture', attended by over 170 people.

Abe Moffat, Secretary of the Scottish Area NUM, spoke on the last night, an evening's entertainment of drama, song and poetry by Scottish miners and their friends.

One of the committee members was very insistent that the festival should not only provide a platform for 'Hamish folksy finds'. However, as things turned out, it was the Oddfellows' Hall Ceilidh, drawing on native Gaelic and Lowland Scots folk singers, which drew the most appreciative comments from the press. One critic even asserted that the most interesting musical experiences of the entire festival period were not to be found on the 'high heid-yin' (or official) side of the event but on the non-official side. The singing began at 7.30pm and finished, rather hilariously, about two o'clock in the morning. It was an event of incalculable importance, because from it sprang a hundred other fruitful cultural enterprises in subsequent years. Instead of 'Muckin' the Byre' in white tie and tails and Kelvinside accents, there was the glorious singing of Flora MacNeil and Calum Johnston from the Isle of Barra, John Strachan singing the classic ballads 'Clyde's Water' and 'Johnnie of Breadislee', the artistry of Jessie Murray, a Buckie fish-wife whose incomparable 'Skippin Barfut Throw the Heather' enjoyed its city debut at the same 1951 Ceilidh. Over from Glasgow to witness the event was the Communist Party cultural stalwart Norman Buchan, who was overwhelmed by the Ceilidh. He said he had never heard anything like it, and afterwards admitted that his folk

---

[5] *Ibid.*, p.10.

song enthusiasms and his resolve to propagate authentic singing styles among West Country children dated from that moment. In the festival programme I wrote:

> In Scotland, both north and south of the Highland line, there is still an incomparable treasure of folk song and folk music. Very little is known to the ordinary Scottish public, and even less to the world public which is patron to the Edinburgh International Festival. What is known is often irredeemably spoilt by normal 'concert-hall' technique and arrangements.
>
> The main purpose of this Ceilidh will be to present Scottish folk song as it should be sung. The singers will all without exception be men and women who have learnt these splendid songs by word of mouth in their own childhood, and who give them in the traditional manner. This fact alone will make the *People's Festival Ceilidh an absolutely unique thing in the cultural history of Edinburgh.*[6]

To explain the background of this truly fabulous event, we must go back six months, to February 1951, when I received the following letter from Ewan MacColl, the brilliant singer/playwright and Communist Party activist, who was the intrepid 'battle-post' of Joan Littlewood's Theatre Workshop. 'Dear Hamish' he wrote,

> Just a brief note – there is a character wandering around this sceptered isle at the moment yclept Alan Lomax. He is Texan and none the worse for that. He is also just about the most important name in American folk song circles. He is over here with a super recording unit and a girl, Robin Roberts, who sings like an angel. Columbia Gramophone Co are financing his trip. The idea is that he will record the folk singers of a group of countries (he has already covered Africa – America – the West Indies – the Central European countries). And Columbia will produce an album of discs – an hour for each country. He is not interested in trained singers of refined versions of the folk songs. He wants to record traditional style singers doing ballads, work songs, political satires, etc. It occurred to me that you could help him in two ways.
>
> 1.   Record some your soldier songs and add any other songs you know. You sang some to me in the little café opposite the Epworth Hall.

---

[6] *Ibid.*, p.8; see the coverage of the first People's Festival in the *Daily Worker*, 22 and 31 August, 10 September 1951.

2.   Introduce him to other Scots folk singers. You know the kind of thing he wants: bothy songs, street songs, soldier songs, mouth music, the big Gaelic stuff, weavers' and miners' songs, etc.

This is important, Hamish. It is vital that Scotland is well represented in this collection. It would be fatal if the 'folksy' boys were to cash in. If you can help, write to him – Alan Lomax c/o BBC, London. He intends coming to Scotland in about a week's time.

Do try and help.
Yours aye, Ewan.

P.S. If and when you meet him, get him to sing some of his American coal miners' songs. They are terrific.[7]

I dropped a note to Alan – a member of the US Communist Party – and in the summer of 1951 spent two or three months with him collecting folk songs, especially in the Scottish North-East (Aberdeenshire, Moray, etc.), and most of the singers we found expressed readiness to make the journey to Edinburgh, to appear at the Ceilidh I was already planning. It will be seen, therefore, that the powerful stimulus behind the whole People's Festival enterprise was that splendid character Ewan MacColl. Although born in Salford, Ewan – real name Jimmy Miller – was the son of two formidable working-class Scots. His father was an iron-moulder from Falkirk, his mother from Auchterarder, and (a fact I can vouch for) a really bonny singer. Ewan knew all about German agitprop troupes and had formed the Red Megaphones in Salford ('A Propertyless Theatre for a Propertyless Class') named after a German communist troupe from Red Wedding. So the People's Festival could claim a distinguished ancestry – both Gramsci, and the KPD's *Das Rote Sprachrohr!*

Encouraged by the success of the first People's Festival, the committee immediately began to plan for the 1952 event. This time it ran for three weeks, from 17 August to 7 September, under the banner 'That the People's Voice May Be Heard and the Needs of the People Met'. The committee appealed in the *Daily Worker* for new songs, poems and plays, and the festival included a 'People's Art Exhibition', including a 'People Like Us' photography exhibition. There were poetry readings by Sydney Goodsir Smith, Alexander Trocchi, Norman McCaig and Sorley MacLean; a series of lectures (including James Gibb on Beethoven, Desmond Greaves on James Connolly, myself on Scottish folk song, Ewan MacColl on MacDiarmid, and MacDiarmid himself on David Lindsay and on the 'Radical

---

[7] Ewan MacColl to the author, 16 February 1951; see Hamish Henderson, *The Armstrong Nose*, Edinburgh: Polygon, 1992, pp.46-47.

Tradition in Scottish culture'). We had an ambitious programme of foreign films, including the award-winning Italian neorealistic masterpiece *Bicycle Thieves*, the Russian classic *That Others May Live*, and the first full-length film from the new China, *Daughters of China*. There was also a People's Festival Ball; a series of Beethoven Concerts; and three plays, *Flatter No Flesh* by the People's Festival Players. *Out of Bondage* by Lanark CLP and a new Theatre Workshop production, Ewan MacColl's *The Travellers*. The festival concluded with a day conference on 'Our Cultural Traditions and Their Advancement Today', and among the speakers were Hugh MacDiarmid, Ewan MacColl, Naomi Mitchison and several Labour MPs.[8]

There was now no question but that the Ceilidh had to be one of the central features of the festival. By this time Hugh MacDiarmid had generously acknowledged the wisdom of our approach to the festival questions and had accepted the post of People's Festival Chairman. Furthermore, as 1952 was also the year of his sixtieth birthday, we resolved to dedicate that year's Ceilidh to him. In the event, this second Ceilidh was an even more resounding success than the first one. The aim was again " to present the finest flower of our folk song tradition", but this time the emphasis was "upon young singers who are carrying on the splendid tradition in its integrity". "We are convinced," I wrote in the programme, "that it is possible to restore Scottish folksong to the ordinary people in Scotland, not merely as a bobby-soxer vogue, but deeply and integrally."[9] The veteran Barra singer Calum Johnston again sang splendid Gaelic songs and played the pipes; the famous Lewis sisters Kitty and Marietta MacLeod enthralled the audience with 'Cairistiona' and 'Agus Ho Mhorag; an excellent bothy ballad singer from the North East called Frank Steele sang 'Come All Ye Lonely Lovers'; the young Arthur Argo, great grandson of the famous Aberdeenshire folk song collector Gavin Greig, sang 'The Souter's Feast' in a boyish treble; 18 year old Blanche Wood sang songs she had learned from her aunt Jessie Murray; and Jimmy MacBeath gave of his best with 'Come All Ye Tramps and Hawkers' and 'The Moss o' Burreldale'. Hugh MacDiarmid, in whose honour they were performing, had been invited to sit on the platform, and at the beginning the entire audience rose while Calum Johnston played 'Blue Bonnets over the Border' as a tribute to Scotland's greatest living poet and most celebrated Borderer. MacDiarmid was obviously deeply moved and at the end of the Ceilidh he rose to propose a vote of thanks to the performers.

> As you all know, my personal vanity has always been notorious –
> but it is quite unequal to the present occasion. I've been absolutely

[8] See the coverage of the second festival in the *Daily Worker*, 27 August, 1, 5, 6 September 1952.
[9] *Edinburgh People's Festival 1952*, programme, p.13.

overwhelmed by the honour that has been done me and by the honour that the various artists, and this magnificent audience, have done to themselves, and to Scotland, in doing it.

It would be wrong of me, even in proposing a vote of thanks, if I didn't point out that our tremendous treasury of folk song in Scotland, whether in lowland Scots or in Gaelic, is a treasury that has been occluded, very largely for political reasons, from the knowledge of the majority of our people. This Edinburgh People's Festival, and the movement in which my friends on the platform and others in the audience are concerned, is a re-assertion of that tradition, against the tide of all the things ... all the cultural enemies that are besetting us at the present time.

One thing must have struck you, I think, in the programme tonight – that is, the extent to which all the items on the programme have been correlated to the lives of the common people, to the work of common people, the daily darg of the common people.

We are not going to be taken from that – we're not going to be persuaded by the advocates of snob art, that some mystical palaver is better than that which comes from the working life of our own people. [10]

Unluckily, Ewan MacColl's The Travellers played straight into the hands of the right-wing minority on the committee – two vociferous ladies who almost from the start had claimed to identify Communist Party propaganda in even the most innocuous events. Drawing on Theatre Workshop's travels in the New Democracies, The Travellers was the subject of an emergency committee meeting called at the insistence of the same ladies in October 1952. [11] The result was that in December 1952 the Scottish TUC placed the festival on its long list of proscribed organisations and withdrew its support for future festivals. Two weeks later the Scottish Labour Party declared that association with the festival was incompatible with membership of the Labour Party (despite the fact that the chair of the festival committee, councillor Jack Kane, was also chair of the Labour Party in Edinburgh). [12]

Thus the two main financial props of the enterprise were knocked from under us at a blow. This was in spite of – or possible because of – the staunch outspoken support of Hugh MacDiarmid, who was later to rejoin the Communist Party in the wake of the Soviet invasion of Hungary. In 1950 I had been expelled, probably under US pressure, from Italy, where as a guest of the PCI, I had been lecturing on folk song traditions; apparently

---

[10] Cencrastus, no.48, Summer 1994, p.9.
[11] See Joan Littlewood, Joans Book, London: Methuen, 1994.
[12] The ban was reported in the Daily Worker, 1 December and 17 December 1952.

folk song was now deemed a subversive activity even in Scotland. Despite this disabling setback, the committee prepared to plan for a People's Festival in 1953, holding meetings at factory gates and building sites to raise support, interest and money. Organised by Norman Buchan and myself, the third festival was inevitably a much smaller event. Hitherto the *Daily Worker* had maintained an even-handed approach to the 'two festivals'. Now it only mentioned the International Festival (which it pointed out was 'neither international nor Scottish') to pour scorn on the way 'Edinburgh breaks into tartan' once a year to the 'rustle of crisp dollar notes'.[13] Theatre Workshop returned with two new plays, adaptations of *Lysistrata* and Molière's *Le Malade Imaginaire*; the Glasgow YCL Choir sang and Ewan McColl gave a memorable three hour performance of unaccompanied folk song. The 1953 Scots-Irish Ceilidh was in many ways the most memorable of all, principally because it was the one which introduced the recently discovered Jeannie Robertson (universally acknowledged now as the greatest Scottish ballad singer of the twentieth century) to a wider public. It also featured the renowned Tennessee diva Jean Ritchie, singing her own people's version of 'Guide Me O Thou Great Jehovah', a truly glorious, spine-tingling rendering.

The People's Festival limped on into 1954, supported largely by contributions from personal well-wishers, but later that year was forced to acknowledge defeat. However, the spirit of the festival continued in the Scottish Folk revival which it had helped to start. And the far-off repercussions of those early proposals from the cultural committee of the Communist Party can still be felt in the Fringe today.

---

[13] For coverage of the third festival in the *Daily Worker*, see 17, 21 and 29 August, 1 and 4 September 1953.

'Dunking their Heels in the Corn and Custard' : About Alan Lomax in Scotland

Ewan McVicar

It is hard to explain to people who were not around then how important the American Alan Lomax was to the Folk Revival in Britain. In Ewan MacColl's autobiography, *Journeyman*, he titles a chapter 'Enter Alan Lomax'. In it he says,

> Lomax is a folklorist, collector, cultural anthropologist and innovator and explorer of virtually unknown territories and a seminal force in the realm of ideas.[1]

In an essay on 'Recording in Ireland with Alan Lomax' in 1951, Robin Roberts says,

> Later, there were those who complained that Alan had roared through Ireland like Attila the Hun ... had not spent enough time with the people to understand them properly and he did not speak Irish. ... Now, of course, the collection is cherished in Ireland. He could not have foreseen that he started something that would blossom into a revival of the music...[2]

The collection referred to is *Ireland, World Library of Folk and Primitive Music – Volume II*, issued on Columbia, and recently reissued on Rounder Records, as part of a wildly ambitious and exciting project, not just to reissue the old classic and massively influential records that Alan Lomax compiled and edited, but also to get out on CD as much as can be issued of his field recordings. The modest eventual target was over 150 CDs.

---

[1] Ewan McColl, Journeyman, Manchester University Press, (new ed.), 2009, p.261.
[2] Robin Roberts, booklet for Rounder Records CD 1742 'World Library of Folk and Primitive Music: Ireland'.

Lomax – MacColl – Henderson

Alan Lomax started young, working with his father John Lomax, then with others. With a fascinating scholar called Mary Elizabeth Barnicle, in 1935, he recorded in the Bahamas. A favourite of mine, out of many now issued on Rounder, is a CD called *Deep River Of Song Bahamas 1935*, beautiful chanteys (that is how they spell it) and anthems from Cat Island and Andros Island (the home of king-of-them-all guitarist Joseph Spence who was then, I suppose, too young to record for Lomax). The album includes an electrifyingly different version of the anthem made internationally famous by the Incredible String Band, 'I Bid You Goodnight'.

Volume I of the *World Library of Folk and Primitive Music* was England, and Volume III was Scotland. Alan Lomax had come to Scotland in June 1951. He had already met and collected songs from singer, songwriter, actor and playwright Ewan MacColl. He and director Joan Littlewood were the "leading figures" of Theatre Workshop. MacColl had in turn met Hamish Henderson through Theatre Workshop's visits to Edinburgh. MacColl alerted Henderson:

> There is a character wandering around this sceptred isle at the moment yclept Alan Lomax. He is a Texan and none the worse for that, he is also just about the most important name in American folksong circles. [3]

MacColl asked Henderson to help with singers and songs, warning that "it would be fatal if the 'folksy' boys were to cash in." Lomax and MacColl were co-operating in various ways. Indeed, they planned to write together a "ballad opera based on the folk music of Britain," to be set "on Kendal Moor, near Manchester, during the Industrial Revolution."[4]

The astonishing harvest that Lomax garnered in Highland and Lowland Scotland in 1951 is still being distilled and bottled. He donated copies of the 25 hours of recordings to the University of Edinburgh, to become the cornerstone of the sound archives of the School of Scottish Studies. Henderson was his guide for much of the trip, and in 1951 Lomax wrote expressing appreciation:

> I've been travelling the roads of the world, hitting the high places and low places, the rough and the smooth, for about twenty years, recording folksongs and ballads from all sorts of people, but I have never had such kind and warm-hearted treatment from anywhere

---

[3] This and other 1951 letters quoted from are in Hamish Henderson, *The Armstrong Nose: Selected Letters of Hamish Henderson* (edited by Alec Finlay), Edinburgh: Polygon, 1992.

[4] *Scotsman* article, August 1951.

as from the people of Scotland... It makes all kinds of difference when you're a long way from home, to be treated like you were a member of the family.

Lomax recalled in a 1994 Radio Scotland McGregor's Folk programme, "It was a fantastic experience, because instead of going along the road and talking about ballad theory, I went along the road and he sang every inch of the way." Henderson's comment was more barbed. "Lomax's tape recorder was called a Magnecorder, and it was a colossal uncouth beast of a thing. It came in two huge halves. I found myself not really so much a guide as a coolie for him."

In 1951,   Alan Lomax cut an astonishing swathe through traditional song and music areas of Scotland, from Barra to Aberdeen and from Portsoy to Edinburgh. The wonders and wealth of song he found and preserved for us are still being mined today. The singers he recorded in 1951 included John Strachan of Fyvie, Flora McNeil and Calum Johnston of Barra, Jimmie MacBeath of Portsoy, Jessie Murray of Portknockie and many other fine singers from the Western Isles and the North-East. He recorded pipers PM Willie Ross and PM John Burgess, and accordionist Jimmy Shand.

One blazing highlight of 1951 was the first Edinburgh People's Festival Ceilidh, organised by Hamish Henderson and featuring Flora MacNeil, Jimmie MacBeath and John Strachan. Lomax was there to record it.

Later in the 1950s, Lomax recorded not only songs but their life stories and some traditional tales from three of his best-known informants – Jeannie Robertson, Jimmy MacBeath and Davy Stewart.

Calum MacLean was Lomax's guide in the Highlands and Hebrides, and Hamish Henderson took him through the North-East. The introduction to Volume III says that Lomax "had originally intended to give Scotland a modest corner on the album entitled *English Folk Songs*." Hamish and Calum put him right. The range of the 43 Scottish tracks is astonishing – the Selkirk Town Band and citizens, Ewan MacColl, Flora MacNeil, pipes and waulking and milking and buttermaking songs.

Collecting in North-East Scotland

Alan Lomax's recordings of Scots song (as distinct from Gaelic song) are dominated by singers from North East Scotland, an area of mostly low lying fine farming land that has the grey granite city of Aberdeen at its heart, the rich North Sea before it, and the rocky almost peopleless Highland Massif at its back.

The land is rich in song. The pre-eminent authority on ballads, Francis J Child (1825-1896) of Harvard, selected many Aberdeenshire versions as his 'A texts'. Gavin Greig (1856-1914), the pioneering North East collector and commentator, worked with Rev James D Duncan (1848-1917) to amass from singers and informants an astonishing 3,500 texts and 3,300 tunes of "the older popular minstrelsy of the district". These include not only thrilling and highly informative multiple versions of 'Child Ballads', as identified and codified by F J Child, but songs of farm work, of sea and army life, love and longing and much else.

The songs of farm labour, the 'bothy ballads', are a distinctive creation of the North East. There are two types, those written by farm workers and telling in detail of the work and the character of the farmer, and the broader theatrical humour of the music hall style compositions of professional entertainers. The emphasis is more on text, and slight variations on the same tunes appear repeatedly, but the North East tunes have vitality and sweetness too.

Alan Lomax recorded many songs and stories from well known singers – Jeannie Robertson, Davie Stewart, Jimmy MacBeath and John Strachan. But he also recorded other less-documented singers in The North-East. Here is just a partial list:

* John Mearns and his wife singing duets and solos
* Willie Matheson singing only one verse of each of 23 songs
* Young Blanche Wood singing Portnockie songs
* Bob Cooney with 'The Wee Toon Clerk' and 'The Road To Dundee'
* 'Lordie' Hay gives 'The Bonny Lass o Fyvie', 'Jock Hawk's Adventures in Glasgow', and 'The Tarves Rant'
* James Wiseman [of Portnockie?] gives a fine Codlins song
* Archie Lennox, grandfather of singer Annie Lennox, gives 'Come Up And See Ma Garret' and 'I Have Never Ever Blacklegged In My Life'
* John Mearns' son Jack and a group of Aberdeen school pals sing street and play songs and game lyrics
* George Chalmers sings 'I'm A Handsome Young Widow'
* Dave Dowman sings 'Auld Maid In A Garrett'
* Bill Finney sings 'Drumdelgie'

The North-East Singers

When Alan Lomax visited Cedar Place, a mile north of Aberdeen city centre, to record the well-known sweet-voiced bothy ballad singers John Mearns and his wife, Alice, he also recorded their son Jackie Mearns (age 10 at the time) and a group of his young friends who lived and played together in the street – Pat and Jennifer Cushnie; Jim and Willie Hunter; Jack and Kathleen Mearns; Norma and Tom Watt; and Arthur, Christopher, and Gwen Ronald, who "lived round the corner." Jack Mearns has vivid memories of the day:

> Alan was unaccompanied on his visit to my parents' flat in Cedar Place, a quiet cul-de-sac in Aberdeen. The children were recorded in the street outside my home and my parents were recorded within our home. . . . When Alan was trying to record us singing and skipping, someone always tripped on the rope. Alan then arranged for two children to 'Caw the Ropey' [turn the rope] while the remainder sang. . . . I saw that he had a guitar in his campervan. After all the recording was over, and in response to my constant pleading, my father eventually asked Alan if he would be willing to play for us. Alan immediately agreed and retrieved his guitar. He sat down on the piano stool and started singing an up-tempo American country song. While he was singing he stamped loudly on the floor with his foot. My brother and I were mortified because, as we stayed in an upstairs flat, we were never allowed to make a noise with our feet. My father always reminded us that "It was Mrs Brown's roof." Our horror quickly changed to sheer delight to see that Alan was being allowed to do what we children were forbidden to do.

Jimmy MacBeath

Jimmy MacBeath was born in a thatched cottage on Church Street in the fishing village of Portsoy on the Banffshire coast, on August 30, 1894. He died in January 1972 in Tor-na-dee Hospital, Aberdeen, and was buried in Portsoy. For most of his life Jimmy footslogged the roads of Scotland and beyond, earning pennies from street singing and shillings from casual labour, living in 'model' public lodging houses.

> Jimmy was much affected by the reception he got [at the 1951 Ceilidh], and at the end of the show he informed the audience that this was his 'swan-song', the culmination and the conclusion of his singing career: for reasons of ill-health and age he would never be able to sing at a similar function again. (He was to visit Edinburgh and sing at my ceilidhs for close on another twenty years.)[5]

In the 1960s, Jimmy began to be recorded commercially and to sing in folk clubs and festivals. Alan Lomax described Jimmy as "a quick-footed, sporty little character, with the gravel voice and the urbane assurance

[5] Hamish Henderson, 'Jimmy MacBeath', in *Alias MacAlias: Writings on Songs, Folk and Literature* (edited by Alec Finlay), Edinburgh: Polygon, 1992, p.165.

that would make him right at home on Skid Row anywhere in the world." In November 1953, Lomax recorded several hours of Jimmy singing and talking. Much of this has been issued on the albums *Jimmy MacBeath: Tramps & Hawkers* [Rounder CD 1834] and *Two Gentlemen Of The Road* [Rounder CD 1793] – with Davie Stewart.

A newspaper article about Jimmy suggests he left home as a young man because he was unable to live with his mother's strict house rules and her house-proud attitude, which saw Jimmy having to take off his shoes every time he went into the house. Listen, however, to how his voice softens when he talks of his mother's singing (disc 2, track 2). Peter A Hall has written:

> He began work at the age of 13 at a farm a few miles inland at Deskford. For his six months feeing he got £4, payable at the end of the six months. He started to learn the store of bothy ballads that were to become his trademark. At school he [had] put by snippets of playground lore and at home listened to his mother singing old ballads like 'Lord Randal' and broadside pieces like 'The Butcher Boy'.[6]

Jimmy left farm employment and began a life of casual employment and wandering. His use of time periods and place names in the varying accounts of his travels that he gave to Alan Lomax and others is often inconsistent, but his first long walk from Inverness to Perth (as detailed on disc 3, track 5) seems to have happened in about 1908. In the First World War, Jimmy served in the Flanders trenches with the Gordon Highlanders and later in Ireland with the Royal Army Medical Corps. Then he returned to the road. In turn he was dishwasher, fruit picker, kitchen porter; but in addition he had his songs. Developed first in the bothies and later under the tutelage of old timers like Aul Jock o Blyth and Geordie Stewart of Huntly, Jimmy's compelling voice and style were soon to be heard in the streets of the larger Northeast towns, at the markets and fairs, around the countryside and in every welcoming pub and bar.

He travelled not just the roads of Scotland. He went through England to the Channel Islands, and later to Nova Scotia, where he found the French Canadian girls "too verocious, like they were hot in the blood." Most of the time he lived in 'model lodging houses', doing casual work and singing for money at fairs and feeing markets where he would find an eager paying audience.

An obituary article by Raymond Anderson gives a warm appreciation of Jimmy's latter years. In 1951, Alan Lomax and Hamish Henderson

[6] Peter A Hall, Notes to the LP Jimmy MacBeath, *Bound to be a Row*, Topic 12T303, 1978.

were collecting songs in Turriff, and veteran bothy singer 'Lordy' Hay recommended they seek out Jimmy, who was based at the time in the North Lodge model lodging house in Elgin.

Alan Lomax wanted Jimmy to go to Turriff with him, but the singer was very apprehensive about this, as the unappreciative police of that town had told him never to set foot in it again. But he decided to take a chance and was put up in one of the best rooms of Turriff's best hotel – all at the expense of Columbia Records.

The very next year he was off to London to record for the earliest folk series on television. Jimmy was now popular in folk clubs throughout Britain and he also sang abroad. But money never remained with him very long, it just slipped through his fingers. This travelling minstrel sang in many unusual places – at wakes in Ireland and at silent movies in place of a piano. He is probably best known for a song he got from Geordie Stewart – 'Come All Ye Tramps and Hawkers'.

Ironically, towards the end of his life, Jimmy got more invitations to sing at clubs in England than in Scotland. In his late life bronchitis left him fighting for breath, but he could astonish people by bursting into 'Come All Ye Tramps and Hawkers' moments after finding it difficult to breathe. "The sight of a stage would work wonders with Jimmy," said Hamish Henderson. But if Jimmy ever played any of his records at the 'model' lodging house, the other men soon told him to turn it off. Few of them liked his songs. There he was looked on as a lost character. Possibly even the last of the characters who used to be well known in the 'model.'

I recall well how delighted and impressed the 1960 audience at the Glasgow Folk Club were with Jimmy's singing, but more vividly how astonished and embarrassingly grateful Jimmy was to receive the sum of eight pounds, more than he had ever before earned from an evening's performance.

Jessie Murray

A fishwife living in the North-East port of Buckie, Jessie would have trudged from door to door, 'a little lady' dressed all in black wearing a black shawl, a basket of fish or shellfish on her back. She was a fisherman's widow aged at least 70 in 1951, and died in the 1950s.

> I always remember Jessie Murray, and she came forward and gave a little curtsey to the audience. And she sang 'Skippin Barfit Through The Heather', and of course these were songs you had never heard, and clearly the whole audience had never heard either.[7]

---

[7] Janey Buchan, Radio Scotland 1994.

Jeannie Robertson

Jeannie Robertson was born as Regina Christina Robertson into an Aberdeen Traveller family in 1908. Her father was a piper and her mother a singer with a huge repertoire of songs and ballads. She lived at 90, Hilton Street in Aberdeen, where a plaque now commemorates her. Like many of the Scottish Travellers from Aberdeen, Glasgow and Ayrshire, she went to Blairgowrie for the berry-picking season.

Hamish Henderson, himself born in Blairgowrie, frequently went there to track down the best singers and collect their songs. In 1953, following a recommendation from Bobby Hutchinson, he appeared at Jeannie's doorstep in Aberdeen. According to legend, Jeannie was reluctant to let him in. She challenged him to tell her the opening line of, *The Battle of Harlaw* (Child ballad No 163) and he complied. She asked him in and sang the ballad for him.

Thus, she was 'discovered.' Hamish invited her to sing at the Third People's Ceilidh at Edinburgh Festival. Alan Lomax was impressed by her singing. In November of the same year she was staying in his London apartment. In preparation for a TV appearance in the series *Song Hunter* about Lomax's work made by a young David Attenborough, Jean Ritchie, Margaret Barry and Isla Cameron were also there. They swapped songs with each other, while the tape rolled. Many of these 1953 recordings were issued as *The Queen Among the Heather* in 1975, reissued more recently as a CD. In 1958, Hamish Henderson recorded her in Edinburgh. Those recordings were issued as *Up the Dee and Doon the Don* on the Lismor label.

Jeannie Robertson also sang at the inaugural Blairgowrie Festival in 1965, alongside Jimmy MacBeath and other tradition bearers whose singing came entirely from the oral tradition. Her 1968 appearance at the Festival was issued as part of an anthology on the Topic label.

In the same year, Jeannie was made an MBE for services to folksong, the first folksinger and the first traveller to receive this honour. She died in March 1975, having passed on her songs to her daughter Lizzie Higgins, her nephew, the storyteller, ballad singer and piper Stanley Robertson, the late Ray Fisher, Andy Hunter, and Jean Redpath.

She was inducted to the Scottish Traditional Music Hall of Fame:

> Jeannie Robertson is a monumental figure in Scottish traditional song whose influence and importance as a preserver of folklore will sustain for as long as traditional ballads are sung.[8]

---

[8] http://www.tradmusichall.com/jeannierobertson.htm

Davie Stewart

Davie Stewart was born in 1901 in Windmill Street, Peterhead, a major fishing port in northeast Scotland, to a Scottish Traveller family, the Stewarts of Buchan, Aberdeenshire. He died in October 1972 while on a visit to the Folk Club in St. Andrews.

Davie's father and grandfather were both called Robert Stewart and were travelling tinsmiths and hawkers. His father "could sing, but he was mostly a piper."

> My father . . . took a fisher-hoose, like off the fishermen. . . . He used to gae awa herrin fishin wi the fishermen from Peterhead and Fraserburgh.

Davie attended schools in Aberdeen, New Blyth, and Fraserburgh. In spring and summer the family would take to the roads of the North. Davie began to earn money by singing for money when he was very young.

> I was about six when I started getting fly for it, you see, and I went away mostly on my own, maybe going away for a week or a fortnight and my people always wondering where I went to. I'd go to other Travellers and live wi them. I went to school when I was four years old and I left it when I was nine. When I was nine year old I went away from home and sometimes I worked wi the farmers, and sometimes I was hawking; sometimes I sung and sometimes I begged. I used to go to the farm house door and sing a songie or twa, and the old woman would come out and gie me a piece and jelly [bread and jam] or a bowl of milk. Then the ploomen used tae take me down to the bothies and I used to sing in the bothies wi them, in fact, I learned a lot of songs off the ploughmen.

When Davie was 13, the First War World War started, and he was determined to enlist, as all his cousins were doing. He joined the Third Reserve Battalion, the Gordon Highlanders, and twice his father produced Davie's "birth lines" to prove he was underage, and "I got tooken back." The third time, at age 15, Davie succeeded. He was wounded three times serving in France. He had been taught by his father to play the Highland pipes when at home, at about age eight and too small to hold a full-sized instrument properly, so his father had bought a "half size" set for "aboot five bob." Like his father had before him, Davie became a piper in the Gordons. "I was so thickheaded I couldn't learn music, so I used to sit back and hear them playing and I would just pick it up."

When he came out of the army, age 21 or 22, he began to play "boxes" – first melodeon and then the accordion, in a style perhaps derived from pipes technique, with an approach to accompaniment on the bass buttons that was sometimes unusual, sometimes downright sketchy, and on occasion doggedly dissonant. He played at markets and fairs in Aberdeenshire, at farmhouse doors, and in bothies until 2 in the morning, when he would pick up more songs. Sometimes he earned money by hawking and tinkering, sometimes by seasonal farm work.

"Maybe I would work for a week or two or three at the hay at this farm, then maybe I did his turnips, then maybe I would come back for his potato picking. In between jobs I did busking to make up my living." For many years Davie travelled Ireland, where he made music, married, and raised a family. At last in 1950, family needs took him from the road. "We come back again to Blairgowrie, Scotland, for the berries. And I says to the wife, says I, 'We'll have to try and settle down.' She says, 'Yes, we're getting older now, and it doesn't do to be runnin about like this, rearin family – getting proper schoolin.' So we went away to Dundee and got a house in Dundee." In March 1962, Davie moved to live in Glasgow. Although commercial recordings of his singing were issued and he was invited to perform in folk clubs and was a favourite and feted guest at festivals, he could between times be met busking for coppers along the "back courts" behind the massed three or four tenement flats that lined the canyon streets of the city.

John Strachan

Born 1875 on the Aberdeenshire farm of Crichie near Fyvie, John Strachan died in 1958 on the same farm. A wealthy farmer, he "took a kindly paternalistic interest in the welfare of his fee'd men," and was a highly knowledgeable champion of the songs of farm life and old ballads. "John Strachan says he's a farmer. Really he's a poet, and chronicler – with all the best bits of Buchan stored in his head."[9]

John Strachan's *Portrait* CD shows the richness of his versions of songs, which led the American collector James Madison Carpenter in 1930 to invite John to visit Harvard College, but to his regret John did not go. "I wis pretty busy, I'd a lot o' farmin to do."[10]

---

[9] Alan Lomax, BBC Radio, 1951.
[10] Hamish Henderson, 'John Strachan', *Alias MacAlias*, p.200.

Blanche Wood

Brown-haired and bonny Blanche Wood. Hers was the clear bell-like voice one hears so often in the North."[11] Blanche is a K-Nocker, of the small fishing village of Portknockie, five miles east of the port of Buckie. In 1951 she was 18, and in the Ceilidh sang songs her aunt Jessie Murray had taught her. Blanche's father was a fisherman, and named a new boat for her, *The Girl Blanche*, launched by Blanche herself at age 15.

Blanche married Robert Allen, who sawed the keels for fishing boats, but by 1961 the boatyards had shut and they moved to Edinburgh, where they still live. Blanche and her sister formed a singing double act which toured working men's clubs in Scotland and England, singing 'more modern songs.'

The Alan Lomax Collection

The new issues of material Lomax recorded are under the banner of *The Alan Lomax Collection*, gathering together his "field recordings, world music compilations, and ballad operas". One element is the *Portrait* series of "brilliant artists and heroes of traditional music". The first two *Portraits* were of Scotland's treasure Jeannie Robertson and Irish street singer extraordinary Margaret Barry. The recordings are of

interviews as well as songs. Only four of the eighteen Jeannie Robertson tracks have been issued before. Jeannie talks about her mother's singing style and makes her own observations on some of the songs.

While these *Portraits* were greeted with delight, they nonetheless ran into some severe criticism, from song experts who know how to pick over the bones, about some aspects of the transcriptions and notes. The most obvious problem area on the Jeannie Robertson album was the transcription of 'The Battle of Harlaw', in which several placenames are misunderstood. "Did ye come aa the way" becomes "Did ye come o'er the Wye". "It's there they met Sir James the Rose, wi him Sir John the Graeme" turns into "It's there they met Sir James O'Ross, who answered John the Grame". Not close enough for a dowt, let alone a cigar. The recording shows another aspect of Lomax's approach. Rather than visit and do a pressured recording in the singer's home, he took Jeannie down to stay with him in London in 1953, and recorded her singing and talking over several days. He did the same with Jimmy MacBeath and Davie Stewart, in 1957.

---

[11] Alan Lomax, BBC Radio, 1957.

Lomax, however, recorded John Strachan, Buchan farmer and repository of wonderful versions of ballads, in John's home in Critchie near Fyvie in 1951. These latter recordings were made jointly with Hamish Henderson, and are among the many gems on the first 24 tapes in the sound archives of the School of Scottish Studies, copies of those Lomax recorded during his 1951 Scottish trip. The critics who hammered the quality of the sleeve notes on Jeannie and on Margaret Barry also had a dig at Hamish Henderson, niggling as to why he gives in print two contradictory accounts of when and where he met Davie Stewart. In fact this is a problem created by whoever indexed Hamish's book *Alias McAlias*. In the index two different Davie Stewarts – one the singer, boxplayer and piper who lived in Dundee, another a younger piper from Perthshire way – are conflated [an unpleasant thing to do to any piper].

But these critical nitpickers did me personally a great favour. Because they swung their hatchets so vigorously and comprehensively, when the next set of *Portraits* were on the production table, *Portraits* Series Editor Matthew Barton and Collection Producer Anna Lomax Chairetakis were casting around for someone Scottish to do the transcriptions and notes for the *Portraits* of Jimmy MacBeath, Davie Stewart and John Strachan. I was invited to undertake some of the work. Not the accounts of the singers though – these obituaries had already been written magnificently by Hamish Henderson, and are included in *Alias MacAlias*. I found myself the startled custodian of a dozen CDs of song, tunes and conversation. Not just of MacBeath, Strachan and Stewart, but also such legendary names as John Mearns, Willie Mathieson, Blanche Wood, Jessie Murray, Lordy Hay, Jimmy Shand. Also on Lomax's tapes are a raft of songs from Ewan MacColl (listed under his original name, Jimmie Miller), and from Hamish Henderson himself.

The North-East material is of course problematical to transcribe, and some critic will complain that an Invernessian like me should not have been entrusted with the task. In my notes on the songs I leaned heavily on the work done by the editors of *The Greig-Duncan Folk Song Collection*. Their comments on the texts of versions saved much time, and also helped with identifying 'standard texts'. My transcription of the songs was made far more confident by checking them against transcripts made of some of the songs by staff of the School Of Scottish Studies archives. Both Jimmy MacBeath and Davie Stewart played fast and loose with the words of their songs. Davie in particular was hard to transcribe with complete confidence. As Hamish Henderson says,

> His attitude to his text and his tune was highly fluid and improvisatory [...] Davie also had the tendency to fill in partly remembered lines with meaningless syllables.[12]

On occasion he could trip himself up in royal style. He introduces 'The Laird of the Dainty Doonbyes', chases all round his accordion till he finds the tune, though he mislays it again on occasion, without ever losing spirit and energy. Then, when approaching the end of the song, he pauses briefly, and seems to mix up lines from two very different songs for, instead of placing the castle keys into her hand, Davie puts another of the laird's most personal possessions there instead.

The new releases contain other material stronger than it was possible to include in the 1950s. Jimmy MacBeath tells of a sexual encounter with two 'very veracious' French girls during his soldiering days in the Gordons in the First World War. John Strachan sings verses of 'The Ball of Kirriemuir', highly concerned lest his wife overhear: "Oh, if she kent that I sang you yon song, I couldn't stay wi you." Jimmy tells of a time at Keith Show when he sang a startlingly basic version of 'John Anderson My Jo', and, "I was just ta'en up next morning. And I got fined five pound or sixty days." The fine was paid by a butcher fan of Jimmy's. Jimmy MacBeath plays up his wild and woolly image of life on the road and street, and claims to have been chased through the streets and washing houses of Peterhead on another occasion for singing 'McCafferty' in the Landgate. He says he got fined ten shillings. Lomax asks "What would happen to you if you sang it in the army?" Jimmy replies, "Ah, I'd get worse. I'd get shot."

The tapes were transcribed in the USA in the 1950s, in the Library of Congress and not by Lomax himself I should think. Here is where the odd misunderstandings occur. Jimmy is asked about bothy songs. He replies,

> The real name is bothy ballad songs ... they originated frae the corn kist, I suppose, a lot of them when they were singing in the stables and duntin their heels against the corn kist, ye see.

The US transcript has "it originated from the corn and custart ... dunking their heels against a corn cest." He also defeats the transcriber with a song "about the Rossy – For John had to bring me along, through rain and sleet and snow." You may have recognised that in search of Rothesay the singer "wandered though the Broomielaw, through wind and rain and sleet and snaw."

---

[12] Hamish Henderson, 'Davie Stewart', Alias MacAlias, p.168.

Of course the great strength of all three singers is in the fine and vigorous versions of Child ballads and bothy ballads they sing for Lomax. John Strachan's fine versions of ballads are widely respected, and he has appeared on various anthologies, but this will be the first disc of his singing to appear – there is/was a cassette of him issued by Peter Kennedy's label. Jimmy gives a wonderful (and convincing this time) account of songs being made in front of the bothy fire, and the words being burnt into the wood of the mantlepiece with a red hot poker.

I also faced the problem of translating cant songs. I still cannot find out what the word 'stollage', used by Davie in a song called 'Last Nicht Ah Wis In the Granzie', means – probably something to do with food. Jimmy sang the well-known cant song 'Hey Barra Gadgey Will Ye Jazzafree?' for Lomax, but explained that the cant of 'the travelling class' is different from "the real Romany cant. You couldn't do the real Romany cant, because it's very very very difficult to understand." The tapes solve a few problems. Even the experts say they do not know exactly where Davie Stewart was born. He told Lomax that Windmill Street in Peterhead had that honour.

Another album is a double CD of Jimmy and Davie talking. Jimmy tells of 'The Horseman's Grip and Word', and the life of the farm, Davie of adventures with carts and horses during his years in Ireland. Another is of children's songs. J T R Ritchie's two books of Edinburgh children's song, based on his collecting work with the children of Norton Park School, were reissued very recently by Mercat Press. He and some of his informants are there on Lomax's tapes, along with songs and rhymes from North-East kids.

The 1951 Edinburgh People's Festival Ceilidh

And there is a selection from the incredible 1951 Edinburgh People's Festival Ceilidh, complete with the warm, incisive and instructive introductions of Hamish Henderson himself. He begins by saying,

> The great thing about the Buchan songs, I think, is their fine rumbustuous qualities, and the first song that you're going to hear from Mr Strachan tonight is the 'Guise O Tough'.

Sadly, John Strachan was not in his best voice that night, although that did not diminish the exhilarated enthusiasm of the audience. The ceilidh featured Jimmy MacBeath, Flora MacNeil of Barra, Pipe Major John Burgess, John Strachan, Calum Johnston, and Jessie Murray of Portnockie and her niece Blanche Wood. Hamish says that Jessie Murray "was born at the very hour and minute, she tells me, of the Tay Bridge Disaster, so as she came over the Tay Bridge today she got a fleeting feeling she might not see the ceilidh." Ewan MacColl was there that night. So was Norman Buchan, and he wrote often of the excitement of the occasion, and the thrill of hearing Jessie Murray sing 'Skipping Barfit Through The Heather'. The ceilidh was due to end at ten pm, but continued 'up the road in St Columba's Hall' at an additional charge of two shillings. The Rounder recordings will cost you a little more than that, but what price would be too much to hear such singers now?

Note:
Rounder has issued CDs from the Lomax Scottish recordings of each of the main singers he encountered in Scotland, and various compilations [http://www.culturalequity.org/], but most of his work has never been commercially available. The Kist o Riches website has thousands of hours of recordings from the School of Scottish Studies, but these omit their copies of the Lomax recordings. 30-second clips of each of his Scottish recordings can be sampled at [http://research.culturalequity.org/get-audio-ix.do?ix=session&id=SC51&idType=abbrev&sortBy=abc].

The Singer behind the Song and the Man behind the Microphone

Margaret Bennett

In all my travels, I have never met such genteel, winning and genuinely cultured people as these Hebrideans – nor have I heard anywhere folk songs of such fine quality. It angers and saddens me to think that the money and the trouble that go into launching one new battleship or bomber could guarantee the security and the perpetuation of a singing style like this, that in another generation will have disappeared (as so much has already irretrievably vanished from the rest of Britain.)

Alan Lomax, *A Ballad Hunter Looks at Britain*, 1957[1]

There is a well-known old Gaelic proverb that runs, *'S e obair latha a toiseachadh'* (the day's work is the getting started). Often it is supported by words of encouragement, along the lines of, 'once you get going, you'll be all right...' In 1951, by the time the People's Festival Ceilidh came around in August, Alan Lomax had been in Scotland for over two months, and had wasted no time in 'making a start'. His journal shows that, after recording Jimmy Miller (Ewan McColl)[2] and his mother in Cheshire on June 13, he left England and headed to Edinburgh. Having already met Hamish Henderson in London in March, Lomax anticipated an inspiring work partnership. According to his biographer John Szwed, "A few hours' discussion with Henderson made Alan realize that Scotland was far more than just an other region of Britain, and filled him with the fire he needed not only to collect the songs of Scotland but also

---

[1] Alan Lomax, radio script 'Songs from the Highlands and Islands of Scotland', co-presented with Hamish Henderson, programme 6 (of 8) for the BBC series, *A Ballad Hunter Looks at Britain*. Recorded Nov. 22, 1957, transmitted by the BBC Home Service on Dec. 6, 1957.

[2] Ewan McColl had written to Hamish in February to introduce him to Lomax, whom he described as 'just about the most important name in American folksong circles. He is over here with a super recording unit.' The letter is published in *The Armstrong Nose: Selected Letters of Hamish Henderson*, ed. by Alec Finlay, Edinburgh: Polygon, 1996, p.46.

to write a Scots ballad opera."[3] The meeting (as well as the man) left a lasting impression on Lomax, as he recalled in his journal:

> The conversation was extremely important... Hamish feels that Scotland is the most interesting and important place on earth, with a real live people's culture, now on the march, and I must say, he made me share his feeling... He also made me sure that the ballad opera job was worth doing in Scotland, as a sort of declaration of Scots independence – giving Scotland the recognition it deserved.[4]

Within two days in Scotland Lomax had recorded three of the people who were to feature in August's 'People's Festival Ceilidh'. One was a seventeen year-old piper, John D. Burgess, and the other two were Gaelic singers from the Isle of Barra: Calum Johnston (age 60, who worked as a draftsman in Edinburgh) and a young woman called Flora MacNeil (age 23).

Edinburgh Castle seems to have been the venue for the Burgess contribution, as the same reel-to-reel tape includes pipe band music recorded on the esplanade, followed by a few more solo tunes. In conversation, Burgess spoke of his teachers, Pipe-Major James Gordon of Edinburgh (also a dancer) who taught him from when he was "a wee boy till the age of nine," after which Pipe Major Willie Ross took over. He gave Lomax an introduction to 'MacIntosh's Lament',[5] then,

when questioned about his own formidable achievements, made little of winning the two of the most coveted awards in piping by the age of sixteen. Nevertheless, Lomax clearly knew that he was in the presence of prodigious talent, noting in bold letters on the tape-box: **excellent**.

On 15 June, his second day in Edinburgh, Lomax was taken to record Calum Johnston who, he noted, lived at 19 Bangholm, Ave., Edinboro [sic]. The Gaelic songs from Calum and Flora were the first of

---

[3] John Szwed, *The Man Who Recorded the World*, London: Heinemann, 2010, p.263. McColl also set up the meeting with Lomax and Henderson in London, March 1951.

[4] From Alan Lomax's field Notebook, March 1951, quoted by Szwed, op cit, p.263.

[5] To introduce Lomax to *piobaireach*, Burgess played only the *urlar*, the 'ground movement', with none of the variations.

many he recorded on reel-to-reel tapes during his monumental visit to Scotland. Naturally, their native Island of Barra would be high on the list of places he should visit; he jotted down 'leads', not only from Calum Johnston (whose sister Annie lived on the island), but also from Hamish Henderson and Calum Maclean.[6] Lomax's hastily written notes are, at times, barely legible but, as far as his recording mission was concerned, they are quite clear and specific. Anticipating the uncharted territory, not to mention driving a hired car, he writes (for example), "Within a mile of the bridge over the ford – ask Eochdar Hall, 1st petrol pump after causeway." Calum Maclean's advice was particularly important, as he himself was well-known in the Uists and Barra and widely regarded with enormous affection. Lomax listened carefully and wrote in his notebook: "When I arrive [in Barra] go to Mary Gillis whom C.M. will have written..." There follows a list of contact names as well as reminders such as "First Mate Donald Joseph MacKinnon lovely singer – on boat – speak of Calum." And, as fortune should have it, Calum also had a brother in South Uist, Dr Alasdair Maclean, the local GP, who shared his devotion to Gaelic tradition.

Exactly a week after arriving in Scotland, Lomax set off for Skye on Monday, 18 June, stopping overnight in Uig (more recordings), before sailing to the Outer Hebrides where he was to record the bulk of his remarkable collection. While sailing to North Uist he wrote:

> June 20.
> While the Lochmor cruised down the Eastern shore of the Hebrides, I sat in my tight cabin below decks and typed. Letters to Australia. Duties. Contracts. A bloody awful business. I'm sick of possessions....
> A ½ hour out of Loch Boisdale and the outpost of the Gaelic world. A fine afternoon. Round the horizon all kinds of weather. A great mountain of cumulus to the East matching & overshadowing the low rock of green & grey that is Uist [?] to the West. Long low clouds running over the island. And back toward the sun round puffs of white scudding before the sun.

---

[6] Gaelic folklorist Calum MacLean (1915-1960) began his intensive training and fieldwork with the Irish Folklore Commission in 1942. In 1945, he was sent to the Hebrides by the director, Professor Seumas Delargy (his mentor), who recognised the urgent need to record the Gaelic traditions of Scotland before they might be lost. Transcriptions of his remarkable recordings (made on an Ediphone) amount to more than 10,000 manuscript pages. As he had completed this before Lomax's 1951 visit, his generosity in helping Lomax can only be measured beside his devotion to Gaelic tradition.

The Hebrides is hard old rock. Worn down now by wind & water & time, nearly into the sea. Barely a skin of green & brown moss for a cap & a covering....

A few days later he is excited as he writes,

"... had a great kaylay [sic] which ended at 3 a.m. Beautiful sounds of Hebridean group singing... like a community sing but magnificent with old tunes and antique communal spirit..."

Within one week, Lomax recorded over 250 Gaelic songs, some centuries old, others composed within the decade, as well as snippets of local history and several traditional stories. Not only were his recordings groundbreaking in content and clarity, but also they succeeded in capturing the essence and ambiance of lifestyles and communities as they were in 1951. The Gaels themselves may never again sing, or hear the songs, in these natural settings captured on Lomax's tapes – the old-style taigh ceilidh was alive in these kitchens, and the way of life was reflected in byre, barn, by the stack-yard, out in the fields, or aboard a fishing vessel or rowing boat.

Lomax's style of collecting, which often saw him move on immediately after a fieldtrip, was very different to that developed by Hamish Henderson, who often kept in touch with folk who had sung for him. Considering the geographic range of collecting that Lomax did, however, it is small wonder that he scarcely gained a reputation for keeping in touch. It would be a sorry mistake, however, to underestimate his efforts to understand and get to know the singers, musicians, storytellers and oral historians he recorded. He did what he could as time and opportunity allowed. Though Lomax recorded an impressive number of singers and songs, as he took his leave he realised he had heard only a fraction of the wealth of tradition that existed. About to leave Barra, the 36 year-old folklorist scribbled a note expressing his awareness of the sheer volume of Gaelic tradition that could (or should) be recorded, if only he had the time: "I've been in the British Isles 6 months. At this rate I'll be 70..."

Having spent only one week in the Outer Hebrides, it was time for Lomax to leave. His journal, scribbled in a spiral-bound reporter's notebook, evokes an image of him standing on deck, leaning on the rail as islanders do, watching with nostalgia as the land disappears into the distance. On the steamer crossing he reflects on his first impressions of the Hebrides, admits his dreadful doubts and negative feelings, and rejoices in the transformation that began as soon as he stepped ashore. This was an experience that was to leave lasting impressions, not only on Lomax, but also on the world of Scottish folk music:

> We have left the land – the little harbour of Loch Boisdale. The last thing I saw of my friends were Mrs Maclean in Green and [??] in Dark Blue running up the hill to the hotel ... and the car. The harbour suddenly became small impersonal and empty – and I had first seen it five days ago – a stage set, a cold and uninteresting – straggling grey buildings set among grey-green and [??] hills. And indeed I was hurt by the sight of Loch Boisdale as I came in on this boat, wishing I had not come, feeling the old strain on my heart. Then on the pier, Dr Maclean[7] – he was a little man in a green suit brushing his unruly hair with stubby fingers and beside him a winsome, really winsome girl [my God this thing is rolling] ... and he came up to the side of the boat as we were hauled sidewise to the pier & said, 'Is this Alan Lomax?' And I exclaimed, 'This is Dr Mclean!' and I came ashore [to ?] smiles. ... Already in the docks he found a singer for me – McKinnon,[8] mate ex the ship on which I had sailed & whom I had not found because I was heartsick anxious & bored, but he agreed to come sing that night ...
> [Now] Off to Glasgow ... from the purest place the sweetest people I've ever met. Hope some of its lodged in this [?r?] heart.[9]

Back on the mainland, he resumed his busy schedule, planning ahead and keeping in touch with the BBC, contacts in London, Paris, as well as with Columbia Records. He spent time in Glasgow, where he recorded the outstanding voice of Kitty MacLeod from Lewis, a Mod gold medallist and popular singer, who was well-known to the BBC. Kitty was also very much part of the vibrant cultural scene that embraced Hamish, Norman

---

[7] Dr Alastair Maclean was the brother of folklorist Calum Maclean.

[8] He refers to Donald Joseph MacKinnon, whom Calum had already mentioned to him before he set out. Donald Joseph MacKinnon had a phenomenal repertoire, and to this day, is regarded as one of Gaeldom's finest singers and exponents of Gaelic song.

[9] Instances where I was unable to understand a recorded voice or make out the handwriting in Lomax's notebooks I have indicated by question marks and square brackets.

MacCaig, Sorley Maclean, Sidney Goodsir Smith and many others.[10] In Edinburgh, before heading to the North-East with Hamish Henderson, Lomax took the opportunity of getting back in touch with John Burgess, picking up from where he left off. This time, on 11 July, he also interviewed the young piper's teacher, Pipe Major Willie Ross, Director of the Army School of Piping at Edinburgh Castle. Naturally, he asked him to play some tunes. Sixty years on, the P.M. Willie Ross tracks, particularly the marches, should be of considerable interest to new generations of pipers, especially competition pipers. When you listen to the tempo of these marches, (such as 'Bonnie Ann' and 'The Duke of Roxburgh's Farewell to Blackmount'), it is clear that here is a soldier who has had to march for real, no hanging about, for the pace is brisk, with a sense of purpose about it. Today, these are particularly important recordings, as they demonstrate the extent to which piping traditions change over the years.

On 14 July, the eve of his recording trip with Hamish, Alan Lomax made his way again to Calum Johnston's house, where Flora MacNeil also turned up for the ceilidh. By this time, he had seen their island, met their people, heard some of their songs, and learned about the tradition. As anticipated, he recorded a few more songs, (including Flora's now famous track, 'Mo Rùn Geal Òg'), and on this tape he also asks Calum about the way of life. The following is a verbatim transcription of this interview – the scene is Calum Johnston's house in Edinburgh; the tape-recorder wheels are running, and so the folklorist begins:

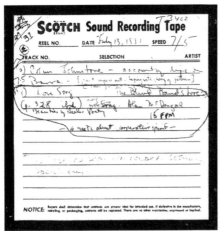

Alan Lomax: How big a place was it that you lived on, how big a croft? Where was it?

Calum Johnston: Oh just the croft that you've seen in the glen there. We used to keep two cows and then there'd be two stirks and a pony.

Alan: How much land was there?

Calum: Well in acreage it's difficult to say, about six or seven acres perhaps altogether. There wasn't very much.

---

[10] Kitty had attended the University of Edinburgh and shared classes with Norman and Sorley. (In their year, it was Kitty, not the poets, who won the University's gold medal for Celtic.)

Alan: What did you raise on this?[11]

Calum: Oh we just raised – we had two cows for providing milk and butter and there were some sheep and the pony was for work on the land, manuring the land and carrying the peats and things like that. And of course, a croft like that wouldn't keep a family going, somebody had to leave home and work elsewhere, you see. Some of my sisters were away and my brother – eventually he was a sailor; he also started in square rig. Eventually he landed in Australia and from there to Tasmania where he was a light-keeper for many years and he died there.

Alan: You didn't see him again?

Calum: I didn't see him again, no. He left shortly before I left. I left home when I was about sixteen years of age. He was away before then.

Alan: Always sending money back?

Calum: Yes, that's so and keeping the place going. While my sister Annie was a teacher – she helped to keep the place going also, and other members of the family also.

Alan: How many of you were there?

Calum: There were seven of us.

Alan: You were the oldest though?

Calum: No, I was the second youngest. You've been to our home – well, Mrs Simpson who is there, she was the oldest of the family; then there was another one, Mary, who is dead, then there was Roderick, who is also dead. Then there was Annie, then there's [??] – and I and Theresa. There were two boys and five girls. There was another boy, actually the oldest of the family – he died at the age of sixteen of blood poisoning.

Alan: Now tell me, Calum, how did your mother raise you? I mean was there discipline in the house?

Calum: Oh, very strict indeed, oh yes.

Alan: How did she maintain it? Can you remember anything that happened to you?

Calum: I can't remember anything in particular; but I always remember that a lecture from my mother was much more severe than if anybody was to take a stick to you. I'd feel a lecture from her much more severe than if I'd got a thrashing. She didn't thrash me, but she gave me a good lecture.

Alan: What would she say?

Calum: Well she would tell you of the faults of your ways and

[11] In the USA the word 'raise' is used in connection with crops (as in 'we raised wheat') as well as livestock. This usage may have been totally unfamiliar to Calum who instantly changes syntax to respond.

how it was quite wrong and how it would disgrace the rest of the family and all the rest of it. She would make you feel just like a worm for doing anything that was wrong, and, well to me, it was much more effective than if I were to get a thrashing for anything.

Alan: Was she a woman that worked hard all the time?

Calum: Oh yes, she was a very hardworking woman; never idle at all. Well, at that time she worked on the croft, of course, and she milked the cows and attended to them in everything. And in the evenings she carded and spun and made cloth. There wasn't an idle moment at all in their lives. They were all the same, the women at that time; they were all the same, working all the time. Of course, working that kind of work they treated it as a recreation. They didn't consider it as work. It was a pleasure to them. They took a pleasure in their work, especially the work of the cloth, the carding and spinning and all that. They had a pride in it and they took a pleasure in it.

Alan: Did they express this pleasure in any way?

Calum: Oh yes. Well, the greatest pleasure that anybody can get is to see the completion of his work. And then when they saw a beautiful piece of cloth or tweed after it had been made, well that was their reward for the labour they had put into it.

Alan: The object of waulking the tweed was to make good strong clothes for the men?

Calum: For the men, yes. At that time practically all the cloth that the men wore were made by the women, by their wives and their mothers. And even the fishermen – they always had to get blue cloth; and that blue cloth that was made for the fishermen – it was so thick that they never wore an overcoat with it, as no rain would go through it. It was warped for a whole night. You know, when cloth is made it has to be shrunk, what they call *luadh*. Well, for ordinary blankets and the like of that, an hour or so's work would be sufficient. But for the fishermen's blue cloth it was a whole night. They would start the *luadh* perhaps at six in the evening and wouldn't be finished until 10 at night, with songs going all the time while they were shrinking it. When that was shrunk to that extent nothing would go through it.

Alan: And they were proud of the way it felt.

Calum: Oh yes, they had pride in their work. The better it was, the more pride they could take in it, and then, of course, the praise of the neighbours, if it was forthcoming, was payment for all their labours.

Alan: How would you describe Barra to someone that's never seen it, Calum, the way it looks to you now?

Calum: Yes, well, to a stranger, when you're going there, it seems a very barren island – seventy-five rocks you might say. I'm sure that's how you felt about it when you approached it. And you'll get there; there are certainly very lovely beaches, sandy beaches, and the like of that. The vegetation in some parts is meagre. But I think that the great attraction in Barra is the warmth of the heart of the people when you get to know it; because if you get to know them, they'll take you to their heart, and it's that I think, that makes the place likeable to strangers, much more than the island itself. Because if you take away the people I think it would feel very cold.

Alan: Yes I think so.

Calum: 'Cos it is naturally barren. There are no trees or things there to make it beautiful except just what nature has made of the beaches and the little bays and the like of that. But I think the whole attraction is really in the way the people make a stranger welcome if he tries to understand their ways. It's the understanding between the people of the place and the strangers who go there.

Alan: And do you find this quite unique, this Barra feeling?

Calum: I shouldn't think so. I think that in most of the Highlands you got the same thing. Perhaps not so much nowadays as perhaps fifty years ago. Of course the Highlands were known for their hospitality to strangers, but that is dying out now – the change of times –of course, that is the trend of things nowadays. You get all kinds of strangers, of course.

Alan: How about among themselves, is there the same warmth as among strangers?

Calum: Oh there used to be, at any rate. I don't know that it's so evident now as it used to be. At one time they worked in a community as you might say – the best idea of communism as you might call it. They all helped each other.

Alan: Tell me how that worked.

Calum: Well, say at the time of peat cutting, you would call on perhaps half a dozen of your neighbours and you would say to them, "I'm going peat cutting tomorrow, will you come and help me?" and they'd say, "Yes, we'll be delighted." And they would go. Well perhaps next week it was their turn. They would call on you and you would also go to them. And you got your peats cut in one day, you see, and the next person had the same experience, and you got on that way. And the same with many other things.

Alan: With other jobs?

Calum: Yes, at the harvest time, of course, when they were cutting the corn everybody was busy; but if anybody was behind the others they wouldn't think anything of going giving him a hand for a day – the like of that. Also, well all the little things that are in the life of a community. When I was a young boy if my shoes needed mending I would just go to a neighbour's and I would say, I'd say to him, "My shoes are needing mending." And he would say, "Oh have you got any leathers?" I'd say, "Yes." "Oh well," he says, "I'll sort them for you in a few minutes." And he would. Of course, all these people were very expert at these acts that are necessary for carrying on life, as you might say; mending boots or mending anything, they could turn a hand to it. As a matter of fact I could do it myself when I was fourteen and fifteen; I could sew a patch on a shoe or anything like that. But the jobs I couldn't do, I went to somebody who could do, and he would even leave what he was doing himself, he would stop it, and he would do the thing that I wanted done, and I went home quite happy – and, well, perhaps I could do something else for him in return. If there was a sheep lost in the hills or anything like that, and I was a young boy and he was an old man, well I went with my dog to try and find that sheep for him. That was all just in the day's running. At the time of shearing sheep, or the like of that, well the young fellows, they liked the job and they only wanted just an opportunity of doing it.

Alan: Was there any such thing as hunger, did people go hungry?

Calum: Well I don't know of it. No, I cannot say there was, and if it was known that anybody was hungry, he wouldn't be hungry for long. The neighbours would provide. I've never known a time when there was general hunger. No, I don't think anybody really suffered from hunger. The times were hard, certainly, but I don't think anybody would suffer through hunger in a community like what was in the isles when I was a boy. It would be unthinkable for anybody to feel hungry and others having something that would help.

Alan: Was there ever any crime on the islands, any violence at all? Do you remember a murder or fights?

Calum: No, no! Well fights were quite a natural thing at times. In those days, well especially on market days, all differences were settled; fights were quite common when they got some whisky in their inside and the rougher element of them got the upper hand, so to speak.

Alan: What did they fight about? Girls?

Calum: Oh, about anything at all, just differences of opinion.

Alan: Were the fights just with fists, no knives?

Calum: Yes, yes! No, no knives, that would have been quite out of line altogether. But I remember – to give you an idea of the spirit of these times, I remember the Rev Dr Neil Ross who was a Skye man telling me that there was a young man in their own place, he was going to the market this day – to the fair, as they called it, and the ambition of lots of these young fellows, just as they were coming out, was to have a good fight just to prove their strength. And he said, "I'm going to the market day today," he said, "and I'm going to have a fight supposing nothing came home of me except the two braces!" You see, when young fellows feel their strength coming on they want to use it very often. But in that respect they're getting much more sensible nowadays.

Alan: Tell me, what about courtship; at what age did young fellows and girls begin to have a look at each other?

Calum: Oh, I don't think that's ever changed very much.

Alan: Well, it varies in different parts. Did you have your sweethearts by the time you were twelve?

Calum: Oh yes, when you are at school you begin to take a fancy to this one and the next one.

Alan: How did courtship go on in Barra when you were a boy? When did courting couples get a chance to see each other?

Calum: Oh, well, when you got to be 16 and 18 you were allowed to go about with a girl without being chastised

Alan: Would you be chastised before that?

Calum: Oh, when you were fourteen or so you would be chastised for winking at a girl.

Alan: But when you were fifteen you'd go to dances or what would be –?

Calum: Oh yes, you'd take them to dances and walk home with them and the like of that. And you were allowed perhaps to stay out a little later at night.

Alan: How late at night would that be?

Calum: Oh well, it all depended on the restrictions at home. If you had strict parents they would want you home at 10 o'clock. But after you got to be eighteen and twenty, well you could make your own time, so to speak, you were getting out of their control by that time.

Alan: Did the songs have a lot to do with courting? I mean were there a lot of songs, which were sung at courting parties, or sung by boys to girls, or by girls to boys?

Calum: No, no.

Alan: Lots of them are about love, you know.

Calum: Yes, but I don't know if any fellow just in cold blood would start singing a song to his sweetheart. They would sing them in companies. Of course, she could take what she liked out of the song. She could feel that it was being sung to her. That was the way it went, I think.

Alan: And what about with the girls?

Calum: Oh the same thing happened there. They would sing at ceilidhs and the like of that.

Alan: And the girls and the boys were both very shy at that time – got embarrassed very easily. Do you remember any occasion like that?

Calum: Yes, yes, that's right; but no, I don't.

Alan: And courtship talk – was it very poetic like the songs, or were they restrained in their actual conversations?

Calum: [laughing] Now you're trying to make me give my life experience.

Alan: No, but the songs are very, very poetic and –

Calum: Yes, but it would all depend on the person. You see, some people are poetic in their ways and some aren't. So I suppose that would all depend on the person; because, you see, even amongst us there were just as many duds as there were poetical persons, artistic persons.

Alan: Calum, what would you say is the main sort of feeling that the music has for you, different from other music.

Calum: When – well, the Gaelic songs are very – I can make myself cry. I don't think I could feel the same in any other language. Of course, Gaelic is nearer to my heart than English is. There's a depth of feeling in these songs that I don't think I could get in any other music. It wouldn't be the same to me at any rate –

Alan: You were talking about decorations – how you fit them in.

Calum: Oh, yes. Well, as for the traditional singer, see – that also depends on the person. There are some people who would sing a song to you just in a straight line, bare notes, as you would say. There are others who would colour these, still keeping to the melody, but colouring the notes with graces or, as we would say [translated from Gaelic], 'putting a taste on it' – [tape runs out][12]

In 1951, this was a way of life, and even of singing, which most Gaels took for granted. There was nothing unusual about any of it, as my own memories of growing up in Skye in the fifties confirm: lighting the tilly-lamp at dusk; families and communities planting potatoes in spring; going

---

[12] I would like to thank Jennifer Meiklejohn for helping me to transcribe this tape.

to the peats in May; hoeing turnips and turning hay in summer; singing at milking; churning butter; lending a hand, no matter how small that hand may have been. Electricity came not long afterwards, and, though it changed some aspects of life, much remained the same, particularly the daily routine of house and croft. A light bulb in each room was the main difference, and while some homes acquired an electric cooker or 'ring', there was no question of people buying appliances such as fridges or washing machines, and television did not make its appearance until after I had left home in the mid-sixties. Single-track roads seemed perfectly adequate for the few folk with cars and for the service buses that stopped in every passing place.

If anyone told us in the fifties that this way of life was likely to disappear, we might have paid no attention. In the late 1980s, however, when the last of my uncles sold his cows, it was even too late to take a photograph of him milking – we had seen it all our lives and suddenly it was gone. Ended. Worse, he told us, none of the neighbours was milking, and the new generation had long since discovered the supermarket. When Lomax suggested in 1957 that, in another generation all of these will have disappeared,[13] surely he could not have meant that people would forget the context of the songs – even the sound of milking?

This year, 2011, celebrates not only the sixtieth anniversary of Lomax's Scottish recordings, it is also the 125th anniversary of the 1886 Crofting Act. To mark the occasion, a two-day event was held in Skye, bringing together crofters from all over the Highlands and Islands as well as over a hundred pupils from schools participating in a three-year project, 'Crofting Connections'.[14] It was an exciting two days, as youngsters (with their teachers) from Lewis, the Uists, Ardnamurchan, Argyll, Orkney and Shetland met with crofting children on the Isle of Skye. As part of their programme included a two-hour session of 'stories and songs of crofting', it seemed the perfect opportunity to teach a range of work songs, including two milking songs recorded by Alan Lomax.

The children, ages 9 to 17, included several talented singers, musicians and dramatists representing both Gaelic medium, and 'spik yer ain tung' schools. They all had learned how to plant potatoes and were learning how to grow crofting produce, make butter and cheese and even butcher a pig. When I played Alan Lomax's 1951 recording of Kate Nicolson singing as she milked her cow in her byre in South Uist, I asked, "What's she doing?" Not a single one could identify the sound of milk in a bucket and, even more surprisingly, neither could any of their teachers, mostly under-

---

[13] Lomax, *A Ballad Hunter Looks at Britain*, 1957; see opening quotation from his script.
[14] Under the direction of Pam Rodway, it is jointly run by the Crofters' Federation and the Soil Association and supporting the 'Curriculum for Excellence'.

40s, and all born long after 1951.

After a very brief explanation of hand-milking (demonstrating the actions), I taught them the song, which they were soon singing, keeping perfect time to a backing track sampled from Mrs. Nicolson's milking. "Now then," said I, "when we sing it for all the crofters we'll ask them to do the actions – let's see how they get on!" There was a certain glee as the sceptics anticipated failure, then, much to their amazement, all the old-timers immediately went into action, hands milking invisible cows. Afterwards, however, the same crofters confirmed, that they hadn't hand-milked a cow in years.

Going back many years before Lomax's visit, islanders had been accustomed to tourists asking obvious questions and even tolerated those who confidently offered advice on how to improve island life (with a view to their own retirement in your beautiful island). Alan Lomax offered no advice but, knowing that he might never have the opportunity of returning, he listened carefully to the singers he recorded. Nevertheless, he was not without his critics, mostly oblivious to the pressures of time and travel. Listening to Lomax's field tapes, however, there can be no doubt from the actual recordings that he had a genuine interest in getting to know the singer behind the song, the role of song within the home and community, the customs and attitudes of the people, as well as the values which sustained their way of living.

It seems curious, to say the least, that the more successful a project may appear, the more criticism it attracts. John Swzed addresses the fact that "not all the Scots scholars appreciated Lomax's work," adding that: "Even the BBC people could find something negative to say about Alan. One executive in Scotland called him the Harry Lime of folk song."[15] Avoiding the 'any fool can criticise' line, Swzed concludes with the estimation of one who actually worked with Lomax and knew his Scottish fieldwork and recordings better than any: "Hamish Henderson, on the other hand, later recalled Alan's work in Scotland as being of the highest quality." Ever one to consider all aspects, Hamish addressed some of the criticism:

[Alan] brought to the task a ruthless readiness to do things with his bare hands that most orthodox folklorists would not have handled with two thicknesses of kid gloves. For example, when in Northeast Scotland, he got to grips with the social and political set-up, did his best to explore the often grisly reality of hardship and oppression which lay behind the songs, and thus came in conflict with the safety-first BBC producers who like to trail a wreath of late roses over the stark cadaver of the old system. Alan

---

[15] Szwed, op. cit., p. 265. Harry Lime was the villain, played by Orson Welles, in Carol Reed's film version of Graham Greene's *The Third Man*.

did not regard folksong as 'something on the side'; he viewed it as an integral part of the life of the community involved, and he enlisted wide reading and lively intellectual curiosity towards the exploring of all its various ramifications. His ruthlessness and intolerance of anything smacking of humbug earned him enemies... However, my own feeling is that Alan is, in his own way, a man of genius.[16]

Lomax was also a man ahead of his time. Had he not recorded conversations such as the one with Calum Johnston, the general insight into Gaelic songs would be all the poorer. How well did he know the singer behind the song? If that conversation alone is anything to go by, he possibly found out more about the singer in 26 minutes and 24 seconds than some folk find out about their neighbours in 26 years – possibly more than the singer anticipated telling him. If we sense Calum shifting in his seat by the last searching question, he may even have been relieved it was time for another song.

Kishmul Castle, Isle of Barra,
drawing by Alan Lomax, 1951.

---

[16] Nat Henfoff, 'Profile: Alan Lomax', (p. 77) quoted by Szwed, p. 266.

Orain Floraidh
The Songs of Flora MacNeil

Peter Urpeth[1]

Flora MacNeil's second recording of traditional Gaelic song for Temple Records, *Orain Floraidh* (COMD2081), is not only a recording of great emotional depth and subtlety, it is a recording that extends our knowledge and understanding of this most beautiful of musics and, perhaps, its finest living exponent. For the 13 tracks of this set provide ample evidence that, while a substantial proportion of Flora's repertoire originates in her native Barra, an important element of her work belongs to the neighbouring islands where, in isolation, the song culture of the Southern Hebrides developed along distinctive lines. While for many this distinction may be viewed as an exercise in hair-splitting, the reasons why distinct variations of the 'same' songs came to exist within such close localities, is deeply rooted in the history of the people of Barra, Mingulay, Vatersay and Bernaray, Eriskay and South Uist.

While reactionary historians (such as *The Herald*'s Tory convener, Michael Fry) are busy attempting to belittle the nature and extent of events in the nineteenth and early twentieth centuries that collectively became known as 'The Clearances', the songs on this CD, their nature and survival within Flora's family, provide a substantial insight into the traumatic history of the region and how that impacted on people and songs alike. The greatest defence against reactionary historians (who come to prominence, sadly, when their target culture is at its lowest ebb) is the fact that the *cultural document* exists, passed down through generations, and its lessons cannot be denied. The songs of the Gaelic oral tradition cannot be taken out of the mouths of those that sang the songs and passed them on. The songs cannot be separated from the singers

[1] This article first appeared in *The Living Tradition*, and is here reproduced with the kind permission of its editor, Pete Heywood.

who choose to preserve them, adapt them and value them individually. They had their reasons. For much of the following biographical information I am indebted to the genealogist Cal MacNeil of Kentangavil, Isle of Barra, whose invaluable work and dedication has greatly assisted in unravelling Floraidh's branch of the MacNeil family tree but, more importantly, Cal has also assisted in unravelling large sections of *history geno* of Flora's music – the points and places in time where songs and people may have met and how, as a consequence, the songs of long ago came to accumulate in Floraidh's repertoire. Further, recordings such as *Orain Floraidh*, when *read* in the broad context of history, may provide some pointers as to the way forward for the 'tradition' of Gaelic song. At present this tradition is, in many respects, in healthy condition, but anyone close to the singers and musicians who currently sustain *the tradition* will know that it is riven with difficult and probably destructive disagreements about the soul and sanctity of the music. In an interview conducted in Flora's home in late 1998, this writer was struck by a very simple-sounding revelation. Flora spoke of how, as a very young child, she was aware that her family were great preservers of the region's tradition of song. In some regards, Flora can recall being slightly embarrassed at that young age of the 'old-fashioned' nature of her family and upbringing – Flora's feelings were doubtless fuelled by the awkwardness she felt when being encouraged by her primary school teacher to come to the front of the class and sing for her contemporaries.

However, curiosity about the origins of these feelings led this writer to Cal MacNeil's kitchen, a place where the question "does this feeling of Flora's have any greater significance; could it be an indication that Floraidh's music is rooted in something deep within the history of her family?" was met with an immediate and unrestrained "yes". There is no better evidence of this than on track 11 of *Orain Floraidh*, Floraidh's beautiful rendition of 'Seathan, Mac Righ Eireann' (Seathan, Son of the King of Ireland'). In her sleeve note, Floraidh states that she acquired this song from the singing of a cousin of her mother's, Mary Johnstone, and that Mary sang this as a lament. Floraidh also informs us that in Carmichael's *Carmina Gadelica*, this song is listed as a waulking song. Floraidh sings it as a lament. Tender, intimate, it is a giant of a song that recollects the life joys of one who now mourns.

Mary Johnstone, Flora once told this writer, would visit the MacNeil home in Ledag, Castlebay, and join in the informal hearthside singing. But when it came to Mary's turn to lead on a song, she would be implored by the others present to sing 'Seathan'. It had a special magic – and probably, for Mary, this magic was more than a quality of the melody: it was rooted in the significance of the song and its survival in a culture that had endured the worst forms of adversity. It is not overstating the case to claim that 'Seathan' embodies the emotions and spirit of many who, like Mary's parents and grandparents, had been forced to live in increasingly marginalised circumstances before leaving Barra to settle on Mingulay. Mary had learnt the song from the oral tradition; those who she picked it up from had similarly learnt it through the oral tradition. The origins of its sorrow and its survival, for it is a very ancient song, must surely, therefore, be rooted in the histories of those that preserved, shaped it and valued it.

Mary Johnstone was, as Floraidh identified, a cousin of her mother, Ann Gillies (born in Gearradh Gadhal, 1889). At the time Floraidh heard this song from Mary, it had come full circle. Mary was the daughter of Angus MacNeil, Floraidh's maternal grandmother's brother. Mary Johnstone (as she became through marriage) learnt this song during her childhood on Mingulay, where it was sung as a lament. Mary's grandparents were Neil 'Beag' MacNeil (1815-1883) and Catherine MacNeil (1824-1901), neither of whom were originally native to Mingulay but settled there later in life after being moved-on from their original habitation in Barra. Neil 'Beag' was born in Gasbhal, Barra, was dispossessed of the family land and moved to the small neighbouring Island of Bernaray, and thence to Mingulay. Catherine MacNeil was born in Borve, Barra. Her passage to Mingulay is unclear, but it is there that she lived with her husband Neil 'Beag', and where she had her children.

However, while the experiences of Mary's parents were extreme and insecure, the true picture of marginalisation in this branch of Floraidh's family comes in the history of repeat moves endured by Mary Johnstone's paternal grandparents, John MacNeil and Christine Campbell. John MacNeil died in 1818. The first records of his life show that he lived in Tangusdale, an inhospitable and rocky glen above Nask and Castlebay, on the road to Vatersay. Today, ruins of small houses can still be found in this high, remote and barren place. Archaeological records show that settlement of the glen has been sporadic over more than a thousand years. In comparison to the richly fertile pastures of Barra's West Coast and the machair land of Vatersay, it is poor and unproductive land that would not have provided anything like an adequate living for a family. Unable to survive in Tangusdale, John and Christine MacNeil moved on to Gashabhal and Kinloch. Christine, whose date of birth and death is not known, may have been significantly younger than her husband, or some fate befell him that prematurely ended his life, for at his death in 1818 his son Neil 'Beag' was only three years old and with his mother, Christine moved from Mingulay to Berneray. (As stated above, Neil Beag subsequently returned to Mingulay). During her life, Christine lived in Tangusdale, Gasbhal, Kinloch, Mingulay and Berneray – many would say a series of moves to ever more marginal lands. It is from these origins that Mary Johnstone, and subsequently Floraidh, acquired their version of 'Seathan'. Perhaps, the poetry of 'Seathan' was itself particularly meaningful to those whose lives were marred by poverty and insecurity of tenure, as it contains refrains that reflect on memories of better times past:

Seathan, Mac Righ Eireann

Hu ru o na hi ho ro
Hu ru o nahi ho ro
Tha Seathan an diugh na mharbhan

(chorus)
Sgeul is olc le fearaibh Alba
Sgeul is olc le luchd a leanmhuinn
Sgeul is ait le luchd an t-sealga
Bannsa Seathan a'faibh sleibhte
Mise lag is esan treubhach
Cota ruadh mu leth mo shleisne
Is iomadh beinn is gleann a shiubhail sinn
Bha mi'n I nan cailleacha dubha leat
Bha mi'n Sleibhte nam ban buidhe Leat
Bha mi'n Eirinn an Coig Mhumha leat

Dh'eisd mi ri Aifrionn sa'Chill Chumha leat
Seathan mo ghille greine
Och dh'am dheoin gundo ghlachd an t-eug thu
Dh'fhag siud mise dubhach deurach
Cha toirinn do lagh na Righ thu
Cha toirinn dhan chro naoimh thu
Cha ghibhtinn do Mhoire mhin thu
Air eagal's gun caillin fhin thu.

Seathan, Son of the King of Ireland (translation)

Hu ru o na hi ho ro
Hu ru o na hi ho ro
Seathan tonight is dead

(chorus)

A sad tale to the men of Scotland
A sad tale to his followers
A joyous tale to his pursuers
I and Seathan crossing mountains
I weak, but Seathan strong
A russet coat around my thigh
Many a glen and ben we travelled
I was in Islay and Uist with you
I was in Iona of the nuns with you
I was in Sleat of the yellow haired women with you
I was in Ireland in the Province of Munster with you

I heard mass in Cill Chumhe with you
Seathan my brightness of the sun
Woe is me that death has caught you.
And that has left me sad and tearful
I would not give you to law or king
I would not give you to the Holy Rood
I would not give you to the gentle Mary
For fear that I would lose you myself.[2]

On *Orain Floraidh* there are two songs that Floraidh states came from her Aunt Mary Gillies. Mary, along with Floriadh's mother Ann, was the daughter of Neil Gillies (1811–1890) and Flora MacNeil (1816–1872). They married in 1833 and, like Floraidh's maternal great grandparents, were resident in Mingulay. The songs contributed to the family's treasure chest by her great-great-great grandparents (mother's paternal side) are also of great interest, for this chapter in the family history is also one of great poverty. John MacNeil (1776–1857), Floraidh's great-great-great grandfather, is recorded as having lived in Tresibhig and Uidh (both Vatersay), and subsequently Mingulay. Standing on the shores of Tresibhig today it is still possible to see where small dwellings once stood and where cultivation of the land took place. Small areas of softer,

---

[2] Translation by Donalda MacKinnon, taken from the sleeve notes of *Orain Floraidh*.

greener grass can be found, but little else remains. On a sunny day in July it is possible to think of this location as a fine place to contemplate settlement. However, the locality suffers from excessive exposure to the ravages of the Atlantic. For most of the year, those forced to live here would be trying to scavenge an existence in the most arduous of circumstances, the unrelenting gales and stormy seas rendering any attempt at settlement almost impossible. From here John and his wife Mary moved to the equally testing surrounds of Uidh, where in 1816 they had their daughter Flora. From Uidh, the family moved to Mingulay. In this interconnected history of songs and singers, it is interesting to note that the informal ceilidhs that Floraidh so enjoyed as a child were largely the preserve of female members of the family and friends. The maternal link to Mingulay therefore greatly extended the influence of the song tradition of Mingulay and other islands south of Barra in Floraidh's own repertoire. Of all the songs on *Orain Floraidh* that Floraidh directly connects with family members, not one song is attributed to the paternal side of the family, while Floraidh attributes some songs of the twentieth century to male singers.

The paternal side of the family, although resident in Berneray in the eighteenth century, moved to Barra circa 1830 and remained resident there. However, Floraidh's family could not have been great bearers of the tradition simply as the result of the influence of the maternal side of the family and, although the paternal family was resident on Barra throughout the Clearances, it is plain that they endured great hardship in the multi-divided crofts on Balanambodach and Brevig on the less fertile, thin soils of the east-side of the Island. It would, of course, be wrong to suggest that only the most melancholy of songs was valid in this sad history. This is simply not the case. However, the variation in songs over time can be attributed to the divergent histories of their singers. Sometimes, as in the case of 'Seathan', the variation is stark, and one can only think that Carmichael's version arose from circumstances within the tradition quite distinct from those that shaped the version Floraidh first encountered in the early 1930s.

The Scottish Folk Revival: Reflections and Perspectives

The Poets and the Folk Revival: A Reflection

Adam McNaughtan

It has long been a commonplace of Scottish literary history that there has never been a wide gap between our art poetry and folk poetry. This held true of the Makars, of the sixteenth and seventeenth century courtly poets and of the eighteenth century's Ramsay, Ferguson and Burns. In all these periods there was a tradition of poetic song to parallel the oral tradition of folksong and the ballads in print of the hack writers. Following Burns there was an explosion of poetry and song of country life and description. There were competent songsters such as Tannahill and Motherwell, the latter drawing on a close acquaintance with the oral tradition; the success of Burns may also have been one factor in the rise of the ballads of farm life, the bothy ballads which had their beginnings in the early years of the nineteenth century; there was also a large number of poetasters who vainly sought fame in Burns's wake. Scotland was then ripe for the literary back to the land movement which swept industrial Europe in the latter half of the century.

In no other country has this movement been denigrated as it has in Scotland under the name of the Kailyard, largely because elsewhere there were major authors turning out literature of contemporary life, which dealt unsentimentally with issues of international import. Scandinavia had a vast 'couthy' output, but it also had Ibsen, Strindberg, Hamsun, Bjørnson. England could boast an array of poets and novelists who overshadowed the sentimental storytellers of rural idyll. Scotland's most gifted writers either contributed to the idyll, or wrote in genres which serious literary critics were prone to dismiss: historical romances, boys' adventures and drawing-room comedies.

With the twentieth century came a marked reaction to the Kailyard. Hugh MacDiarmid distrusted the simplicity of lyric and song. He began first by writing lyrics which were intellectual rather than sentimental, giving a cosmic sweep even to eight-line poems. He then declared that the lyric was incapable of handling the issues of the twentieth century. There was an end to a tradition of poetic song. In his 'folk-song flyting' with Hamish Henderson, he also made a sweeping dismissal of the traditional songs and the songs being written by young people in the Revival. It is of the nature of flyting to be sweeping and extreme. He later praised the work of the School of Scottish Studies and paid tribute to the 'genuine' ballad-singing of people like Jeannie Robertson.

The poets of the second wave of the Scottish Cultural Revival all recognised MacDiarmid as the sole begetter of the movement. Some followed him slavishly into plastic or dictionary Scots; some were inspired to write in their own dialect; others acknowledged the importance of his break with nineteenth century forms, but chose to write in English. None gave up writing short lyric poems but few wrote songs, even though several of them had an advanced musical education. How were they affected by the Folk Revival which began with the opening of the School of Scottish Studies in 1951? The question arises from my coming across the name of Norman MacCaig among the treasures of the *Tobar an Dualchais* website.[1]

In 1952, Norman MacCaig was recorded singing four of the Muckle Sangs at the School of Scottish Studies. This was in the middle of a nine-year period when he published no volumes of verse, having forsworn his first two books because he felt that the complexity of their imagery made them nigh incomprehensible. It is tempting to speculate that his encounters with folk-song – he is also on record as a popular performer of 'The Keach in the Creel' at the Bo'ness Rebels' Ceilidhs[2] – were a contributory factor in his journey to lucidity that began with the 1955 volume, *Riding Lights*. The rhythms of the ballad with its fixed stresses and variable unstressed syllables might also have influenced the sprung rhythms of his later, carefully disciplined, free verse. On the other hand, the sureness of his free verse rhythms might have come from his familiarity with the scansion of Latin hexameters with their mixing of triple feet and spondees – the 'strawberry jam pot' and 'hickory dickory dock' of schoolboy mnemonics.

MacCaig's imagery is bolder and more demanding than that of the folk-poet. Lord Beichan's eagerness and haste are concisely expressed in:

> He has hied him swiftly doon the stair,
> oot o' fifteen steps he has made but three.

---

[1] www.tobaranddualchais.co.uk
[2] *Bo'ness Journal*, cited in Ewan MacVicar, *The Bo'ness Rebels*, Linlithgow: Gallus, 2008.

But the poet frequently compresses his metaphors into a single word, the recognition and expansion of which unites his readers to him, as in his image of the kingfisher's flashing speed over the water:

> That kingfisher, jewelling upstream,
> seems to leave a streak of itself behind it
> in the bright air.

MacCaig's song repertoire and the tempo at which he sang suggests that he was greatly influenced by Ewan MacColl's appearances at the early People's Festivals. In 1952 he sang 'Kilbogie', 'The Broomfield Hill', 'The Jolly Beggar' and 'The Keach in the Creel'; it is no surprise that the table-turning humour of these should appeal to Norman. In 1954 he was recorded for the Archive singing 'Hey Ca' Thro', 'Kissin's Nae Sin', 'The Burning of Auchendoun', 'The Dowie Dens o' Yarrow' and 'The Wife of Usher's Well'. His texts for the ballads showed an acquaintance with Keith and Greig's *Last Leaves of Traditional Ballads*[3]. Four of the 1954 songs were published in MacColl's *Scotland Sings* from 1953.[4]

Norman was even seduced into joining his friends from the Bo'ness Rebels in celebrating with a song the retrieval of the Stone of Destiny in 1951, using the Scots so often noted as absent from his poetry:

> A chiel cam doun tae London toun
> An nicked awa wi the stane, man.
> A lassie cried oot, "I'll gie ye a haun,
> Fir it's ill tae dae it alane, man
>
> A chiel's awa, a chiel's awa,
> A chiel's awa wi the stane, man.
> A lad and his lass made His Worship an ass,
> An' nicked awa wi the stane, man.[5]

The 1952 recording was not the first MacCaig record preserved in the Archive. In 1951, Alan Lomax taped Norman playing the pibroch 'Rorys' Lament' on the fiddle. According to Dr John MacInnes, who recorded the 1954 session, he was "a brilliant exponent of Scottish fiddle and pipe music," with a particular skill in adapting the pibroch for the fiddle.

---

[3] Gavin Greig and Alexander Keith, *Last Leaves of Traditional Ballads and Ballad Airs*, Aberdeen: The Buchan Club,. 1925.

[4] Ewan McColl, *Scotland Sings*. London: WMA, 1953.

[5] *Rebels Ceilidh Song Book*, Bo'ness Rebels Literary Society. [1953]

Although others have experimented with pibroch along the same lines (and possibly with other instruments) MacCaig, so far as I am aware, is the musician who must be remembered as the pioneer and precursor of them all. His skill was such that the fiddle adaptation actually sounded like pipe-music made distant and fine."[6]

It is no surprise then that the pibroch and the fiddle should figure in his poetry, or that he should find such an affinity, both socially and in performance, with Aly Bain.

SHETLAND REEL
For Aly Bain

The fiddle bow slides and hops and dances
At a speed that should sound hectic but doesn't.
Down-bow becomes three up-bows in places
I would never have thought of, following
The jags and curves of the tune as though it were
Helicoptering at a hundred miles an hour
Along a drystone dyke on a humpy landscape.

The result – a tune: a witty celebration
Of nimbleness and joy, fit to be played
In a tenement room, in a hall, in the lee
Of a Shetland peatstack where the Aurora
Remembers its other name, the Merry Dancers.

Another of the poets who appreciated pipe music was Robert Garioch, who celebrated the vitality of the early festivals, official and People's, in 'Embro to the Ploy':

The Epworth Haa wi wunner did
behold a piper's bicker;
wi hadarid and hindarid
the air gat thick and thicker.
Cumha na Cloinne played on strings
torments a piper quicker
to get his dander up, by jings,
than thirty u.p. liquor,
hooch aye!
in Embro to the ploy.[7]

6 Dr John MacInnes: 'MacCaig and Gaeldom', in Joy Hendry and Raymond Ross (eds), *Norman MacCaig: Critical Essays*, Edinburgh: Edinburgh University Press, 1990.
7 Robert Garioch, *Complete Poetical Works*, Edinburgh: Macdonald, 1983, p.15.

Luckily he does not specify which fiddler was playing MacCrimmon's 'Lament for the Children'. Robert Garioch Sutherland, when he returned to Edinburgh after some years as an English teacher in London, found congenial employment with the Scottish National Dictionary at 27 George Square. He also found time to help with transcription work in the School of Scottish Studies' Archive. His transcription of Jeannie Robertson's 'Silly Jack and the Factor' was published in *Tocher* no. 6.

Like MacCaig, Garioch was a more than competent musician. He had been a cinema pianist in the thirties and during his time in an Italian P.O.W. camp played piano in the camp orchestra. Like Norman, and indeed MacDiarmid, he considered the *piobaireachd* the height of Scottish artistic accomplishment. MacCaig set the *piobaireachd* alongside the works of Bach; MacDiarmid wrote a 'Lament for the Great Music'. Garioch, however, did not think that the great pipers were all dead.

> Here comes the unco ferlie of the pipes,
> the first of the grace-notes, like a precious stane,
> gale-force music, delicately ruled,
> a thrawn, strang Clydesdale; the horseman kens the word.
> Allanerlie the great highland pipe can mak this soun,
> this rattle of reedy noise, the owretones brattlan thegither,
> wi maybe a swirlan danger, like musardrie of maut.
> Piobaireachd adorns tragedie wi maist sensie jewels.
> (From *The Big Music*)[8]

The 'horseman' in this poem is the piper. Garioch, in close touch with Hamish Henderson during his time in George Square, was aware of the kind of control that 'the horseman's word' gave to its possessors. They were even able to put a bridle on the De'il, as in the poem, 'Weill Met in Buchan', dedicated to Hamish. Perhaps the most apposite verse was the one relegated to the notes in the *Complete Poetical Works*. The speaker/horseman has managed to get on the Devil's back:

> I spier'd him gin he'd gree to gie's his crack,
> seean it wes some field-wark I wes on,
> caa cannie while I held the microphone,
> and tak tent no to coup me frae his back.

---

8 *Ibid.*, p.144.

Of all the poets, Robert Garioch, when writing in his native Edinburgh Scots, was closest linguistically to the Revival songwriters, and many of his topics could have been chosen by those songwriters. The only piece for which he indicated a tune, however, was 'The Wark o the Polis':

> I wes luikin at the miners on the TV,
> sic a lot o miners ye nivver did see,
> bit they wirnae howkin coal firtae warm you and me --
> they were owre busy fechtin the polis.[9]

Because of my own shortcomings I'll pass quickly over the Gaelic poets active in the Fifties. Sorley MacLean was important to the School of Scottish Studies both as the brother of Calum, the School's first fieldworker, and as a repository of island lore himself. Iain Crichton Smith has few references to song in his poems, though in his first novel, *Consider the Lilies*, those who bid farewell to the emigrants cleared from the land take up the Gaelic words of the 'Old Hundredth', and one of the emigrants sings "An Quebec chaidh mi air tìr's thug mi sgrìob feadh an àit", (At Quebec I went ashore and I took a walk through the place). Smith also managed to work in a memory from his own Lewis childhood of young folk dancing at the crossroads to the music of the accordion, though the novel was set some decades before the accordion came to Britain. Professor Derick Thomson of Glasgow University, the last surviving poet of the generation and an important historian of Gaelic culture, had little contact with the School, but was well aware of folksong scholarship; his mother's songs had been collected in the 1930s by the Finnish folklorist Otto Anderson.[10] He himself is featured in an Archive recording as the main guest at a Heretics' reading in 1971.

Two other Glasgow-based poets had equally little to do with 27 George Square. Edwin Morgan, Glasgow's, and then Scotland's, first laureate, was well aware of the folksong movement. He was aware of, and had a go at, almost every verse form from the traditional sonnet and translations of Old English heroic verse to science fiction and Concrete Poetry. In his Glaswegian version of Cyrano, some of the chorus songs were hard to shake from one's mind and could well have been used as protest songs. At least two of his poems were set to music by Archie Fisher (in a style more contemporary than traditional). But his recognition of the Revival is clearest in his sonnet on Matt McGinn, where Matt in his life and his songs, is seen as a Glaswegian Omar Khayyam:

---

9 *Ibid.*, p.207.
10 Maurice Lindsay (ed.), *As I Remember: Ten Scottish Authors Recall How for Them Writing Began*, London: Hale, 1979.

We cannot see it, it keeps changing so,
All round us, *in and out, above, below,*
at evening phantom figures come and go,
silently, *just a magic shadow show.*[11]

Maurice Lindsay, a violinist and music critic with the *Glasgow Herald*, and a prolific poet and anthologist, had little time nor patience with any except classical music. Yet in his final anthology, the 420-page *Edinburgh Book of Twentieth Century Scottish Poetry*, which he compiled in association with Lesley Duncan, we find Hamish Henderson's 'Flyting o Life an Daith' and 'Farewell to Sicily', McGinn's 'Coorie Doon' and 'The Big Orange Whale', and my own 'Oor Hamlet' and 'The Jeelie Piece Song'.

The years hae gi'en me the gift o sang
Though cuist in a minor key.

Such was Helen B. Cruickshank's own assessment of her place in the Pantheon, but she was the kindest of hostesses and a friend to younger poets, informally and as secretary of the Scottish branch of P.E.N., the international writers' association. She was a friend also to those who arrived for the People's Ceilidhs, because she undertook to find accommodation for many of them and her home was the venue for the After-the-Ceilidh ceilidhs. There the traditional singers met with members of the audience and with performers from Theatre Workshop, and there Hamish Henderson and Ewan MacColl had one of their frequent castin-oots. Hamish accused Ewan of hogging the stage and Ewan replied that folk would rather hear him than the rum-soaked voices of people like Jimmy MacBeath.

Helen rightly identified her gift as one of 'sang'. Many of her titles include references to song: 'Song of the Shepherd of Gruline', 'Leebie Sings', 'Ballad of a Lost Ladye':

O siller, siller shone the mune
And quaiet swung the door,
An' eerie skraighed the flaughtered gulls
As she gaed by the shore.

Many like that one are eminently singable. However, the poem that will preserve her memory at festivals and folk clubs is 'Shy Geordie', in the setting by Jim Reid:

---

11 Edwin Morgan, *Sonnets from Scotland*, Glasgow: Mariscat Press, 1984.

Up the Noran Water
In by Inglismaddy,
Annie's got a bairnie
That hasna got a daddy.[12]

Finally, the 'reporter' who recorded MacCaig's four ballads in 1952 deserves a mention, though he is often regarded more as a folklorist who wrote poetry than as a poet who was influenced by the folk movement. William Montgomerie was already well-known for the two volumes of Scottish nursery rhymes, compiled with his wife, Norah, which the Hogarth Press had published in the Forties. They would go on to publish collections of folk tales. He completed a post-graduate thesis on Scottish Ballad Manuscripts at the University of Edinburgh and contributed numerous articles on ballad history to learned journals. Though never on the staff of the School, he was a frequent and welcome visitor and, especially during his time in Angus, a busy fieldworker. On the same tape in the Archive as Norman MacCaig's book-based ballads are to be found the songs of the Cargill family of Auchmithie in Angus, including some memorable verses for Child 73, known to Jessie Cargill as 'Sweet Willie and Fair Annie':

Some said it was the sun risin,
Some said it was the moon;
Some said it was Fair Annie
Comin to see Sweet Willie's weddin.

Another of his prizes was included in *Tocher*, Vol.1 no.44. 'The Navvy' celebrates the men who built the mid-nineteenth century waterworks in Dundee. Its tune, a variant of 'The Enniskillen Dragoons', suggests their nationality.

Success to the Navvy wherever he may be!
May fortune attend him and good times may he see!

Dundee was the second of Montgomerie's three cities. He began his life in the East End of Glasgow and spent the latter part of it in Edinburgh. His first two volumes of poetry appeared in 1933, *Via*, and 1934, *Squared Circle: A Vision of Cairngorm*. They show the same kind of double allegiance to city and country as MacCaig. *Via* is a book of short Glasgow poems; *Squared Circle* finds him alone in the mountains in a series of six longer unrhymed poems, each with a mountain location indicated. The Glasgow

---

12 Helen B Cruickshank, *Up the Noran Water, and other Scots poems*, London: Methuen, 1940.

poems are in English, in traditional forms, sonnet, triolet, not of the MacDiarmid school nor of the New Apocalypse:

GLASGOW STREET

Out of this ugliness may come,
Some day, so beautiful a flower,
That men will wonder at that hour,
Remembering smoke and flowerless slum,
And ask – glimpsing the agony
Of the slaves who wrestle to be free -
"But why were all the poets dumb?"

Like MacCaig, he draws on music and birds for his imagery. For example this image from 'The Gull and the Crow', a poem of some 180 lines, might suggest a kinship with MacCaig:

This vision is an appetite – a gull –
A winged hunger with appraising eyes,
Evaluating all things; life and death
Divided to the taste of its desire.

However, the poem is visionary in a way that might have made MacCaig 'phone a taxi', as he threatened to do when faced with White Goddesses.

Bill Montgomerie's third book did not appear until 1972, but he had continued to write and publish in all the Scottish poetry magazines, and from 1977-1982 he exercised an influence as one of the longer-serving editors of *Lines Review*. The 1972 volume of poetry, *From Time to Time*, contained poems from all periods and from the three cities. It seems appropriate to end with lines from a poem which, dedicated to Robert Garioch, brings together poetry and folksong:

And later Scotland sang to me.
Jeannie in Aberdeen and Belle
in Blairgowrie of the Berryfields
singing without book or songsheet
their heirloom Lallan songs and ballads.
The Arbroath fishwife who
collected songs and in her basket
wild flowers of the Angus glens
and the young women of Auchmithie
laughing

who swept me from house to house
without knocking
to listen together to
the centuries-old ballads
of their ancients.[13]

13 William Montgomerie, *From Time to Time: Selected Poems*, Edinburgh: Canon-
gate, 1985.

The Survival of Folk Music in Scotland:
A Personal Comment

Jean Bechhofer

To obtain a comprehensive over-view of the folk music 'revival' in Scotland, I commend you to Ailie Munro's splendid book,*The Democratic Muse*.[1] My intention is to present you with a personal memoir.

I can look back on more than 60 years of exposure to folk music. Indeed, I claim notoriety from having been a dancing member of Tom Anderson's Isleburgh Concert Party, while I was still at school. In the late 1940s I also encountered Patrick Shuldham Shaw who had visited Shetland as a collector of songs and traditional tunes. Of the former there were a few, mainly lullabies. Tunes were another matter entirely, as the predominance of Shetland fiddle music is well known.

Music was very much part of my teenage years, but the nearest I got to 'folk' was a love of Vaughan Williams' translations of English traditional folk melodies into his symphonies. I recall that my favourite tune as a little girl was Percy Grainger's 'Country Gardens'. I was told that my maternal grandfather had been a keen singer of Irish songs. Years later I learned that his family had come from Limavady, and I have a few prized pieces of Beleek china as proof.

Perhaps it was in my genes, but I had loved the modal Irish air 'She Moved Through the Fair' long before I learned to sing it. The version I sing is not the poem written by Padraic Colum, but a brisker version I got orally from Sean Cannon. Puzzled by certain words, I did some research and found a version in Kennedy's *Songs of Britain and Ireland*. This account

---

[1] Ailie Munro, *The Democratic Muse: Folk Music Revival in Scotland*, Edinburgh: Scottish Cultural Press (2nd ed.), 1996.

had lines such as 'Dew falls on meadows and moss fills the night' and 'The glow of the Grecian hearth'. I reckoned that *moths* were filling the night and a Gaelic speaking friend suggested that the glow came from the '*gruchia*' or reflection from pots on the fire, rather than from a classical marble mantelpiece.

At the time of the People's Ceilidhs in the early 1950s, instrumental Scottish folk music was alive and well, although for most people that meant primarily dance music. Required Saturday evening listening on the 'wireless' featured, and still does, Scottish Country Dance Music. Posh folk dressed up for Highland Balls, and still do. Informal dances in village halls and student hops kept social dance alive. More recently, a younger generation discovered that Stripping a Willow with a Dashing White Sergeant could be far more fun than bobbing up and down on the spot.

So why the need for a 'Folk Music Revival'? Was it near to death or extinction – no, that was not exactly so. I think survival is a better term. Survival against the odds.

During my years as a student in Aberdeen there was no University Folk Club, although there was a dimly lit smoke filled jazz club where I was thrilled to hear Josh White, who was our Honorary President. There were many varied opportunities for singing. I particularly enjoyed honing my close harmony skills in the student coffee shop, and in student shows.

Bothy ballads and street songs still featured in relaxed student pub evenings with what little breath we had left after hill walking and climbing with the Lairig Club, as well as in rural community pubs and family parties. This became quite apparent as the folk festival movement gathered pace in the 1960s and '70s. Many singers who became professional performers have spoken of their early exposure to a wide range of songs at family and Hogmanay parties. Certain family members could be relied upon to produce 'their' song at the drop of a bunnet. Over the years, I have heard reluctant singers, coaxed to perform at impromptu gatherings or sessions, produce local versions of old sangs and ballads.

I was aware of other pockets of work-related song. Ewan MacColl wrote about the herring gutters, or Fisher Lassies, although he did not emphasise how much they sang as they worked. As a student travelling south from Lerwick to Aberdeen in the 1950s, I was frequently kept awake by whalers en route to the South Georgia whaling grounds. Much later I re-discovered their songs on A.L.Lloyd's *Leviathan* LP and wished I had listened more receptively.

Song and singing were generally less prominent everywhere in the 1950s. Few of the Muckle Sangs were then widely known or sung, but there was much Tartan Nostalgic Tat and Bowdlerised Burns on offer. After graduating, I spent a couple of years in Dumfries, again before the establishment of the Club at The Globe. I was once asked at very, very short notice to deputise for the pianist at an extremely formal Burns Supper. With no opportunity to rehearse, all I can say is, I never, ever wanted to attend a Burns Supper again. And did not until nearly twenty years later I went to that of the Edinburgh Folk Club, and have only missed one there since. Here was a night for folk where Burns himself would have felt welcome. One triumph of the revival has been to rescue Burns from idolatry and welcome him back to the people.

The end of the 1950s a was fruitful time for the re-discovery of the power of folk music for me and many others. The protest movement in America had spawned a generation of new writers. Collectors like Alan Lomax published, for instance, *The Penguin Book of American Folk Song* (as opposed to Les Barker's '*English Book of Penguin Folk Song*'!). This intrigued me because of the obvious cross-over and relationship to our own heritage. Then, in the UK, folk clubs arrived, skiffle gave way to folk and blues – and guitars sold like hot cakes. I was now in London, and was taken by a Scottish friend one Sunday night to a north London pub where 'The Ballad and Blues' club met. I still treasure my membership card for 1959. On that first night, I heard Ewan MacColl, Peggy Seeger, Isla Cameron, and Séamus Ennis. Not a bad line-up.

By the beginning of the 1960s, I had moved to Cambridge where there was not yet a folk club nor, alas, the now world-wide regarded Cambridge Folk Festival. In summers spent in Cornwall, I did eventually find folk music at the legendary Pipers Club, established with others by Brenda Wootton who had 'rediscovered' old songs, and wrote quite a few new. I started doing floor-spots with up and coming artists such as Jasper Carrot, Decameron and Michael Chapman, to name-drop a few! However, I was aware that community singing in male voice choirs, and church groups was still very common in Penwith. Round about this time I was introduced to Norman Buchan's *The Little Red Book*. Although I did know many of the entries, it was a revelation, and still is. I lend my precious copy to NO ONE. It is priceless. The influence of people like Hamish Henderson and Norman Buchan had of course spread widely. They had made available a kist of sangs for young singers such as the Fishers, Hamish Imlach, Jean Redpath and Iain MacKintosh.

Frank and I relocated to Edinburgh in the mid-'60s but did not get immediately caught up in the very lively Edinburgh folk scene which by then was well developed. I was mainly singing bairns to sleep. I relied on the radio and our LP collection to expand my own small repertoire, hitherto mainly kids songs. Though I ought to mention that was when I came under the spell of Tom Paxton, a man who treasures his Scottish roots. I do recall being very impressed by The Bitter Withy whose short career set a high standard for later vocal groups. I would go to the odd concert, and took my young six-year-old daughter to hear The Spinners and The McCalmans – was that why she later latched on to punk?

Clubs were being set up throughout Scotland. A few of these clubs survive today, but others have come and gone. The Edinburgh Folk Club, which I discovered in 1974, through an advert in the local library for The Shetland Fiddlers of Leith, had been established in 1973. A previous club, The Buffs, which had been around long enough in the '60s to become a legend, had had to shut down due to licence difficulties. The EFC became and still is a major part of our world, although in the '70s we did attend The Triangle, The Fuzz Club and The Crown on occasion. EFC's theme song should perhaps be 'We will Survive', but that is another story!

Survival is a key word for an important category of Scottish music, the Muckle Sangs. These were largely preserved by the travellers, by a few source singers who have been the tradition bearers and now, by a new generation of singers. For me, the ballads represent basic human experience, emotions, history, and memories. Each culture and community has stories which frequently mirror issues and concerns world-wide. They are songs which often have hidden messages, warnings or observations of human frailty. As a psychologist married to a sociologist there is much grist there for our mills!

I know that, because the oral tradition was paramount for the travellers, Sheila Stewart is most concerned that their heritage is not being passed on through her family. However the mammoth task of editing and printing the *Greig-Duncan Collection*[2] will surely ensure the future of much of our Scottish heritage. These eight volumes have pride of place in the middle of my rather large collection of songs, ancient and modern. Collectively, we owe a huge debt to Emily Lyle who took over the major task of co-ordinating the editing of the manuscripts on the premature death of Patrick Shuldham Shaw. The *Greig Duncan Collection* tells us *what* people sang but not *how* they sang. We now owe a further debt to the work of those who have recently made available, in digitised form, thousands of oral recordings in The Kist o' Riches compiled by the School of Scottish

Studies. Hopefully some of the songs written by today's singer-songwriters will also survive, even if only to document the issues which bothered us in the late twentieth and early twenty-first centuries.

A major difference or development which I have observed over the years of the revival has been the increased emphasis on, and improvement in, the standard of instrumental playing. Where once music for dancing restricted the style, length and interpretation of composition, today we have bands and performers whose style has earned them the freedom to make arrangements which are more equivalent to those in 'chamber

[2] P. Shuldham Shaw and E B Lyle (eds), *The Greig-Duncan Folk Song Collection*, 8 vols, Edinburgh: Mercat Press, 1981-200.

music' and demand an attentive audience. Sometimes enthusiasm overtakes experience, but there is no doubt that the standard of musicianship has risen and is still rising due to increased opportunities provided by college and conservatoire teaching. However, it is best not to forget that the source singers and carriers of the stream of the remote and recent past, had both experience and commitment. Today the best young performers choose to be mentored by them.

Apart from many years as a committee member of the Edinburgh Folk Club, while I was a member of the Fringe Society Board in the 1980s, I had a role in promoting the interests of folk music on the Fringe, and did a fair amount of table thumping at Board meetings. By then the 'revival' was alive and kicking with very different material and artists touring both sides of the Tweed. When I first got caught up in the folk world, piping, fiddle and accordion, and Gaelic song kept severely to their own spaces in the Scottish 'House of Music', even though occasionally sound drifted through from adjoining rooms. That attitude has now largely gone. 'Aabody talks tae aabody', and even sit beside each other at the Trad Awards! Seriously, this rapprochement will be a major factor in the continuing survival of what never really went away.

As a result of the many developments in performance, presentation and repertoire, venues and clubs have had continually to consider how they present themselves to a paying audience. There are now free sessions in many pubs and settings which vary in standard from OK to professional. These provide a challenge, but one which needs to be met, and should be met since venues have to take into account the changed nature of folk music and its revival/survival while retaining the informal camaraderie which is a feature of its appeal.

As well as becoming involved in club management, my husband Frank set up The Bechhofer Agency in the 1980s, originally to assist artists from outwith Scotland who were keen to widen their acquaintance with northern areas. As a result we have experienced a certain amount of stress from time to time, but gained a huge amount of pleasure and satisfaction from the contact with a wide range of musicians, singers, instrumentalists and promoters. Our involvement in revival/survival has indeed been a major source of personal enrichment throughout our time in Edinburgh.

Corner House Café

Alastair McDonald

On receiving the news that folksinger Ray Fisher (1940–2011) had passed on, my thoughts went, unbidden, immediately to a venue called the Corner House Café on Trongate, Glasgow, over half a century ago. It was the first 'folk club' I'd attended, having served my two-guitar-chord apprenticeship with skiffle groups various, elbowed my way into a jazz band, been given an LP of *Pete Seeger & The Weavers at Carnegie Hall, New York* and, as a result, desperately attempting to get a noise like the 5 string banjo out of 4 strings & a plectrum (!!?), had taken up with fellow skiffler Nigel Denver to explore '...the folk scene'.

The first impression was one of complete wonderment at being allowed in to something special. The night, as I recall, was kind of overseen by Morris Blythman, school teacher, poet, songwriter & active promoter of the John MacLean society – and someone with whom I had the privilege to work, laugh, cry, share and drink over many later years.

Running alongside the folk clubs that were (gradually) springing up around the country was another equally exciting event called the 'Ballads & Blues' concert. The Corner House Café folk club was a relaxed listen on non-licensed premises and on various nights you could hear Ray & Archie Fisher, Bobby Campbell (all later to become the Wayfarers), artist & teacher Josh McRae of TV, radio & record fame (and owner of the first Gibson guitar I ever clapped eyes on), actor Roddy McMillan, accompanied by Jimmy Reilly on the guitar, Jeannie Robertson, Joe Gordon, Calum Sinclair and far too many more than we have space to mention here. Robin Hall & Jimmie McGregor along with Rory & Alex McEwan, Cy Grant and others were introducing the viewing public to this new & musically uncluttered style of entertainment on the TV programme *Tonight*, so in all sorts of ways the so-called 'folk revival' was taking hold.

The Ballads & Blues concert was a splendid affair in a quite subtly different way. Being a theatre presentation it tended to be more 'formal', but the variety of musical styles showed how broad the music of folk could be, with no pigeon holes. For instance, there was Forrie Cairns' Scottish All-Stars scything their way through the opening set with some trad jazz (the folk music of the American Blacks), followed by a bothy ballad or three from The Reivers (who appeared on the STV show *Jigtime*); some American blues and folk songs from a skiffle group, tuning in with the hit parade of the time, and, rounding off the evening, was another blast of jazz to send us home happy, uplifted and with a feeling that we had learned something, too.

It saddens me that what is called the 'folk scene' today can be so picky about what is good, right and proper. For just one instance, Pete Seeger largely introduced us to a song by José Martí of Cuba, 'Guantanamera'. That was considered an acceptable song until The Sandpipers got a hit with it (having cannibalised Seeger's inbuilt personal musing on the song), and after that it became a no-go area, being regarded by the 'real' folk scene as 'commercial' – how can a good song become bad just because it got something on its shoe?

For myself, I'll never forget meeting Belle, Sheila & Cathy, the Stewarts of Blair(gowrie) in the early 1980s at the Dundee Music Festival. They were really kind, welcoming and encouraging to me personally, and I am so grateful to them, especially since I was held in distinct suspicion by the 'folk' world because of, presumably, my TV appearances with people who wore (gasp!) TARTAN (eeuuggh!).

Belle (looking magnificent in a Stewart tartan dress!) told me they got really bored with people who only ever wanted to impress them with their knowledge of 32-verse ballads, while seemingly uninterested in other traditions, notably the Music Hall tradition. Lots of bothy ballads and songs grew out of the desire for folk simply to be entertained, and what could possibly be wrong with that? A lot, it seems, in the mind of the 'traditionalist'.

Another belter for me was wondering why in the all-embracing 'celtic' explosion there was no sign of American traditional jazz – a music learned by slaves from their Scottish/English/Irish plantation owning masters and evolving into the 'Dixie' jazz music of today. I took a demo CD of an all-Scottish bunch of guys playing the Black roots music to a 'celtic' record label. They listened politely and said, "No thanks Alastair, I think we're going to keep things Scottish." "Fair enough," says I, "got anything else coming up?" "Yes," says he proudly, "a SALSA band!"– Where are you supposed to look?

In conclusion, it was maybe not the worst of times to grow up, when people liked a thing just because it appealed to them, without the need for neat compartmentalisation.

Landscape with Fiddles

Jim Gilchrist

This response to Paddy Bort's request for a few thoughts on the folk revival is a very personal one, and duly idiosyncratic, though I comfort myself with the thought that what we call the Scottish Folk Revival itself is a large, energetic and vastly multifaceted entity – not unlike Hamish Henderson, whose memory this Carrying Stream Festival has celebrated these past ten years.

I have to declare certain credentials here. Around the earlier years of the revival, in the Fifties and Sixties, I was not taking too much notice. Like many others of my generation, my earliest passing exposure to Scottish music would have been through the Saturday night strains of 'Kate Dalrymple' on the Scottish Home Service. The great Jimmy Shand and his ilk did not stand a chance, however, as the late Sixties saw me, like many of my peers, in thrall to the guitar rock of the Yardbirds, Stones, Cream, etc, that and the odd Sibelius symphony (this last thanks largely to Ken Russell's great mid-Sixties BBC series of TV documentaries on composers). Some of my mates went to folk clubs, but what I tended to regard then as three Arran knit sweaters singing 'The Wild Rover', as lampooned later by Billy Connolly, did not hold water.

Gradually, though, I started wagging a curious ear towards folk music – largely through the instrumental rather than the singing side, attracted more by the Corrie's pioneering instrumentation on TV than by the songs themselves, and later by the folk-rock excursions of Fairport, Steeleye, and others. There were some distinct near-Damascene moments, however. I particularly recall listening to the Dubliners' 1967 album *A Drop of the Hard Stuff*, which a friend had bought largely on the back of the group's unlikely 'Seven Drunken Nights' pop chart success. Still the songs remained secondary – it was Barney McKenna's banjo solo, 'Colonel Fraser', then John Sheahan's fiddle joining him on 'O'Rourke's Reel', the whole ensemble echoing into the sunset, that really made me sit up. A few years later someone played me the live Gaiety Theatre recording of Sean O'Riada's old Ceoltóirí Chualann and the magnificent ÓNeill's March' sounding as if from a long way off but strangely familiar, inducing a similar jolt of inexplicable connectivity.

But also, along the way, while playing that old Dubliners LP, it was a salutary revelation to discover that my mother, third-generation Irish, who grew up in what was very much a Scots-Irish-Italian community in the Grassmarket, knew some of the words of 'The Rising of the Moon' that Ronnie Drew was roaring out on my borrowed vinyl. It started to dawn on me that what we called 'folk songs' possessed a life of their own, and a circulation not circumscribed or requiring endorsement by the business of being recorded.

Then there was seeing Alan Stivell on *The Old Grey Whistle Test* – a Frenchman, for God's sake, who played bagpipes and harp, and accompanied by rock musicians. That much used and abused 'Celtic' word started to impinge.

Curioser and curioser, it seemed, and by the time I migrated from the west to Edinburgh in the mid-1970s, I was hooked and my folk music education greatly furthered by Edinburgh Folk Club in its George Square incarnation, where one could enjoy wonderfully intimate performances by everyone, from tradition bearers like the Stewarts of Blair to an emergent Battlefield Band. There were also some salutary folk festival experiences, most memorably, I think, Newcastleton in the hot summer of '76, pipe tunes and the screich of swifts mingling of a hot evening in the back yard of the Grapes, ballads from both sides of the Border and Northumbrian pipes burbling sweetly, along with an ecstatic canary, in a back room. Then there was an unforgettable (despite the mass hangovers) Inverness, the year of the Bothy Band and much else. Studious extracurricular activities, naturally, took in Sandy Bell's, where one might hear the likes of the Cunningham Brothers, Aly Bain and Cathal McConnell, the McCalmans or whoever was about.

But I should not labour 'the good old days', because while you could enjoy Scottish music if you knew where to find it, it was still regarded very much as 'minority interest' music (and let's not forget the vigorous box and fiddle clubs, which tended to go unacknowledged by the folk revivalists in those days, but which, instrumentally, were carrying the tunes like no-one else). If not quite a desert, the Scottish cultural scene could be arid. I always remember the Scottish academic – in charge of producing *teachers*, God help us, who once drily assured me, "of course, there *is* no culture in Scotland."

Mind you, the folkies themselves were not always the greatest champions of the Scots muse. I remember Sandy Bell's going through a phase, in the late Seventies and early Eighties, when you would be hard put to hear a Scots tune at a session, as frantic fiddles reprised tracks from the latest Bothy Band or Chieftains album. Strathspeys? What were those?

When this present event's predecessor, the long defunct Edinburgh Folk Festival, was first mooted, with support pending from City of Edinburgh Council, back in 1978 I recall certain toon cooncillors complaining that, in terms of bringing in business, such an event would simply attract those they dismissed as 'the knapsack brigade'. Clearly, this was long before Glasgow's Celtic Connections jamboree could inject an estimated £11.9 million into the economy of the Dear Green Place.

The Scottish musical landscape I survey today has changed immeasurably over the past three decades or so. Active interest in traditional music has never been greater – on the instrumental side at least, with impressive numbers of youngsters learning fiddle, pipes or harp, with organisations like the seemingly unstoppable Fèis movement seemingly producing legions of impressive young players and singers from the Highland and islands and elsewhere.

Thirty years ago, simply trying to get a modest element of traditional music into schools was a major challenge, and the idea of a BA degree course in Scottish Music at the RSAMD (sorry, Royal Conservatoire of Scotland!) or a dedicated National Centre of Excellence in Traditional Music at Plockton High School would have been deemed as fantasy fiction, along with such an unlikelihood as the Scots Trad Awards, a glitzy 'folk Oscars' bash. (At the same time, one can't help wondering where on earth all this emergent talent will find employment.)

Meanwhile the advent of the wired world has opened up levels of access and communication unimaginable even 20 years ago. What might that much sung seer, Thomas the Rhymer, have made of an astonishing facility like the Tobar an Dualchais/Kist o Riches online archive of some 11,500 hours of recorded Gaelic and Lowland songs, tunes, tales and reminiscences, enabling anyone with internet access anywhere in the world to invoke the voice of a tradition-bearer – long departed, renowned singers such as Jeannie Robertson or Willie Scott or some unknown but richly endowed islander, out of the ether, as it were?

While making my first tentative forays into the folk scene, I was invited to write my first occasional reviews for The Scotsman – which of course had carved a very honourable niche for itself in the annals of folk music coverage through Alastair Clark's ground-breaking 'Sounds Around' column, at a time when no other papers bothered with regular coverage of such 'minority music'. As an example of changing times, one of my earliest reviews for the paper, back in the late Seventies, was of a public recital presented by the Royal Scottish Pipers' Society (RSPS), a rare event in those days. I reported the event in glowing terms – it featured, after all, two late greats, John D Burgess and Donald MacLeod, playing for public entertainment, no less, rather than for competition judges. I also had the temerity to comment that such events should be a lot more commonplace. Some time later the RSPS repeated the imitative and I duly reported that as well, repeating my opinion that there should be more such public showcases for good piping – which prompted a somewhat harrumphing letter from a military gentleman suggesting that I had made my point and should ... well, pipe down. If anyone had mooted the idea then that Glasgow might sustain an annual week-long festival of piping, featuring a wealth of well-attended concert and recitals, as a countdown to the World Pipe Band Championships, as it has done for the past seven years, they would have been laughed out of court.

The whole face of Scottish piping has changed vastly over those years, with the impact of folk bands using pipes, and fair exchange between the folk scene and what was once a very separate piping establishment. Plus there has been the catalytic effect of the 'cauld wind pipes' revival: what at first may have appeared an esoteric interest in Scotland's forgotten bellows blown bagpipes has developed into a genuine renaissance.

Fiddling, too, appears to be flourishing, although the sheer ubiquity of recorded music raises some concerns about how distinct regional styles might fare. Of particular interest – affecting piping, of course, as well as fiddling, has been the 'discovery' by Scottish enthusiasts of the vigorous fiddling, piping and step-dancing traditions among the Gaelic diaspora of Cape Breton Island, which has seen many younger players here striving to emulate the driving, dance-related style, with strathspeys hammered out as if there were no tomorrow. It is fascinating, and great fun, although I would not like to see the currently less trendy north-East 'high style', with its elegantly beautiful strathspeys and particularly slow strathspeys, become neglected.

If I may indulge a certain bee in my bonnet, strathspeys in general tend to be too often shunned by many younger players in favour of break-neck jigs and reels. There is nothing new in that, mind you: as far back as 1903, Highland fiddler (and angling innovator) Alexander Grant of Battangorm – 'Sandy Battan', as he was known – formed the Highland Strathspey and Reel Society to preserve what he regarded as the old styles of Highland fiddle playing, particularly the strathspey, which he feared were slipping away.

It will also be interesting, a few years down the line, to see just how many of the countless new tunes being composed in this current hotbed of instrumental creativity will have what it takes to endure, and embed themselves in the repertoire.

There is definitely a healthier and less compartmentalised atmosphere, with numerous fusion exercises – 'orchestral' and other large-scale folk works, some of which work better than others, similarly with often lively collaborations between folk and jazz musicians or with elements of rock or electronica.

Coming back down to earth, and indeed grass roots, however, the current Gaelic cultural resurgence, particularly through the energetic Fèis movement, appears to be producing legions of fine young players and particularly singers. Emerging Lowland Scots singers seem less than prolific, particularly in the male line, though we have such impressive young exponents as Siobhan Miller, Shona Donaldson and Lucy Pringle.

In the Lowlands, organisations such as the Traditional Music and Song Association (TMSA) and Edinburgh Scots Music Group (which arose out of the phenomenal response to the Adult Learning Project) have played an important part in nurturing emerging talent, though have been stymied over the past couple of years by cuts in Arts Council funding. There does remain the concern that dare not speak its name (no-one wants to risk being misconstrued as anti-Gaelic), that the official status granted to Gaelic, and the associated arts funding that attracts, is creating a disparity between financial support for Highland-Island and Lowland music activities. It remains to be seen how Creative Scotland, which replaced the Scottish Arts Council, may take this on board, and what effect the Scottish Government's Traditional Arts Working Group, whose report and recommendations were published at the beginning of last year, might have and what action Creative Scotland takes on them.

Certainly, while the big events such as Blàs Highland festival and Celtic Connections play an important role in providing a showcase (and also in commissioning new works), the teaching and promoting of grass roots music has to remain at the very heart of traditional music, to protect the 'seed corn', without which the higher-profile and burgeoning scene would not exist.

Of course, regardless of fluctuating finances and cultural trends, folk will aye sing. Hamish Henderson – a folklorist who unearthed and celebrated, as only he could, the wealth of Scottish folk song as a *living* tradition, rather than indulging in the 'last leaves' obsequies of an earlier generation of collectors – held that the 'carrying stream' of folk song continued to flow underground, even if the 'overground' looked less evidently healthy. One suspects that he might not have been too preoccupied with funding issues.

Amid all the musical sophistication, the fusion exercises, the festival stages, there remains the simple, crucial act of someone – practised performer or otherwise – standing up to sing a song. Over the past three decades I have come to appreciate, much more than I once did, that the sang's the thing. A few years back, I was at the Border ballad competition at Newcastleton when an elderly man whose name, sadly, I've forgotten, got up and sang 'Johnnie Armstrang'. He maybe did not have the greatest voice doing, but he declaimed that muckle sang, with its timeless and fatal dialogue between reiver and king, with smeddum and utter self-possession, and all the while the rain was drumming off the hall roof – a factor which the judge, Mike Tickell, conceded, definitely enhanced the atmosphere of the performance. Such unlooked for moments come without price.

Despite these uncertain times, I cannot help thinking of a remark made by Dr Joshua Dickson of the RSAMD at a conference of Gaelic and Scots song held at the ever-buzzing Sabhal Mòr Ostaig on Skye last year. He came out with the intriguing tale of an Oban woman who, banned by her father from learning the pipes as a girl, nevertheless absorbed so much of the music that she not only sang pipe tunes in her own personalised *canntaireachd*, the vocables used to transmit pipe music orally, but composed melodies in the idiom.

As Dickson observed, "Music, like the truth, will out."

Piping and the Folk Revival

Gary West

The only instrumentalist to appear on stage at the first Edinburgh People's Festival Ceilidh in August 1951 was the piper John D. Burgess. At seventeen years of age, John was just starting out on his long and illustrious career, although he had already taken the piping scene by storm. Recognised by the great pipers of the day as a child prodigy, the previous year he had become the youngest player ever to win a coveted Highland Society of London gold medal at the Argyllshire Gathering in Oban, following that a short time later by repeating the feat at the Northern Meeting in Inverness. Under the guidance of the greatest teacher of his day, Pipe Major Willie Ross, this young Edinburgh Academy pupil had that rare talent of being able to combine lightning-fast fingers with a musical maturity that belied his youth, and which was soon to earn him the reputation as 'King of the Pipers'.

It may be no surprise, then, that John Burgess was invited to play that evening in the Oddfellows' Hall. He had, after all, already shown that he was capable of taking the stage in any company with no fear, and that he could have the audience in the palm of his hand within minutes. And yet in some ways it *is* a surprise, because for almost two centuries the highland bagpipe had been viewed as an instrument somewhat set apart, and certainly not flowing in the same carrying stream as 'folk music'. A combination of competition, military patronage and musical literacy had set highland piping down its own path, one in which the concept of 'tradition' appeared to mean very different things to different people. This is a point taken up rather convincingly by William Donaldson in his book *The Highland Pipe and Scottish Society,*[1] in which he argues that the way an

[1] William Donaldson, *The Highland Pipe and Scottish Society, 1750 – 1950: Transmission, Change and the Concept of Tradition*, East Linton: Tuckwell, 2000.

art form is allowed to develop depends to a large extent on the attitudes of both performers and patrons to the very concept of *tradition*. And in the case of highland piping, their respective attitudes were diametrically opposed. In short, the performers up until the late eighteenth century saw their tradition as a living, developing art, showing no signs of decadence and moulding their practices to their own tastes, functions and accepted localised cultural conditions. The patrons, though, took a very different view. Following what Donaldson calls the 'MacPherson paradigm' – the attitude to tradition which was crystallised in the Ossian controversy – he argues that the cultural string-pullers of the day and especially the members of the Highland Society of London and its Edinburgh sister institution, took an altogether more pessimistic line on the progress of tradition. To them, it was axiomatic that tradition is eroded through time, and that by definition, the further back in time one looks, the purer the art form must have been. That frame of mind, and its lasting influence on the whole cultural context of piping, is what set it apart, shutting it off from the wider landscape of folk music.

It seems to me, therefore, that John Burgess's appearance on the Oddfellows' stage at the People's Ceilidh was an important step towards the eventual snapping of these constricting tethers. The public celebration of the highland bagpipe as belonging to 'the folk' alongside both Scots and Gaelic song and devoid of formalised judging, had been a relatively rare occurrence in Edinburgh during the preceding century and a half. As Hugh Cheape recognises: "The constraining fences, erected and policed by the social oligarchy, now appear to be down and the pastures are open to all to roam and graze freely."[2] The re-orientation of piping towards 'the people' was, I suggest, at least partly instigated that night in August 1951.

John Burgess himself went on to greatly influence today's piping generations, inspiring many younger players with his dexterity, his lightness of touch and his instantly recognisable style. He was something of a hero figure to my own generation, and particularly to the most innovative of them all, the late Gordon Duncan. I well recall Gordon's father, Jock Duncan (himself on the bill of the sixtieth anniversary of the Ceilidh), driving Gordon and myself to hear John play a recital in the Weem Hotel in Aberfeldy. We were young teenagers, and we were both just completely blown away. Gordon often reminded me of that night later in life, by which time he himself had embraced the wider folk tradition with wide open arms and to international acclaim, and it is a sad and poignant coincidence that he died in the same year as his hero in 2005.

Many players came directly under John Burgess's guidance and <u>teaching, and one</u> of the very finest of them is representing him at the

[2] Hugh Cheape in *Review of Scottish Culture*, No. 13, 2000-2001, p.141.

ceilidh's anniversary concert: Donald Mackay, former pipe major of the Strathclyde Police Pipe Band. Donald's touch and style owe much to his mentor, and his playing is a tribute to the man who, as Hamish Henderson later recalled, "played us marches, jigs, strathspeys and reels with all the expertise of Auld Nick at Kirk Alloway."[3]

---

[3] Hamish Henderson, *Alias MacAlias: Writings on Songs, Folk and Literature*, Edinburgh: Polygon, 1992, p.9.

'The Past is a Foreign Country...'[1]

Nick Keir

Just today someone brought a video clip to my attention. It was an STV programme from 1986 called *Shindig*, a half-baked TV Musical Spectacular hosted by Sydney Devine. In the programme the door opens onto a sort of Barn Dance Set and some under-rehearsed dancers lollop about for a while doing an approximation of an American Hoedown. A studio audience of pensioners, seemingly bussed in from Newton Mearns, clap along, trying their best to look spry, and eventually Sydney himself takes the microphone to welcome us one and all. "Amongst tonight's guests," he beams, "will be Donny Macleod, The Alexander Brothers and ... The McCalmans." Sydney makes an off-colour joke about toilets and we are on!

It's 'Johnny Cope', and I see The McCalmans as I remember them: Derek Moffat in his pomp, one of the finest singers of Scots Folksong, and Ian McCalman at the top of his game, powerful, relaxed and full of charm and wit. In the middle is a clean-shaven, fresh-faced lad with his dark curls shaped into an unfortunate mullet, his eyes unwrinkled and clear. It is me ... but a me that I scarcely remember. Even with video evidence I am slightly doubtful that I was ever that young, or ever had that much hair, so if I misremember things that happened long before that, things for which there is only my own memory to consult, I hope people will forgive me.

Folk music was very much part of the fabric of everyday entertainment in 1968. My pal Buffy Skinner and I were playing guitars and mucking about, skipping from Beatles numbers to Incredible String Band songs when he put on the Corries LP *Kishmul's Galley*, and I remember being very impressed. I had never heard anything like that before. It was thrilling and otherwordly and distinctively Scottish. Inspired by this, we played on and put together a set which was shamelessly pillaged from our LP collection and even got a few gigs, calling ourselves September Wine after a Dando

[1] "…. they do things differently there." Famous first sentence of L.P. Hartley, *The Go-Between*, London: Hamish Hamilton, 1953.

Shaft number we both liked.

Buffy moved south soon after and, having no confidence in myself as a soloist I let the thing drop. My first experience after that of a Folk Club was when a girlfriend took me to see Rankin File at The Triangle Club off Queensferry Street. I loved the atmosphere and the Country-tinged songwriting of Ian Rankin with Rick Nickerson on bass and Tony Mitchell on guitar. We went back quite a few times and, when I went off to Stirling University, just about the first society I joined was the Folk Club.

Most Folk Club organisers of that era will regale you with stories of getting Fairport Convention for £2.35 and a Fish Supper, but we did have some real bargains ... Our opening act were The Gaberlunzie who were 18 quid and who blew us away with their professionalism and tight harmony singing ... Mike Whellans, Archie Fisher, Billy Connolly, Hamish Imlach, an early line-up of Silly Wizard (featuring Madeleine Taylor and a 15 year-old Johnny Cunningham) all followed, to be joined over the years by The Whistlebinkies, The JSD Band, Contraband, Amazing Blondel, Saffron Summerfield, Matt McGinn and The Great Fife Road Show. Meanwhile in Stirling Town there were 2 folk clubs, The Stirling Folk Club itself (at the Golden Lion in those days), with a guest list much like our own, and the Number 7 which had a slightly more English slant and where we saw Mike Harding, Swan Arcade, Bernard Wrigley and the like.

Quite early on I was introduced to Tony Ireland and we began to jam away on 12 bar blues, and then gradually introduced some self-written songs and Scots trad ones. Tony was a big Rab Noakes fan and one of the first songs we learnt was 'Turn a Deaf Ear'. Before long we were doing a residency at the St Clair hotel in Edinburgh two nights a week. Dagger Gordon was around then too and introduced us to more Scots dance tunes and airs.

Tony and I called ourselves Finn mac Cuill and began to get gigs around Stirling and Edinburgh. Tony was well-connected and sometimes we would play at Ricky Demarco's house or gallery for parties and meet up with people like David Campbell from The Heretics and so on. I was studying English and my Poetry tutor was Norman MacCaig, who was a wonderful performer of his own poems. Now and again we would set off with him to do Folk and Poetry shows for Arts Clubs, travelling back through the night in Tony's ex-Post Office Morris van, and once taking the last train south out of Inverness in a snowstorm, fortified with Lager and a bottle of Calvados we had gathered from somewhere. We also played Ardfern Festival, where The McCalmans famously arrived by helicopter and Finn mac Cuill turned down a precocious 14 year old who wanted to join our band – it was Phil Cunningham.

After University we carried on singing, doing all sorts of gigs, including a variety show with John Cairney, Matt McGinn and the lovely Lesley

Hale. Sometimes Tony or I would stand in as Matt's guitarist, a job a bit like juggling greased eels , so often did he change repertoire and begin songs in keys of his own devising.

Soon we formed a Theatre Group called The Finn mac Cuill Folkshow, adding actor Colin Brown and Actress/Singer Megg Nicol and Actress and Dancer Avril Stewart. We did shows all over the Highlands in association with Pitlochry Festival Theatre and performed at the Fringe in 1975. The Fringe was much smaller then, and there was a wonderful club where you could give a sample of your show for 20 minutes or so in order to encourage people to come along. The show was OK, but there were more problems than we expected and Tony and I returned to a purely music-based act. We made our first album at Maritime Studios in the New Town with first Johnny Cunningham, then new member John Wilson on bass. Johnny was around for much of the recording and often came on tour with us when he was not busy with the Wizard. John Wilson was a real find, a great singer who had been in the band Witch's Promise up until then.

The trio toured for a couple of years, heading to Germany and Holland and picking up quite a lot of gigs in Northumberland where there was a strong scene. I remember going to the Osnabrück Festival, with Archie Fisher travelling in our van, and him teaching me the chords to '1950s Blues' as we trundled along the Autobahn slow lane, being hooted at by impatient truckers. Another festival, this time in Belgium, we were on the bill with my hero Bert Jansch.[2] I was hoping to learn some musical secrets from him but in fact he taught me how to top up your vodka from a bottle of Duty Free under the table, and how to balance a spoon on my nose....

At home this was the era of *Sandy Bell's Broadsheet*. None of us were Bell's regulars, finding it (and the associated broadsheet and early Edinburgh Folk Club) an unwelcoming environment, but we would pop in with Johnny now and again, and sing with Hamish Henderson, both of whom were open and friendly. The *Broadsheet* had slated our first LP, much as it was to do Dougie McLean's song 'Caledonia', but we were soon getting ready to record again.

Madeleine Taylor (the same woman who had been in Silly Wizard a few years earlier) was the best thing that ever happened to Finn mac Cuill, and by rights should now be a recognised treasure of the Scots Music scene. When she joined us, Madeleine brought us a whole raft of new material, and a wonderfully charismatic stage presence. We recorded *Sink Ye Swim Ye* at Radio Edinburgh studios. It was a much stronger album and much of it stands up even today.

---

[2] Bert Jansch sadly passed away while I was writing this piece.

Sadly we never got to release it properly, as the group van was involved in a bad accident. Although no one was seriously hurt, it was enough of a financial and spiritual blow to the band that we called it a day. About a year passed and Tony, John and I were lured back on the road by a promised tour of Germany. It was pretty much a disaster, but a lifeline was thrown by 7:84 Theatre who were looking for musicians for their upcoming tour.

We rehearsed *Joe's Drum* in a church hall in Stockbridge and met a marvellous group of people ... Sandy Nielson, Jimmy Chisholm, Dolina McLellan, John McGrath and Billy Riddoch amongst them. John McGrath was both playwright and director, and was wonderfully open about collaborating, so that I was often given a line or two to work on or asked for a song to bridge a couple of scenes. The following tours were really enjoyable and we were retained for the next production, *Swings and Roundabouts*. Soon after that, Tony Ireland left the band to move to Germany, and we recruited Richard Cherns, later of Runrig. The mix did not gel and quite quickly we called it a day.

By this time I was living in a scruffy flat in Clerk St which became gradually a bit of a folksinger's howff. Christine Kydd, Janet Russell and George (now Georgina) Faux all lived there at one time or another, and it was quite usual to wake up and find a band sleeping in the sitting room. Round the corner in Buccleuch Street was a flat where most of Hom Bru and (I think) Jim Sutherland lived, and along the street were Patsy Seddon and Jack Evans, with John Martin just over the road. I had got a job at Napier by that time and did not even possess a working guitar. I will always be grateful to Janet for virtually frogmarching me to the Waverley Bar and getting me to start playing again.

Janet and I were regulars at the Edinburgh Folk Club at the time it was run by the Bechhofers, and in fact it was Frank Bechhofer who sounded me out informally to ask if I would consider going on the road again, as Hamish Bayne was leaving The McCalmans. To this day I do not know who (if anyone) else was auditioned for the job, but after a while I was offered the position and took it with enthusiasm. We shook hands on it, started rehearsing and fixed a date for the 'handover'. The next week John McGrath phoned to ask if I would like to return to 7:84, this time as musical director. I gulped a bit at the time but have no regrets.

Ian and Derek thought it best to have an album ready for the first gig, so we recorded *Bonnie Bands Again* virtually in secret at Temple Studios and made our debut at Linlithgow Folk Club, which had given both The Macs and Finn mac Cuill so much support. Next we went south to Whitehaven and died flat on our arses at the Folk Club there, but spent the whole of the following day in Kendal honing and rehearsing. A tour of Shetland, basing ourselves at the hospitable home of Rick and Dorothy

Nickerson (the same Rick I had seen at the Triangle in Rankin File fifteen years before) gave us a good run of gigs to settle and polish the show, and we began to plan for the future.

The story of The McCalmans 1982 to 2010 is one that must be told elsewhere but I can remember Derek going AWOL in Hong Kong just before we were due to fly out, landing at Alice Springs in a tropical storm; zigzagging across the Falklands in Chinook helicopters; wild nights at Tønder Festival; sunrise in Africa, and the jeeps clearing the baboons off the runway as we landed in the Masai Mara; gentle autumn mornings in little Danish towns and the kindness of strangers all over the world.

Postscript

It is almost 10 years to the day since Derek died. There are so many stories of hellraising and lost weekends, but put on a CD and hear The Macs at the top of their game and listen to the quality of his singing. My memories may be jumbled and incomplete, but I remember Derek Moffat when ...

Hold The Arts Page:
Personal Reflections on
Twenty-odd Years
(some of them very odd) Covering
Folk Music for the Press

Rob Adams

It is often said that the Scottish press carries too little coverage of the folk scene. I am not so sure. There are days when I think there is far too much coverage of the folk scene.

For example, every time I have been called upon to mark the passing of a musician who has been taken from us all too soon, I have felt that this was coverage we would all rather had not been necessary, and I dare say that on those occasions when a reviewer's observations have, shall we say, stimulated debate, others have found this coverage surplus to requirements.

Obituary duty – or what is referred to with gallows humour in the business as 'delivering to the morgue' – was not on my mind when I started writing about traditional music in the late 1980s. I wanted to write about what people like Johnny Cunningham, Gordon Duncan and Martyn Bennett were doing, rather than what they had done, not through any high-flown notion that evangelism on my part would increase appreciation of their talents. I just enjoyed their music and thought I would enjoy describing it, and if occasionally someone checked them out on my say-so and found that this traditional music thing was not half bad, I did not think anyone would mind.

Newspapers were different beasts back then. For a start they were actually made of paper and could not be accessed from a laptop or mobile phone. Newspaper offices were computerised – a certain Mr Murdoch had seen to that – and the pages were put together onscreen. E-mail was in its infancy, however, and for quite a while I worked with a pen and a notebook and phoned in copy to the copytakers who, let's face it, were not exactly waiting with bated breath for my words of wisdom.

This was pretty far from the 'hold the front page' romanticism portrayed in films of a certain era. It was a lottery. People would always be aghast to discover that filing copy was not a case of reading out a line and having it read back to you. You read out a line, the copytaker said "yep" to nudge you on to the next line, and so on until you reached the end of your story. You just had to cross your fingers and hope that the words would appear as dictated.

Having watched the great London-based Scottish sportswriter Hugh McIlvanney in action on a TV documentary around this time, I very quickly learned to speak as clearly as possible and, if anything, with exaggeratedly careful enunciation, although not quickly or exaggeratedly careful enough to prevent my favourite-ever faux pas. I am by no means claiming to be infallible but this really was a case of 'it wisnae me'.

I had described Hamish Imlach down the line as – and I remember thinking I'd been very particular with this one - "a well-known carouser." Nobody, least of all Hamish, would take issue with this. Hamish liked a drink. Pints would disappear during his sets without him appearing to either drink them or feel any effect from them.

Quite a few people took note, though, when they read the next day that Hamish Imlach was a "well-known carol singer." Hamish was very good about this – so far as I know, he never made good on his threat to include 'Away in an effin' Manger' as a twelve-bar blues in his repertoire. But my face was stopping traffic at every crossroads for days afterwards and for quite some time, having left the venue immediately post-gig, I would approach the nearest phone box with heightened trepidation.

I may even have become paranoid. I remembered the copy taker involved – he was the one whose "yep" was more of a grunt and either he did not like the job or he did not like me. It might have been both, other journos said that their copy provoked the same grunted response, but not long after this debacle I had to file a piece about the great Irish pianist and adventurer within the tradition, Micheál Ó Súilleabháin. And guess who took my copy? Correct: Gunter the grunter. The piece actually appeared more or less as written, but the dictation, including repeated suggestions from my bête noire that Micheál Ó Súilleabháin should change his surname to something sensible like Smith, and spell his Gaelic first name like every other Michael, was pretty damned uncomfortable.

Yet it was not as uncomfortable as another assignment. The Battlefield Band had just undergone some personnel changes that brought an influx of new, young blood in the shape of John McCusker and Iain MacDonald, and their gig in Acharacle Village Hall was deemed by our then arts editor at *The Herald* as an ideal opportunity to introduce the new line-up to our readers. "Stick in a bit of local colour, set the scene a bit," were my instructions. I seem to remember that I was sticking in a bit of local colour and setting the scene for an American magazine as well on the same trip. But that was a doddle; I just had to type that version, fax it and forget about it.

This was early 1991, at the time of the first Gulf War. On the Sunday I got my copy written and, with my hosts presciently telling me that they did not want their phone tied up for ages while I played our man in the Western Highlands, I headed for the phone box in the village. The weather had given us a great Highland welcome, and the phone box was now a kind of red island in the middle of a loch. But hey, your intrepid reporter can cope with puddles, even when theyare ankle-deep, and more, in phone boxes.

I was thirty words into an eight hundred word article when the copy taker first apologised for an interruption from the Gulf and asked me to hold the line. I was maybe fifty words in when the second interruption came from the Gulf and I was asked to hold the line. Paragraph by paragraph we got through the article, with dispatches from our war correspondent arriving with impressive regularity, and I would love to tell you that I had had the foresight to take my wellies on the trip. But I cannot tell a lie. By the time we got to the end of the article, my shoes and socks were sodden and for once in my life I actually found a suitable rejoinder coming from my lips when the copytaker apologised one last time for the interruptions from the Gulf.

"Aye," I said, "that other bloke's filing copy from a war zone but it's me who's had to stand here and get trench foot." At the time this seemed like another example of too much coverage of the folk scene, not to mention my ankles, but I soon got over it.

There were other examples of what might now be considered beyond lo-tech involved in the job back then. Although CDs had been introduced some years earlier, record companies continued to mail out promo cassettes to reviewers. This, apparently, was at the behest of the scribes who supplied the London papers and glossy music mags; it allowed these busy people to appraise new albums on the move via what during my time working in London we came to refer to, in the spirit of political correctness, as a the Sony Walkperson.

This trend of renaming items for fear of causing offence spread to all manner of objects and places and I can remember, having been asked if I had managed to catch up with the latest batch of demo tapes on the Walkperson during a business trip that crossed from the north-west of England to the East Midlands, being able to confirm that yes, indeed, I had been listening to them all the way from Personchester to Peoplesfield.

Nowadays, of course, the Walkman has been superseded by the ipod for playing music and by digital recorders or cameras for capturing it *in situ* (as in every time some twit stands up and takes a photo at a concert, everyone else shouts "situ down"). Before they came in, though, it was quite handy to use a personal cassette player for interviews – providing you did not tape the chats over the latest promo cassettes, which were not always "blocked" to prevent over-recording. By some miracle I managed to avoid this, although I heard a few tales of woe from PR reps regarding other less fortunate scribblers and cassettes that, not being the most physically robust of examples, could come to grief in other ways.

Indeed, compared to some promo cassettes, there are taped interviews that seem to have enjoyed a charmed life: I occasionally come across past conversations such as the one I had with Johnny Cunningham on the day Scotland's match against Estonia was abandoned after three seconds due to the Estonian team not turning up. Johnny, a hopeless Scotophile who was perennially homesick in Boston, was so ragingly jealous when he heard that I was about to watch the football, which he could not access, that I thought it best to phone him back and put him out of his misery when the ref blew for full-time right after kick-off. Johnny did not know whether to be pleased he hadn't missed a whole game or annoyed that he'd missed the shortest match on record.

They are not folk music related but I have also been quite pleased to discover some other tapes that have survived. There is one of jazz guitar hero John McLaughlin, a confirmed espouser of peace, love and Eastern philosophies, calling a certain former bandmate "a [expletive deleted] wally" for not agreeing to reform the band for a charity gig, and another of the truly wonderful Randy Crawford serenading me with a remarkably fine 'One Day I'll Fly Away' unaccompanied down the line while she was, as it were, as jetlagged as a newt.

Promo cassettes of Capercaillie's *Sidewaulk* and *At It Again* by Andy M Stewart & Manus Lunny, however, actually snapped through repeated rewinding, and I was so taken with what was probably the last example of an advance cassette I received, Rounder Records' priceless documenting of *The 1951 Edinburgh People's Festival Ceilidh*, that it attracted the sort of attention normally reserved for vintage cars when I got caught playing it in public. It was one of those releases that merit more than a review and *The Herald* gave it a decent spread with the invaluable help and comments of Ewan McVicar, who edited and annotated it from Alan Lomax's live recording.

This release, with John Strachan, Flora MacNeil, Jimmy MacBeath *et al* singing songs as they possibly had sounded centuries before and Hamish Henderson's revelation that Jessie Murray's birth in December 1879 coincided exactly with the Tay Bridge Disaster (guaranteeing goosebumps for a Dundee boy), could hardly be more different as regards musical style or in its method of production from another release that found traditional music making an arts page take-over bid.

Almost from the first notes Angus Lyon & Ruaridh Campbell's *18 Months Later* struck me as something special. Here was the tradition being both honoured and advanced with skill, love and imagination. It was not, perhaps, as revolutionary as Martyn Bennett's *Grit*, which gained an added emotional quality for me through Martyn's sending different mixes as progress reports (Jeez, Martyn, just how much progress do you want to make?) on its way to being completed to his satisfaction. But, at a rough guess, sixty-five months later, I can still listen to Angus and Ruaridh's wonderful variations on 'Drowsy Maggie', 'Eilidh on the Western Shore' and any of the other tracks and be reminded why I phoned a festival organiser who is, alas, no longer with us and demanded that he listen to the album and book the musicians responsible *toute de suite*, the tooter the sweeter. Actually, that is not as assertive as it sounds – he was a pal and I knew that as soon as he heard the album he would want to include the music on his festival.

Angus and Ruaridh's triumph would have merited major coverage anyway but the story of how the album came to be made – it was recorded on Angus's laptop and one of the components that facilitates this had to be replaced, picked up in Glasgow by a mate, driven to the Mull ferry at Oban, entrusted to a plumber and dropped off at An Tobar arts centre in Tobermory – made it even worthy of the three-quarter page feature it was given and surely would have inspired a broadsheet ballad in days gone by.

It is a wonder also that, unless I have missed them, there are no ballads devoted to another innovation that has arrived during this time and about which I have mixed feelings. I am talking about folk awards. I have no trouble with Simon Thoumire organising the Scots Trad Music Awards because I think he has achieved his aims of uniting a fairly diverse scene and presenting a ceremony that does raise the music's profile, even if it is only briefly once a year. You might actually be surprised at the weight that the words "award winner" can carry with movers and shakers in the media: quite a few articles and appearances have been generated as a result of these successes.

However, what I do find a waste of time – literally – are the BBC Folk Awards. I really should know better by now but every year I receive an email asking for my nominations for the various categories, and every year I spend hours arriving at a personal short list that will be blootered out of the park by what I have come to regard as the unseen committee.

Admittedly, I could spend less time if I did not start playing CDs to remind myself which new songs are the most deserving or which adaptations of traditional tunes or ballads have really stood out in the past year, as one CD leads to another ten and we all know that procrastination is the thief of – och, I'll tell you later. Then there is also what for reasons of self-preservation I'll call research into whether the CDs or performances of choice were released or took place within the time under consideration. Even with a list of possible CDs of the Year from the organisers, this can involve a bit of a trawl – because this list does not necessarily include everything of merit that has been released.

Anyway, form completed, I email it back, fairly certain that my contributions will make not a jot of difference. And almost invariably I am right. As sure as night follows day, the second stage voting form will arrive with a choice of four options in every category – none of which I will have voted for – with instructions to pick one or abstain.

This leads me to think that these people on the unseen committee are truly blessed. At various times over the years they miraculously seem to have heard not one but four traditional singers better than Sheila Stewart, Alison McMorland and Janet Russell; not one but four bands better than Fiddlers' Bid, Session A9 and Jock Tamson's Bairns; not one but four duos better than Angus & Ruaridh, Catriona McKay & Chris Stout and Alasdair Fraser & Tony McManus; and not one but four – well, I think you get the point.

Even when I have spread the betting and included deserving causes from America, Ireland or England as well as Scotland, it has been to no avail – with, I think, the sole exception of the truly wonderful, BBC award-winning Chris Wood.

Thank heavens, then, that at *The Herald* we have our own small rewards system for outstanding contributions, the Bank of Scotland Herald Angels. They only operate during Edinburgh's festival season and, with the way reviews are organised these days – shows have to still be running when the reviews appear –, traditional music can miss out on these Oscars of the Fringe, as we like to call them.

I am proud to say though that the great matriarch of Gaelic song Flora MacNeil has received one, as have Michael Marra and the Vale of Atholl Pipe Band. Alan MacDonald is another piping representative who has been 'Angeled', in recognition of his brilliantly imaginative new settings for pibroch, *From Battle Lines to Bar Lines*.

Oh yes, there's a verb 'to Angel' if we say so, and on a good day I can even conjugate it: angelo, angelare, angelavi, angelatum, if I am not mistaken. But I digress - or as the Germans say, 'Bort'. [Careful now – editor]

Jock Duncan turned up to collect his Angel in front of a crowd of mostly theatre and classical music performers in his famous bunnet and then tore the place apart by singing and enacting his 'Tradesmen's Plooin' Match', complete with phantom and notably disobedient Clydesdales on the chorus. Sometimes, I will admit, there is an element of lifetime achievement behind the award. Well, there are no rules, just pure gut instincts, for guidance. Sheena Wellington, who was given an Archangel, the award that recognises sustained contributions, was recognised for fighting the good fight for traditional music on a squillion Scottish Arts Council panels and elsewhere as well as for her singing in Edinburgh International Festival's Work, Sex and Death song series.

It is always great to hear – and read about – the folky Angels, as one of my colleagues affectionately described them, even if they do not show up to collect them. Adam McNaughtan was a deserving case, both in terms of his sustained contribution to the music and the excellence of one particular performance – his duet with Karine Polwart on 'Oor Gudeman Cam Ham at Een' – but he did not fancy the occasion. So his co-compilers of EIF's political song series, Anne Neilson and Janey Buchan, picked up the award without him.

The Angel that gave most satisfaction, however, was the one we awarded to Gordon Duncan. As I said, there are no rules for these awards and it was unusual to say the least for a performance to be recognised seven years after the event, let alone posthumously. This, though, was a special case and an Angel that, in different circumstances, would have been awarded much sooner.

When Gordon played on the Official Festival's 1999 piping series and unleashed his fantastic bagpipe arrangement of AC/DC's 'Thunderstruck' alongside some slightly more conventional Scottish music that left everyone in the Queen's Hall gobsmacked, he was unlucky because it was the final Friday night of the festival and we had decided the last set of Angel winners for the year the day before.

Even as Gordon incorporated what appeared to be feedback, a whammy bar and Eddie Van Halen-like hammering-on into his chanter skills, I sat there thinking, "Angel him". There was nothing we could do at that late hour, unfortunately, and the assumption was that we'd have plenty of other opportunities to honour Gordon. The opportunity never came during Gordon's lifetime, so the year after he died I went into the first of our weekly Angels meetings determined to put matters right. My colleagues quickly agreed with the idea and we were able to present Gordon's family with his statuette.

Just how much this meant and still means to the family can be seen from the inclusion of a picture of the certificate that accompanies the Angel awards in Gordon's book of tunes. It also appears in the photo collages that are projected above the stage at the A National Treasure concerts held in tribute to Gordon at Perth Concert Hall every September. I always get a lump in my throat when that shot appears. It does not make up for the loss of one of our greatest talents – nothing can – but it is one of these times when I think: we got that coverage right.

Quick Jump To Now

Norman Chalmers

As one of the team who set up the *List* magazine over a late summer a quarter of a century ago, I had the job of pulling together all the information on 'Folk and Traditional Music' that was then taking place in Glasgow, Edinburgh and the Central Belt. Looking over the couple of dozen copies of that first year (1985-86) gives an eerie definiteness to the changing meaning and effect of Scots folk and traditional music as it altered with the socio-cultural evolution of our country up to the present day.

Playing Scottish music with Jock Tamson's Bairns, regularly, and mainly then in Scotland, we were continually brought into contact with artists, journalists, broadcasters, poets, writers and the authentic tradition bearers from all over the nation and, with our own interests in culture, art, history and politics, we became enmeshed in what was going on within the changing Scotland. The Bairns were always an amateur group. We were, and always had been, a part-time democracy, and always did things our own way; but the word 'amateur' has its root in 'amare,' – Latin 'to love' – and is that not the commendable spirit in which to do anything creative, or anything at all?

As Scottish traditional song and instrumental music, both Gaelic and Scots, were 'rediscovered' in the post-war 'Folk Revival,' the rise of Folk Clubs and Festivals gathered apace through the 1960s into the '70s and '80s. 'Sessions' where established traditional singers, fiddlers, whistle players, box and moothie performers would congregate and collide with guitars, mandolins and banjo players, sprouted all over the country. From what had been mostly centred on Glasgow's Clutha Bar and Edinburgh's Sandy Bell's, the new acoustic energy and expanding number of players spawned new playing grounds and also incorporated the revived bellows small pipes, hammered dulcimer, Appalachian dulcimer, sax, djembe and other eclectic instruments into the mix. 'Ceilidh Dancing' exploded into fashion in urban centres. It even became fashionable to carry a fiddle case. The Gaelic revival accelerated, and created the expanding Féisean movement, while the Scots language broke into the classroom – and through the BBC glass ceiling.

As cross-cultural forces pushed for a new Scottish self-respect through the Thatcher years, folk and traditional musicians generally became more identified with Scottish nationality and more expressive of it. Unfortunately, the cultural aesthetic eludes shapeforming and is endlessly mutable, and the emerging desire to pop, swing and jazz up the native traditions evolved a myriad variants. By the time that Scotland's self-determination became more of a conscious desire among its population, on the road to the set-up of the new parliament, the nation's sense of its musical representation, and cultural values, had shifted.

We now have awards, medals and trophies for everything Scottish, amidst post-modern liberalised values that do not segregate value, worth and quality. Becoming famous is seen to invest the wearer with celebrity, some sort of magic power, and is hotly pursued by many of the young players. The near universal socialist outlook of those involved in folk and traditional arts has dissolved into a green nu-eco soup. The sounds of Scotland, often codified as incidental or link and programme music on Scottish TV, rarely succeed in representing the honest sound of Scots traditions, preferring the coddled contemporary surround sound of trippy pop/rock with a fiddle/accordion/bagpipe on top. The nation is now very happy with a song from Eddie Reader and a tune – probably 'Highland Cathedral' – from the Red Hot Chilli Pipers!

Back in mid-October 1985, the powerful Chilean group Inti-Illimani were on their endless world tour, after becoming exiled outside their native Chile when elected Socialist President Allende was murdered with CIA help. Supporting them at their Edinburgh concert was the unique, new all-women Scottish outfit Sprangeen -- with Hamish Henderson in vociferous support! Down in Leith's Shore Bar caroused the Reverend Brothers, who ultimately morphed into Shooglenifty. As Liz and Maggie Cruikshank were ensconced down in Edinburgh's Royal Oak, the Whistlebinkies performed Glasgow's Star Club – Pentangle even played in Greenock's Town Hall. But, that week, the 'Big' Scottish Music event was the so-called Hebridean Halloween at the SECC – with the Scottish Caledonian Strathspey and Reel Society, Moira Anderson and Andy Cameron, and the British Caledonian Pipes and Drums.

Things, though, were slowly changing. A month later, Glasgow Tryst organised a new winter festival to support the Traditional Arts, and included Hamish -- who was given a show of his own: two hours of song, music and poetry and prose. And a few days later, at the Third Eye

Centre (what ultimately became the CCA) the Broadcasting Band was the handle used for the unusual effect of Michael Marra, Jim Wilkie and accordionist Blair Douglas bonding with drums and guitar. Next month, Babbity Bowsters opened, underscored by the Laurie clan's predilection for traditional song and music and, as you will know, they are all still at it, especially on a Saturday afternoon.

The new, contemporaneous Traditional Music Degree courses and other educational awards had started well-intentioned, but de-structuring traditional song and music from its social context puts stresses on its understanding and function. The Scots language is now more often sung, but it is often without a link to its accents and natural expression or, indeed, meaning, and Gaelic song is often unrecognisably pronounced, or even understood by choir members or solo singers. More changes came in later, with the rise of the Scottish Folk Awards annual competitions, the corresponding media attention, and the scramble for uninformed public votes over social media sites and the Web.

The Web has had a complex effect on traditional music. It now takes anyone seconds to find song lyrics or a tune, online, and print it out. Information and history are easily accessed, but its educational flexibility does not compare to its ability to sell, allied to the computer's ability to record, mix and publish your own music, especially online as an MP3.

The rise of World Music as a commercial product has been phenomenal. That does not mean ethnic music from some pure, far away culture. The term describes that syndrome where remotely evolved song styles, instrumental sounds or forms of music are refurnished and burnished to make them appeal to Western audiences, usually by adding keyboards, electric guitar, bass and drums. How long will it be before the ravishing distinctiveness of our world heritages are ground down to lumpy homogeneity?

The Web, and hugely increased number of TV channels, has pushed the music of Scotland/Ireland back towards its descendants in the US and Canada and brings us hosts of transatlantic performers, and the likes and show biz of Transatlantic Sessions, where the plangency of pedal steel or slide blues guitar licks are hardly noticed, and the overall sound and song lyrics become trans-national and usually weaker.

With the popularity and now-fashionable status of acoustic folk and traditional music, there are now so many people playing it, to some degree, that the music itself has changed, and is being reproduced in sessions, bars or kitchen parties with a little understood sense of tempo, rhythm or phrasing, while singing is just being pushed to one side. The older traditions are being displaced as the new generation of singers and players are being acculturated. Scottish traditional music has undergone a similar process to American Country – its emerging function as a commercial entertainment has spawned a Nashville equivalent. The authentic Scots revivalists today are hardly noticed, while the attention-seekers gain large public followings, their music in general becoming deracinated and blander. The performer spends more on dressing for the stage than ever before, seeking media attention of the cheapest kind, and an audience more undiscriminating. The Celtic Connection has its own fragmenting momentum.

But that is not the whole story. There are great young singers emerging, and remarkably skilled and moving young players. There will always appear artfulness and quality, and it behoves us to seek the gold among the dross – to be discriminating, and seek to find the continuity of the Scottish character, and the beautiful and often strange new shapes thrown up by the endlessly enduring Carrying Stream.

Legacies of the Highland Traditional Music Festival 1981 to 2002

Rita Hunter and Rob Gibson

Hamish Henderson, President of the Traditional Music & Song Association of Scotland (TMSA), signed the affiliated member's certificate on 21 April 1984 which recognised the role of the Dingwall festival, rendered in Gaelic, Fleadh Ciùil Bhaile Chàil, in the family of traditional music and song in Scotland.

This conversation between Rob Gibson and Rita Hunter considers the work to secure the taped archive of recordings at the Highland Traditional Music Festival (HTMF), to give the Dingwall event its Sunday title. Securing access for its music for the future reveals the range and effects of a small festival that ran for twenty-one years at a critical time in our traditional music development:

Rob: As the volunteer organiser for much of the time I gathered taped recordings from the sound desk and from subsequent radio coverage of the festival weekends. I was a minor member of the committee stemming from the Dingwall folk club which produced the first festival during a successful weekend in June 1981. The leaders were Easter Ross based musicians Dagger Gordon, Iain MacBeath and Iain 'Physics' Macdonald.

At the time it was felt that a showcase for Highland traditional music would be best staged every two years. From 1983, I led the various teams who turned it into an annual event till 2002. The recordings were made from 1985 and have produced some sixty CDs of music when Rita used a Steepletone 'contraption' to transfer tape to hard drive and CDs.

Fond memories of imperishable music were fuelled by highlights of these 'forty-eight hour ceilidhs', as one young fiddler recalled, in the short darkness of northern summers. A small number of festival regulars shared some of the tapes of these big moments, and participants both on and off stage recalled the eclectic concerts and sessions. Unbundling fond memories from the raw material of unedited tapes was long overdue when we set to work this year.

Rita: Listening to the tapes brought so much to the fore about the HTMF as well as the music. A forty-eight hour ceilidh it certainly was, happy golden years in Dingwall. Listening to the tapes from a twenty or so year distance brought reflections of a very fertile renaissance period of traditional music in the Highlands. Really what it did was bring 'music people' together from all over the Highlands, and this fostered terrific support between the musicians and provided them with a platform and the chance to work on their music.

There were a number of HTMF special touches. Firstly, the idea of creating 'and Friends' line-ups was spawned from talent-spotting in the legendary hotel lounge sessions, and somebody would be invited to put a performance together for the following year – Iain Macfarlane, Kaela Rowan, Janice Clarke etc – these line-ups were really exciting and never disappointed. The festival gave a platform for lovely moments to happen – such as Margaret and Martyn Bennett (aged 13) on song and pipes.

With Highland music at the core, the great Highland bagpipes and Gaelic song were set pieces in each festival line-up. We will never forget the thrill of 3 sets of pipes in harmony – Duncan MacGillivray, Iain MacDonald and Davy Garrett – and the sight of those same three taking up front row seats to be equally enthralled by P/M John D Burgess' festival performance, complete with winks to the young fellas in the front row who were shaking their heads in disbelief at his prowess!

Highland singers, duos and ceilidh bands all gave their best to the festival, and the team experimented with workshops, venues and dances, notably giving Wolfstone their first gig. Phil Cunningham & Aly Bain and Capercaillie gave us sell-out top notch concerts, and listening to Dougie MacLean's Sunday night set, with the packed hall singing every chorus, really takes you back to that night.

As Fèis Rois began to produce teenage groups, the festival invited a young group to the evening concert each year to take centre stage in the proceedings. This became a popular invitation and groups raised the bar annually, giving a first sense of the tradition being both secure for the future and that something exciting was ahead.

We invited guest artists from overseas as 'special treats' for our audience. Unforgettable sessions were delivered by Manus Lunny

& Gerry O' Connor, Tommy & Colum Sands, Andy Irvine, Alasdair Fraser & Paul Machlis – playing from their groundbreaking, newly-released *Skyedance* – and fiddle and balalaika ensembles from California, Russia and Sweden, as well as Alwena Roberts from Wales and David Wilkie's Cowboy Celtic from Calgary – all brought an international dimension to be greeted by that fantastic Dingwall audience warmth.

Rob had close links with Brittany, and these musical friends brought a special insight and respect for the wonderful music of Giles Servat, Triskell and later the fest noz–night dance-band Dremmwel.

The tapes themselves are for the most part in good shape, a few sets are spoiled by some technical hitch on the night, and some are outstanding – like Highland Connection for example – but one thing for certain is that they all capture the magic of the Festival and that special Dingwall Festival warmth as well as some witty repartee from the festival's 'characters'!

It was a great time for music for the Highlands, to bring all the styles and ages together in musicianship, appreciation and respect.

Rob: You mentioned the range of views in the songs we heard which confirms the incipient political nature of folk song. At one afternoon session in 1985 in the Croft restaurant a young man sang of going off to the Falklands war whose recent impact was very personal. Iain Sinclair of Mirk wrote and performed 'The King's Shilling' at our festival. The song exposes the price of soldiering and is as pertinent now as it was then. It was thrilling to hear Karan Casey and James Taylor reprise an all-star version on the BBC's *Transatlantic Sessions* in 2009.

Specific mention has to be made of Iain 'Toots' MacDonald who performed some of his best work at Dingwall. From a searing exposé of child abuse to the loss of hundreds of Lewis servicemen on the 'Iolair' in 1918 his material seriously hit the mark.

As a result he was dubbed 'sing us a happy song' Macdonald. There were lighter moments in the hilarious 'Gig in Ness', however, when he sang his anti-apartheid anthem 'No Fun City' in 1986. The applause reached a crescendo when the British representative of the ANC came to the stage and thanked him for his support. This incident duly appeared on the 8am news on BBC Scotland the next morning. The recording is superb, and the moment that brought committed music and international political struggle together unforgettable.

In those years both BBC Highland and Moray Firth Radio took turns to record concerts for later broadcast. We managed to tape the broadcasts for several years and enjoy the presenters' take on our music.

In the midst of the miners' strike Magpie from the USA sang of anti-globalisation and solidarity, while Gilles Servat from Brittany in 1993 and 2000 explored issues of language, freedom and international concerns which were lapped up by our audiences. Dougie MacLean in 1988 and 1991 explored his own rural muse from Butterstone to Brisbane on the steamy stage at the National Hotel.

The 1991 festival, In particular, led to a seemingly dangerous billing risk: a solo act after various big group sets. Kicked off by young local musicians, the evening hooted up with the first incarnation of Iron Horse which was followed by another first, Jim Hunter and the Thunderbird Band, whose eight local musicians from Glenuig took the audience by storm before the interval. Where could it all go next, I was asked? As Rita mentioned, Duncan MacGillivray, Iain MacDonald and Davy Garrett in harmony piping thrilled us to bits. And finally, the solo set by Dougie MacLean magnetised the expectant crowd as the choruses lifted the rafters in 'This Love Will Carry' and much more.

Rita: Yes, we enjoyed bringing back old friends, and for the Millennium Celebration Festival we had a return visit from Capercaillie in an international line-up in the packed Town Hall.

There is plenty good quality music in the recordings, as well as magic moments and memories, and it would be fitting for a Highland Traditional Music Festival recording to be made professionally from these tapes.

Rob: The festival produced great music, and a fully edited archive will inform a new generation of those twenty years a-growing for Highland music.

The Folk Revival – So Far So Good?

John Barrow

The so-called Folk Revival has been under way, at least in these parts, for a good sixty years now, if we measure from the first Edinburgh Peoples' Festival of 1951 which, in the context of this publication, seems appropriate. One really has to wonder on this measure, however, whether we should be talking about a 'revival' at all. In another ten years' time we'll reach the three-score and ten mark. That is not especially significant, it is just one of those human-scale markers commonly used to mark a passage of time, but 'revival'...? Surely, that is now behind us and we are sailing into open, calmer, less contentious waters with the storms of our cultural adolescence behind us.

2011 is an appropriate time to write about this, to take some stock. In 1980, Polygon published *The People's Past*, a collection of essays from contributors, including Hamish Henderson, to a series of lunchtime lectures held during the first Edinburgh Folk Festival in 1979, which culminated in a conference which gave its name to the book.[1] I wrote the final essay, 'Folk Now'. Thirty-odd years on, where are we now?

Some things are immutable. I wrote in 1979:

> The final contribution to this series of essays is intended as a contemporary view of folk music, with the philosophy that "folk" is to be found in any nation or group of people based on a common root or ancestry. As soon as people congregate, folk exists; the analysts to quantify or qualify the manifestation follow later. Folk is the cultural foundation stone of any people. Without an indigenous culture reflecting or

---

[1] Edward J. Cowan (ed.), *The People's Past: Scottish Folk – Scottish History*, Edinburgh: Polygon, 1980.

transmitting the feelings of the people society would be anaemic with little or no idea of its own significance. Hence the strength of feeling expressed through the medium of folk by, for example, exiles from Chile where the current political ideology is very anti-people.

A second approach to constructing a philosophy of folk is that without an indigenous culture there can be no so-called higher art forms. Here, by implication, the author will risk the scorn of many arty high-heid yins by considering folk as an art form. What can be conveyed through this idea is that if there is a literature, a drama, a visual art and so on, it has to be founded on the bedrock of the nation's expressed culture or exist *in vacuo*. If such higher art forms are imported they have a reduced validity in the context of the nation to which they are brought unless they strike some popular chord. Thus a preoccupation with, for instance, Scottish ballet in its own right is fine, but in a Scottish context it has to be related to the indigenous culture of the nation and should reflect or transmit that, rather than stay comfortably within the traditional offerings associated with such an art form, important though they may be.[2]

These tenets hold today, and indeed why should they not? They are so fundamental that they form a universal truth.

In 1984, the Scottish Arts Council created a working party to report on 'The Traditional Arts of Scotland' which included Hamish Henderson, Aly Bain, and several others, including me. The report opened with a more manageable version of these 'universal truths' which had appeared in *The Scottish Review* of August 1983, *vis*:

My understanding is that indigenous arts of any country are of fundamental importance to the people of that country and indivisibly linked to their sense of nationhood. Without reference to these foundations, any other art forms (whether described as 'higher' arts or whatever) lack a foundation, and will exist rather than live in the hearts of the people. Therefore to have a healthy nation, in all forms of the arts, requires great attention to be paid to the traditional or indigenous arts of that nation.[3]

In a way the Edinburgh Folk Festival came at just the right time. It arose primarily through the efforts of the Scottish Tourist Board (STB) who

---

[2] *Ibid.*, p.206
[3] *The Traditional Arts of Scotland*, Edinburgh: Scottish Arts Council, 1984.

were looking for a way to extend the Edinburgh tourist season, and by osmosis the Scottish season, away from the two month-long summer season, while looking rather enviously at London's 12-month season.

There had been a rather disastrous attempt to run an event in January 1977 and again 1978 using STB funding. The present Edinburgh's Ceilidh Culture event is very similar to that. The great majority of the festival's activity is not funded but participants put on self-funded activities while the City Council provides PR and marketing back-up but, crucially, compared to the earlier event, had a specialist (Steve Byrne of the band Malinky) overseeing how the whole event was run. In 1977-1978, STB coordinated and provided PR and marketing backing but not much else, and while useful that may have been, it was not enough.

The Edinburgh Folk Festival, it was eventually decided, would follow Easter and include two weekends and the four days between so that tourists could come to the city and have plenty of time to spend spending in George Street. A bit naïve perhaps but at least we got a folk festival out of it which ran, or perhaps staggered from financial crisis to crisis, for a further 20 or so years! And douce Auld Reekie got another festival notch on the bedpost! To cap it all, I was lucky enough to be there at the right time to become its first Artistic Director.

In retrospect, 20:20 and all that, should we be surprised that the second half of the twentieth century saw the kind of cultural shifts which led to the rise of such events? I do not think so. After the Second World War, especially in the West and in particular the class-ridden United Kingdom (later to become the Untied Kingdom!), society continued its post-First War re-defining unabated.

Across Europe the allies stationed their armies of occupation up against the Eastern bloc's Western walls. Popular culture, especially in Germany, was influenced by the allies' imports of US and British folk acts to perform in the PXs and NAAFIES which went with occupation. Denmark, perhaps because it was the nearest Scandinavian country to Britain, also to an extent fell under the thrall of British folk acts. The French of course had no truck with this – after all they are French! Other European countries, no doubt changing their societal structures as well, were also less immediately influenced or impressed by this cultural wave. Eventually, however, as you can see today, the influence of so-called 'Celtic music' has been very pervasive, with 'Celtic' festivals stretching away to the horizon in all directions (including Lorient and Quimper in Brittany which began in the 1970s), and if not 'Celtic', then hiring acts from the Celtic homelands and diaspora to appear.

Through the 1970s, Irish traditional music held court in the UK. Hardly surprising, given the great performers like The Chieftains, Planxty, The Bothy Band, De Dannan, The Dubliners and of course, Christy Moore,

Andy Irvine and Paul Brady, with many others showing what could be (in) credibly done with 'your own music'. So much so that direct spin-offs on mainland UK soon came about.

In England, The Old Swan Band, led by Rod Stradling, decided that enough was enough and rode popularly into the fray with a set-list of entirely English country dance music, while in Scotland we began to see the rise of the bands like Battlefield, Ossian, Capercaillie (very young winners of a folk group competition during the Edinburgh Folk Festival), and Silly Wizard (who, by 1978-1979, were felt to be a big enough name to appear in the Usher Hall along with Alan Stivell), joining existing acts like The Corries, The Tannahill Weavers, The McCalmans, Ray and Archie Fisher, Dick Gaughan, Five Hand Reel, The Whistlebinkies, The Laggan and The Clutha. The Boys of The Lough of course already had feet on both sides of the Irish Sea. Even in Wales, not really known even today for its folk music output, there were stirrings as Ar Log began to look at that country's traditions.

Stradling observed quite simply, when I met him in 1976 at Loughborough Folk Festival, that a lot of folk in England, especially the south, had got fed up with Irish music and song. In fact in some parts of England, the ceilidh dance clubs became as popular as the folk clubs at that time, with their presentations of English country dance music.

Up here, in that hot-bed of music and craic in Edinburgh that was Sandy Bell's in the 1970s, the music became increasingly Scottish and less Irish, and bands like Wee Willum, Chorda, and Jock Tamson's Bairns began playing (with a name like 'Jock Tamson's Bairns', could their repertoire have been anything other than Scots!?). Then, towards the end of the 1980s, along came The Easy Club – a quartet (Rod Paterson, Jack Evans, Jim Sutherland and John Martin) who were really ahead of the curve with their very influential folk-swing style of playing.

The 1970s was indeed, in retrospect (there's that 20:20 hindsight thing again) a quite exciting musical decade, at least in folk music (in pop and rock it was a lost decade, as the prog rock bands with their interminably long, boring and pretentious guitar solos led the way; in a way – thank God for punk!). I wrote in 'Folk Now':

> Particularly obvious is the booming interest in fiddle and accordion clubs and Strathspey and Reel societies. Young musicians appear to be less aware of, or perhaps less keen to observe, the boundaries that existed between the traditional music of the pipes and other instruments, with the result that multi-instrumental groups like Silly Wizard, Battlefield and Ossian all used pipe tunes set for other instruments to great effect. In a footnote in the May 1978 edition of the magazine *International Piper* the editor remarks: "Both the

Battlefield and Whistlebinkies use the bagpipe to excellent effect and, what is more, the pipers are of a very professional standard. They also showed that it was quite unnecessary to venture out of the Scottish idiom to combine successfully with other instruments. Their renditions of Strathspeys, reels and jigs were first class." (I reckon that just about says it all.)[4]

We were beginning to be taken seriously it seems!

There have been several important developments in the infrastructure of Scottish music in the past 30 years. First came the Fèisean movement which began in 1981 on Barra. There, the community had become very aware of the fading of their island traditions as the non-Gaelic speaking young children of islanders returning home from working away began to dilute the culture. It was decided that for the first fortnight of the summer holidays there would be a teaching 'festival' to which performers in the role of teachers were invited from all over. It was a bold move, to suggest to the children that they might go back to school as soon as their holidays started, but it worked in spades! Now, guided by full-time staff based in Inverness, there are over 40 such events across the Highlands and Islands and the Central Belt which over the years have produced a great many first class young musicians.

> Around 13,000 young people annually participate in activities supported by Fèisean nan Gaidheal, 5,000 of which take part in the Fèisean themselves. Around 5,500 take part in Youth Music Initiative classes organised by local Fèisean, through contracts with the Highland Council and East Lothian Council. Fèisean nan Gàidheal continues to support the Meanbh-chuileag Theatre Company, which tours schools with plays focussing on Gaelic culture and history, from which around 2,500 benefit.[5]

The National Centre of Excellence in Traditional Music (NCETM) has been hosted by Plockton High School since 2000 and led since then by Director Dougie Pincock, no slouch as a musician himself. Many of their students on leaving go to the Royal Conservatoire of Scotland (formerly the Royal Scottish Academy of Music and Drama, aka RSAMD), which offers the only honours degree in Scottish traditional music in the world, and at which Dougie taught in the early days of the BA course in Traditional Music in the mid-1990s. In 2010, NCETM survived a very ill-judged attempt by Highland Council to kill it off in a money-saving exercise. This idiotic proposal was eventually fought off with help from all over the world and

---

[4] John Barrow, 'Folk Now', pp.215-16.
[5] From Fèisean nan Gàidheal's website: www.feisean.org

the Scottish Parliament. Two steps forward and one back? Let us hope, as indeed it appears, that the future of this very important institution has been secured.

Judging by the above, we had a second revival, it seems, before the first had ended. On the down side, though, the Traditional Music and Song Association (of Scotland), the TMSA (founded in 1966), is now a shadow of its earlier self – and even then it was never really the force it should have been.

In the more day-to-day, perhaps mundane or at least less esoteric, world of running folk clubs, concerts and festivals, the big news in 1993 was the advent of a major festival in Glasgow scheduled for January 1994. And so it was and indeed is. Designed to fill a scheduling gap in the Glasgow Royal Concert Hall's normally quiet post-Christmas period, Celtic Connections burst on to the scene with very few people giving it even a 50:50 chance of success. Aye, January in Glasgow and three weeks long – who's got enough money left after Christmas and Hogmanay to be able to afford that? And so on. But it just shows you what a major arts organisation can achieve when it puts its collective mind to something and, in particular, is prepared to learn. Colin Hind, the festival's director until 2005, was on a steep learning curve from day one and, fair play to the man, his artistic and commercial common sense, allied to the marketing and PR muscle of GRCH, made it all happen.

I have currently in my agency's database about 60 annual festivals in Scotland which are either 'folk' festivals or festivals which regularly include folk music in their programme of more general arts. This is not an exhaustive list but is reasonably complete, ranging from the specialist events like the Scots Fiddle Festival or Ullapool Guitar Festival to those who simply book a string of acts without any apparent theme or links (including one called the Galway Sessions which take place over two weeks in Galway, Ireland and Stirling).

However, I have currently only 26 folk clubs listed in my agency's database. I wrote in 1980:

> Since 1973 there has been a decline in the number of Scottish folk clubs from approximately seventy-five to just over thirty: This is a startling statistic. The most rapid reduction occurred through 1974-75 but it appears now that a stable level has been reached. According to the Scottish Folk Directory – as good a source for this information as any – about thirty clubs or regular folk venues disappeared in the two years up to the end of 1975, with a less rapid decline after this period to just over thirty. It is important to know why this occurred, bearing in mind that the same sort of thing happened south of the border over roughly the same period. No

one has yet produced the answer – although none seem sufficiently concerned to actively pursue the question.[6]

Perhaps there is a clue in another statistic from the database where I have about 200 of what I describe as 'independent promoters' listed, including the Promoters Arts Network across the Highlands and Islands ("PAN members promote events in communities from Bute to Shetland, from the Western Isles to Moray using all kinds of spaces: arts venues and theatres, village halls and community centres, converted churches, schoolrooms and barns." PAN's mission is: "*Supporting the communities of the Highlands and Islands to promote artistic events of the highest quality*").[7] This was not so in 1980, there were some such of course, but 200! No. Another type of venue which was not really on the map in 1980 is the arts centre, often municipally funded. There are about 40 of them in the data base.

On the face of it all, this activity, quite a lot of which was not going on in 1980, looks quite impressive in its quantity (and Lord knows what this equates to financially over a year – worth looking at I'd say). I suspect, however, if you drill down just by attending one or two clubs or concerts you will find that, as the performers seem to get younger, the audiences are often ageing; it is a bit like the bobbies on the beat. Perhaps this is just a phase; I hope so. Even so it would be at least reassuring to see a much wider range of ages at events in general.

Maybe we are in a period of just taking stock of what is on offer. Certainly, in Scotland there are some of the UK's best, most inventive, outward looking and open-minded musicians. Cross-overs of genres have been and are still happening – like just now, Jim Sutherland's Banda Europa, Shooglenifty, Peatbog Faeries or, in the 1990s, the great Clan Alba led by Dick Gaughan, and the Cauld Blast Orchestra.

What will be the next 'big thing'? Or is that the sort of question we ask in folk music (discuss)? We have had the rise of Celtic music and that shows no sign of abating at all. After the musical developments of the previous three decades, it perhaps was not surprising that the Celtic Connections festival appeared in the early 1990s. World Music which came upon us in the late 1980s has perhaps lost some of its 'oomph', and there seems to be less of it around. Maybe it has just become more assimilated and thus less obvious. At the giant Womex conference in Copenhagen last October it was not in short supply elsewhere in the world – and some fantastic musicians to boot. Watch out for Womex, it will be in Cardiff in 2013 and Glasgow in 2014. Great craic!

In 2010 some London-based academics caused a minor stooshie about

[6] John Barrow, 'Folk Now', pp.211-12.

[7] www.panpromoters.co.uk/

how popular folk music was. Professors Sue Hallam and Andrew Creech, from the Institute of Education at the University of London, suggested in their book *Music Education in the 21st Century in the United Kingdom*, that while there is a wider choice of music generally, restrictive play-lists are increasingly limiting musical experiences of young people. "Unless they are introduced to a range of different musical traditions early on when they are still open-eared, young people can refuse to engage with any music other than their preferred genre."[8]

It was quite widely reported that Scottish folk musicians denied this was happening. Karine Polwart apparently said: "Folk isn't only flourishing but people outwith the scene have taken folk music and made it their own. People are hacked off with the commercial music they are getting fed. There's an interest out there for independent grass-roots music with meaning and identity."[9] Well, to be honest, I'm not so sure about the young folks at this very moment.

However, we can also take heart from the present Chief Executive of Creative Scotland, Andrew Dixon, quoted at the Òran 2010 Sang conference at Sabhal Mor Ostaig in Skye as saying: "Creative Scotland will be a rallying call for the cultural strengths of the whole of Scotland. Traditional arts is a key sector and is central to Scotland's international reputation." I do not think I heard anyone in the Scottish Arts Council say that in the 1970s! So that's alright then, I can go to the pub now.

Dare we hope economic data would show that Creative Scotland's rhetoric is not just hollow tub-thumping? Is anyone up for carrying out an in depth look at the actual, rather than imagined or anecdotal, benefits to Scotland's economy arising from what we, and the hundreds of others like us, do in what is still known generically as the 'folk scene'? Such a survey would fill in some of the background of the story of the past sixty years. But it is the foreground where the real action is – in the clubs, sessions, concerts, and festivals where this great music is to be found, and that has not changed so much. It is so much more, enormously more, than 'mere' bean counting.

---

[8] Susan Hallam and Andrew Creech, *Music Education in the 21st Century in the United Kingdom: achievements, analysis and aspirations*, London: Institute of Education, 2010.

[9] Quoted in Robert Dawson Scott, 'Scottish musicians rubbish claims that folk music is dying out', STV, 15 July 2010, http://scotland.stv.tv/culture/traditional/187042-scottish-musicians-rubbish-claims-that-folk-music-is-dying-out/

Hamish Henderson and the Scottish Folk Revival

Hamish Henderson:
The Grand Old Man of Scottish Folk Culture

Christopher Harvie

It was the weekend of the European Union's Edinburgh summit in November 1992. I was in Munich, addressing the English-speaking Union. I knew that a demonstration in favour of Scots self-government was planned in Edinburgh, but was not hopeful. Demonstrations in Scotland, especially after a disappointing election, in which the Conservative government had unexpectedly survived, tended to mean the crowd being outnumbered by the police. But I phoned up my sister, then a social historian at the School of Scottish Studies.

"How many were out?"

"Goodness, couldn't count, maybe 20,000."

"Well behaved?"

"Everyone was, except the politicians. They were at it like cats and dogs."

"Oh God!"

"But then there was Hamish, and he sang 'The Freedom Come-All-Ye'."

"And all was well?"

"Ian Lang (the Conservative Secretary of State) said it was a disgrace to the country."

"What more could we ask for?"

Hamish Henderson was, apart from Glasgow's Edwin Morgan, the last of a generation of great twentieth century Scottish poets. For all the success of political devolution, the 1990s was a decade of loss for Scottish literature. The voices of George Mackay Brown, Sorley MacLean, Norman MacCaig, Iain Crichton Smith and Naomi Mitchison were stilled. Many would argue that a little of the formulaic urban violence of Irvine (*Trainspotting*) Welsh goes a very long way. But though they may not know it, the countless kids who (in Germany as much as in Scotland) thrill to the Battlefield Band, Dick Gaughan, the Tannahill Weavers, Brian MacNeill or Runrig, are Henderson's children, committed to an ideal of Scots nationality which is pacifist, anti-racist and international.

The route Hamish took was not straightforward, but it mirrored his country's awkward history. He had an upper-class education (not unlike Tony Blair, whose Scottish background was totally overlaid by it) at Merchiston Castle School, Edinburgh, and Cambridge. Like so many of his generation, he joined the Communist Party, and his sympathies were with the Spanish Republic, something which led to a fascination with Federico Garcia Lorca and his enthusiasm for the folk culture of Andalusia, and a critique of orthodox Communism's undervaluation of national and regional culture. Even so, he was no dogmatist: he could hold his own, in the pub and meeting-room, notably with the intellectual Tory Walter Elliot, who coined the phrase 'the democratic intellect' to describe the Scottish 'sonderweg', as well as with Glasgow shipyard workers and trade unionists.

The war broke out and Hamish found himself, like many thousands of his contemporaries, in the desert. He became one of the great poets of the Secnd World War, and his *Elegies on the Dead in Cyrenaica*, as much as Wilfred Owen's poems a quarter-century earlier, are an even-handed tribute to the dead of both sides:

There are many dead in the brutish desert, who lie uneasy
among the scrub in this landscape of half-wit
stunted ill-will. For the dead land insatiate
and necrophilous. The sand is blowing about still.
Many who for various reasons, or because of mere
    unanswerable compulsion, came here
and fought among the clutching gravestones,shivered
    and sweated,
cried out, suffered thirst, were stoically silent, cursed
the spitting machine-guns, were homesick for Europe
and fast embedded in quicksand of Africa agonized and died.
And sleep now. Sleep here the sleep of the dust.[1]

No Gods and Precious Few Heroes[2] comes from the *Elegies*: 'They saw through that guff before the axe fell.'[3] The Italian invasion followed, and the bitter fighting from the Sicilian landings up the Apennine chain

---

[1] Hamish Henderson, 'First Elegy', Collected Poems and Songs (edited by Raymond Ross), Edinburgh: Curly Snake, 2000, p.52.
[2] Christopher Harvie, No Gods and Precious Few Heroes, Cambridge: Blackwell, 3rd rev edition, 1998.
[3] Hamish Henderson, 'First Elegy', Collected Poems and Songs, p.52.

– "the last classical war" he termed it – was lightened for Hamish by the Italian Communist partisans, and his appreciation of their learning as well as their tenacity. In particular the ideas of Antonio Gramsci, Sardinian-born leader of Italy's Communists who made his prison-cell his classroom, worked their leaven to make Hamish look for a Scottish culture, not in the high literary style of Hugh MacDiarmid, but in the traditions of ordinary working people and the travellers.

In the 1920s MacDiarmid, in *Contemporary Scottish Studies*, castigated the commercialised sentimentality of Scottish poetry and song. Where Béla Bartók and Zoltán Kodály were researching the folk-music of Hungary, the Scots were contorting their musical heritage into the drawing-room ballads of Marjorie Kennedy-Fraser. It was Henderson and his colleagues from the School of Scottish Studies who, in the 1940s and afterwards, scraped the varnish off, and rediscovered a wealth of music which had remained stuck in the throats of fisherfolk, farm labourers, gypsies and travelling harvesters.

One story has become legendary: how Henderson got to know of a gypsy woman, living in a housing scheme in Aberdeen, who was said to have several of the old ballads off by heart. He turned up on the doorstep, and rang the bell. A woman answered the door. Not knowing what to say, he struck up one of the ballads. "That's dreadful," the woman said, "Come awa' in an' I'll sing it to ye right." The woman was Jeannie Robertson, illiterate, but with the lines of Europe's greatest ballads – thousands of them – in her head. A folk tradition, on the edge of extinction, was rescued

But Hamish with the heavy, old-fashioned tape-recorder, was still Hamish the political activist. Enraged at the élitist nature of the Edinburgh Festival, he and fellow-communists Norman and Janey Buchan and Morris Blythman set up the Edinburgh People's Festival, and involved many American folksingers and researchers like Pete and Peggy Seeger and Alan Lomax, New Dealers and socialists who had been blacklisted because of their politics – the same politics that also informed his famous 'Freedom Come-All-Ye', dedicated to the memory of John MacLean, the Clydeside revolutionary and teacher, first Consul of the Soviet Union in Scotland, who died young in 1923, and 'the blsck boy frae yont Nyanga' – Nelson Mandela:

> O, come all ye at hame wi' freedom
> Never heed what the hoodies croak for doom.
> In your hoose a' the bairns o' Adam
> Can find breid, barley-bree an' painted room.

When MacLean meets wi's freens in Springburn
A' the roses an' geans will turn tae bloom,
An' the black boy frae yont Nyanga
Dings the fell gallows o' the burghers doon.[4]

Much more than the medieval violence of Burns's 'Scots wha hae' or the sentimentality of the Tartan Army's 'Flower of Scotland', this has become the country's real national anthem.

In 1956, like so many other Scots radicals, Hamish broke with the Communist Party because of its support of the suppression of the Hungarian Revolution (MacDiarmid, always given to ruthlessness, rejoined) but was on hand when the Scottish Campaign for Nuclear Disarmament packed the roads to protest at the turning of the Clyde into a nuclear arsenal of unparalleled potential for destructiveness, and when Anti-Apartheid kept vigil against racism and repression in South Africa.

These were the Sandy Bell's years. The Forrest Hill Bar, of whom one Sandy Bell, long years ago, was the tenant, lies between the University and what used to be the Royal Infirmary in Edinburgh. Long and dark, it hosted Hamish, his magnificent russet spaniel, and whoever he had in tow from the centre or who had come in for a talk. "I remember a day in 1981," writes the historian and poet Angus Calder,

> When I dropped into Bell's for a half-pint before lunch and came out dizzy seven hours later. Hamish Henderson had presided over an impromptu colloquium involving Tom Leonard, Cathal the flautist from the Boys of the Lough, and a schoolteacher from Glasgow called Lorna never seen by any of us before nor, by me, since. She and I mostly nodded and smiled while Cathal played, Tom recited stanza after stanza of 'The City of Dreadful Night' and Hamish reminisced, sang, and reminisced more – all serious pleasure, a communion on some high frontier of culture to which Hamish had led us, from which every Scottish century could be surveyed, but also green Ireland, the townships of South Africa, Brittany, Italy, Germany,
> Lorca's Andalusia ... even England.[5]

Out of this period, too, came Hamish's films: *The Dead, the Innocent* on the Italian war, *The Summer Walkers*, directed by Tim Neat, about the last Scottish tinkers and their stories, and John Berger's *Tell Me a Story*

[4] Hamish Henderson, Collected Poems and Songs, p.143.
[5] Angus Calder, 'Introduction', in Hamish hendrrson, Alias MacAlias: Writings on Songs, Folk and Literature (edited by Alec Finlay), Edinburgh: Polygon, 1992.

in which Hamish, fictionalised into a West Highlander, did duty for all the people travelling in a Europe grown material and memoryless, and their struggle to maintain their own identity.

One of several remarkable sides to Hamish Henderson was the man's ecumenical spirit. Good humour, song and learning – capacities, alas, not always encountered in Scottish politics – were always on tap in Sandy Bell's Bar. But these could also intervene helpfully in his causes of home rule, socialism, peace and human dignity. Many in Edinburgh will remember the torchlight procession up the Mound in 1962 to protest against the jailing of Nelson Mandela, not least because Hamish adapted a simple but catchy song of the Spanish republicans:

> Verwoert fears the voice of Mandela!
> Room-ba-la, room-ba-la
> ROOM-BA-LA![6]

and got us all bawling it out.

A decade earlier, when the cause was on the floor after the failed referendum, I had as chair of a session to soothe a Westminster duo at a rally in Edinburgh. Escaping to the bar I found Hamish with Edwin Morgan and Tom Nairn, a heartening *troika*. There were no Tories around, but Hamish affectionately remembered the greatest of them, Walter Elliot. He had been in Paris in 1937, encountered the Secretary of State, and introduced himself. Elliot gave the young Communist lunch, talked about Scottish literature – "He made a very good case for regarding Hugh MacDiarmid as fascist-minded, like Yeats" – and promised that, however impressive the Paris Exhibition was, Scotland had, in the Glasgow Empire Exhibition he was organising, to do better. Hamish never lost that sort of ambition – for everyone.

His *Collected Poems and Songs* were published by Raymond Ross in 2000, two years before he died. In two volumes of essays and letters, *Alias MacAlias* and *The Armstrong Nose* we have a budget of Hamish on history, song, Marxism, travel – by turns comic and heartwarming, bawdy and reverent. And after his death in 2002, Timothy Neat set to work and, eventually, published Hamish's biography in two volumes.[7]

In 1949, the historian E P Thompson, author of the classic *Making of the English Working Class*, wrote to him:

---

[6] Hamish Henderson, 'Rivonia', *Collected Poems and Songs*, p.150.
[7] Timothy Neat, *Hamish Henderson, Vol.1 The Making of the Poet*, Edinburgh: Birlinn, 2007; *Hamish Henderson, Vol.2 Poetry Becomes People*, Edinburgh: Birlinn, 2009.

I greet you with humility, compagno, for you are that rare man, a poet. You have achieved poems out of our dead century ... Remember always who you are writing for: the people of Glasgow, of Halifax, of Dublin ... You, more than any other poet I know, are an instrument through which thousands of others can become articulate.[8]

His eightieth birthday was celebrated in 1999 at the last Edinburgh Folk Festival, in the same year Scotland's Parliament reconvened. A lifelong campaigner for Scottish self-government, Hamish lived to see this dream take shape. He did not live to see another war – 'race and leader, realm indivisible, laboured Augustan speeches or vague imperial heritage'[9] again let out to play. But he remained relevant. The man who fashioned out of 'Lili Marlene' the heartbreaking last lines of 'The D-Day Dodgers'

> Look around the mountains, in the mud and rain –
> You'll find the scattered crosses –
> (there's some which have no name).
> Heartbreak and toil and suffering gone
> The boys beneath them slumber on.
>   They are the D-Day Dodgers who'll stay in Italy.[10]

could also fashion, in the cause of peace, lines which matched those of Homer on Troy:

> There were our own, there were the others.
> Therefore, minding the great word of Glencoe's
> son, that we should not disfigure ourselves
> with villainy of hatred; and seeing that all
> have gone down like curs into anonymous silence,
> I will bear witness for I knew the others.
> Seeing that littoral and interior are alike indifferent
> And the birds are drawn again to our welcoming north
> why should I not sing them, the dead, the innocent?[11]

---

[8] Hamish Henderson, *The Armstrong Nose: Selected Letters* (edited by Alec Finlay), Edinburgh: Polygon, 1996, pp.28-29.
[9] Hamish henderson, 'First Elegy', *Collected Poems and Songs*, p.52.
[10] Hamish Henderson, *Collected Poems and Songs*, p.95.
[11] Hamish Henderson, 'First Elegy', *Collected Poems and Songs*, p.53.

Hamish of the Songs

Maurice Fleming[1]

It is no exaggeration to say that Hamish Henderson changed my life. Nothing extraordinary about this – he did it for many other people. This tall, stooping scholar-gypsy with the throaty laugh and the ready song had a way of colouring one's life and, whether you liked it or not, altering its direction.

We first met on the night of 26 July 1954 when, quite by accident, I found myself sitting opposite him at a dinner in the Adam Rooms of the George Hotel, Edinburgh (I still have the menu!). He was interested to hear that I was a magazine journalist with D.C. Thomson & Co., Dundee, but I was a lot more interested in the work he was doing as a research fellow at the School of Scottish Studies, Edinburgh University.

It so happened I had been listening, intrigued, to a radio series, *As I Roved Out*, in which Peter Kennedy, the presenter, played recordings of traditional songs collected in corners of rural England. I loved the freshness of the unaccompanied voices, the simplicity of the words, and the thought had struck me, "What a pity there are no old songs like these in Scotland!"

Now here was this chap telling me that of course there were, and that it was his job to collect them. And when he learned that I lived in Blairgowrie he told me that all I had to do, at that time of the year when the raspberries were being picked, was to go out into the fields and ask for songs.

---

[1] Maurice Fleming started collecting songs and stories for he School of Scottish Studies following a chance meeting with Hamish Henderson. A selection of the tracks recorded by Maurice can be heard on *Songs and Ballads from Perthshire Field Recordings of the 1950s*, Greentrax 'Scottish Tradition' No.24, 2011 (CDTRAX9024), issued in conjunction with the School of Scottish Studies Archives. This tribute first appeared in the *Scots Magazine* in May 2002, here reproduced with kind permission.

"Go amongst the travellers," he told me, "and here are a few songs to ask for." He scribbled a quick list of titles. At the top was 'The Berryfields o' Blair'.

The following week I wrote him: "You were right! The fields are full of songs. I have found nearly all the ones you asked for – and the woman who wrote 'The Berryfields'.

Before I knew it a tape recorder from Edinburgh arrived at my door and all else was forgotten as I filled tape after tape. Belle Stewart, the singer who wrote 'The Berryfields', and her talented family became great friends and their home in Rattray, over the river from Blair, was a collector's dream house.

Soon Hamish himself arrived in town and a hectic time was had by all. It was at sessions in and out of doors that summer that some of the best material held by the School of Scottish Studies was collected.

Hamish had the gift of making friends of all the singers he met. Travelling people can be severe critics but I have yet to hear one of them miscall him. He was completely at home in their company. Many of them then were what the travellers themselves call 'far back': illiterate, living in tents, their transport a horse and cart. Hamish camped alongside and became one of them (though I never saw him pick any berries!).

I missed out on a historic meeting I would love to have witnessed. A colleague accompanying Hamish arrived at the main door of my Dundee offices one morning and asked to see me. He told me Hamish had been given the address in the city of a traveller singer called Davie Stewart. They were on their way to meet him. He wanted me to come along. I had to explain that my editor would not appreciate my walking out mid-morning to call on a folksinger, however good!

And Davie *was* good. The following year Hamish rang from Edinburgh. Could I possibly go to see Davie (who had no phone) and arrange for him to travel to London to sing and be interviewed by the BBC?

That evening I hurried to his door. Davie was delighted at the news – but could not go.

"Why not?" I asked.

His accordion, on which he always accompanied himself, was where it frequently was, in the pawnshop. I gave him the money to rescue it, and his rail fare, but it was all in vain anyway. He had, at that time, no false teeth and what with that deficiency and his broad Aiberdeen, the English interviewer could not understand a word he said. The broadcast never took place. Worse, Davie got himself arrested in a London street for busking without a licence.

Still, teeth or no teeth, Davie Stewart was, under Hamish's guidance, to become one of the most popular troubadours on the folk club circuit, and something of a recording star.

Hamish's name will be forever closely associated with his work among the travellers, but it should be remembered that he also recorded and befriended many singers and storytellers outwith the fraternity. John Strachan, a wealthy farmer (there were such things then), gave him a rich crop of North-East ballads. Willie Mitchell was a Campbeltown butcher, Willie Scott a Border shepherd.

In Dundee I introduced him to Mary Brooksbank, a one-time mill worker and political agitator. They hit it off right away. Reviewing an album of recordings made at the 1967 Blairgowrie Folk Festival he praised the artistes heard on it – Davie Stewart, Willie Scott, Belle Stewart, Gaelic singer John 'Hoddan' MacDonald. "But", he wrote, "the singer who really steals the show is Mary Brooksbank with her 'My Johnny' and 'The Jute Mill Song'."

He also enjoyed a warm relationship with Jimmy MacBeath, the last 'King of the Cornkisters', who earned a kind of living by singing at markets and fairs and wherever folk would listen throughout the North-East and beyond, as his footsteps led him.

The people I have mentioned – Jimmy, Belle Stewart, Davie Stewart, John Strachan, Willie Scott, Mary Brooksbank and others, were well on in years when they met Hamish, but they all found the latter years of their lives transformed as he gave them an honoured and deserved place in the pubic gaze.

A new song, or version of a song, delighted him. Every time we met he had a recent discovery to tell me about and to sing for my delectation. This he would do no matter where we were, in the street, a pub, a restaurant. I recall a very long version of 'The Hairst o' Rettie' that seemed to last all through a meal in a polite little Edinburgh café.

It was a stroke of enormous good fortune that the School of Scottish Studies had opened in 1951 just when Hamish was considering his future. His temporary appointment as a research fellow was to become permanent. What would he have done, barring that happy accident? He told me he had been tempted to join Theatre Workshop, the company run by Joan Littlewood and Ewan MacColl. At that point they had been considering setting up headquarters in Scotland. When they went back south instead, Hamish decided against it. Had he gone he might well have become a director, an actor, or most likely of all, a playwright.

The Theatre's loss was Folksong's gain. Without his inspiration Scotland's Folksong Revival would not have arrived so soon nor made such impact. It took off with the People's Festivals he ran from 1951 to 1953 when many of us heard, for the very first time, real traditional singing on a public platform. The star of these 'come all ye's' (Hamish's term) was Jeannie Robertson, the Aberdeen singer who was his greatest discovery and was to be acclaimed as one of the world's leading interpreters of the Big Ballads.

He loved these noble songs but could be just as enthusiastic about a humble street rhyme. In the Abbotsford Bar, Edinburgh, my wife mentioned a children's game song she remembered. Nothing would stop him but we had to repair to the School in George Square to record them. By the time we had finished she had recalled and sung some I didn't know she knew!

Hamish was proud of his early beginnings as a boy in Blairgowrie though not very willing to talk or write about them. In an obituary in a leading daily newspaper following his death the writer said that Hamish and his mother had been evicted from their "cottage" for not paying the rent.

The 'cottage' is, in fact, a fine villa in one of the best parts of the town. Hamish told me in an unusually frank letter that it had been leased to his grandfather, a silk merchant in Dundee. He had died without leaving a will. His widow kept on the lease and had her daughter and Hamish to live with her. However, funds ran low when Hamish was six and they had to give it up and move into lodgings. They lived for a time with a family in Glenshee.

Despite these unhappy recollections, he retained a strong affection for Blairgowrie, and I am sure he relished the fact that it was here, years later, that he was to spend some of his happiest and most fruitful hours.

Of course his life was not all ceilidhs, come-all-ye's and roaming the countryside. In his letters he often spoke about the volume of correspondence he had to deal with at the school. Folklore enquiries came to him from all over the world, many requiring time-consuming research. Still, he enjoyed that challenging work, and his university lecturing duties which gave him the chance to communicate his passions to young folk. On top of all that, there were the invitations to give talks, attend conferences, take part in debates, write papers and articles.

His last years saw a rapid decline in health. He made his last public appearance in Blairgowrie at a day of celebration for the local Stewart family and their legacy. He was driven there from Edinburgh for a morning event but then quietly slipped away to be taken home.

Sheila Stewart sang that day a song about her grandfather which she was to sing again at Hamish's funeral in St Mary's Episcopal Cathedral, Edinburgh. It contains a line about old John Stewart which says it all about Hamish, too: 'A man you don't meet every day.'

I won't meet another like him.

Scotland's Internationale

David Stenhouse[1]

On the terraces at Murrayfield they prefer 'Flower of Scotland'. At the
Edinburgh Tattoo, it is 'Scotland the Brave'. In some Scottish towns, they
shuffle to their feet for 'God Save the Queen' and, behind closed doors,
some belt out 'The Sash'.

But on demonstrations and rallies, at sit-ins and ceilidhs, they draw on
a different number from the back catalogue. It is a song of hope and a
song of apology, an anti-war anthem by a one-time warrior. The song is
both lilting and stirring – a song about a better world, sung by those who
still believe in its possibility.

Hamish Henderson, the man who wrote it, played a part in some of the
past century's great struggles. He helped smuggle Jews out of Germany,
oversaw the surrender of southern Italy after the Second World War,
and offered his help to the Italian partisans. He travelled Scotland with a
clumsy tape recorder, making a record of an oral tradition that was fast
slipping away. Folklorist, poet, musician, political activist – a packed life
by any standards. Yet it would be fitting if Henderson's greatest legacy
was a single song.

The song begins, as Henderson tells it, with a long train journey down
from Sutherland one day in the late 1950s. "The wind was blowing fiercely
through the glen and I thought about that wind and imagined it blowing
on through the great glen of the world. The line had been in my head for
a long time but, at that moment, it all came together."

The image of a wind blowing away the old world and carrying the hope
of a new would enter the protest singer's standard vocabulary. It was

---

[1] This piece was originally published in the *Sunday Herald* on 7 Nov, 1999, and is
reproduced with the author's kind permission.

two years before Harold MacMillan would unwittingly use the image to describe the "wind of change" blowing through Africa.

When Henderson was stationed in North Africa during the war, he helped compose bawdy songs to lift the spirits of the men under his command, giving new words to traditional tunes. For 'The Freedom Come-All-Ye', he used the pipe tune 'The Bloody Fields of Flanders'. The new words were not intended to raise martial spirits but to quash them forever. They transformed a war song into a powerful anti-war hymn – the musical version of beating swords into ploughshares.

The musical historian John Purser believes that much of the power of Henderson's song lies in its musical origin. "Hamish was involved in the war and he knew what Scottish soldiers could be like. It is, at one and the same time, a powerful protest against war and a war tune. That someone who had fought in a great war could get the meaning of war so right is amazing," he says.

When Purser devoted a section of one of his radio programmes on Scotland's music to Henderson's song, he interwove it with Scottish war songs, including 'Scotland the Brave'. Henderson's song was there as an ironic commentary but it drew its power from a shared root.

But 'The Freedom Come-All-Ye' is not just a song about war. In it, Henderson faces one of the dilemmas that has so convulsed Scottish thinking: our own complicity in the crimes of Empire. If "broken faimilies" curse Scotland the Brave, it is because that tune carried the occupying Scottish forces into foreign lands, serving the purposes of the British Empire in the countries "we hairriet". And if, by the end of the song, there is reconciliation through marriage and friendship, that is not because the crimes of the past never occurred but because they have been forgiven by a new generation.

The song brings into focus many of the concerns of Henderson's adult life. After the war, Henderson translated the writings of the Italian Communist philosopher Antonio Gramsci into English for the first time. Gramsci's work discusses the revolutionary potential of ordinary people, and Henderson's song is informed by a humanistic faith and internationalism that owes much to the European traditions of communism.

It is a declaration of the brotherhood of man, from a time when such hope was still bright; of international reconciliation when it still seemed possible. But there is a fighting sprit in the song, too. When John MacLean the socialist hero meets with his friends in the final verse, he plans the overthrow of the bourgeois world. When the "gallows o the burghers" fall, it is in the service of revolution.

After the war, Henderson worked as a folklorist, gathering songs and stories from Scotland's oral tradition, and "discovering" some of the greatest interpreters of traditional Scottish song. Though 'The Freedom Come-All-Ye' is literary, it draws on some of the greatest precursors in Scotland's music.

"The images in the opening lines would be familiar to any folk singer," explains the folk singer Adam McNaughtan. "The 'heilster- gowdie' comes from 'Maginty's Meal and Ale', and the 'painted rooms' are from the Jacobite anthem 'The King's Farewell'. But the song is so poetic. It's a literary look at the folk tradition. No-one else could have written it."

'The Freedom' gathered a life of its own. We now live in a time where political songs seem to come from a different era. New Labour dumped 'The Red Flag' for the froth of 'Things Can Only Get Better'. But to those who march for a leftist political cause, 'The Freedom' lifts all spirits.

It was sung in France during the 1968 student uprisings and later at devolution meetings and political protests in Scotland during the 1980s. At countless shivery rallies and rain-soaked marches, 'The Freedom' warmed up frozen throats.

It was sung at the launch of the Scottish Constitutional Convention, where it chimed with Canon Kenyon Wright's declaration that "we are the people and we say Yes." It was sung at vigils and fund-raising ceilidhs. It was missing at the opening of the Scottish parliament but only because Burns's 'A Man's A Man For A' That' stole the show.

But songs have hidden private meanings as well as public, political ones. Appropriately for a song about reconciliation, the song allowed Henderson a poignant posthumous reconciliation with a one-time enemy. Henderson had famously quarrelled with Hugh MacDiarmid over the value of folk songs – songs that MacDiarmid dismissed as peasant art of no political significance

It is a moot point who won that particular exchange. But, in 1984, when a delegation of Scottish cultural activists travelled to MacDiarmid's home town of Langholm to protest against the town council's reluctance to put up a statue to its controversial son, the song that was used to rally the troops was Henderson's 'The Freedom Come-All-Ye'.

So what explains the song's evocative power? After all, leaving aside the complexity of its imagery, it is written in a Scots that many will find difficult to get their tongue around.

"People like the Scots, even when they don't understand it," says magazine editor Joy Hendry. "They like the egalitarianism of its sentiments, but it's a beautiful song too, with its complex ideas rooted in friendship and the image of the trees blooming in a bitter world. The core of its appeal is that desire to set nationalism aside."

Robin Morton, one half of the Boys of the Lough, recalls that "it was performed in the Usher Hall at the time of the Commonwealth Games in Edinburgh. The concert was a great opportunity. It was the first time that

I'd ever had the funds to put on just what I wanted. At the end of the concert, we all played 'The Freedom Come-All-Ye' and everyone was on their feet."

So Henderson's song is at once complex and simple – an apology to those whom we once fought against, as much as a rallying cry to further battles.

When the Scottish Parliament re-opened, there was a nationwide competition for schoolchildren to write a poem for the special day. The vexed issue of the Scottish national anthem was left well alone. In fact, 'The Freedom' is a national anthem in search of a nation. It resembles the anthem of a revolutionary country – all hopes for the future and blanket condemnation of the past.

"It could never be a national anthem," Henderson declares firmly. "It is an anti-nationalist song." If 'The Freedom Come-All-Ye' is reminiscent of anything, it is of 'The Internationale', the communist anthem that was composed to celebrate the Paris Commune of 1871. That song, sung to a stirring rhythm, triumphantly declares:

> So comrades, come rally
> and the last fight let us face.
> The Internationale unites the human race.

A final fight that will end the need for fighting? A war on tyrants and oppression? International fraternity? 'The Freedom Come-All-Ye' is Scotland's Internationale – an appropriate testament to the internationalist who wrote it.

At the Vigil
Hamish Henderson and the
Campaign for a Scottish Parliament

Ivor Birnie

It is not widely enough known that, and how, Hamish Henderson campaigned for many years for a Scottish Parliament. Many a tribute has been paid to Hamish Henderson from all quarters of the globe when he died in 2002. It was an honour to have Hamish supporting the cause and an immense pleasure to have him sharing his views on what he thought was best for the future of his fellow Scots.

When in the General Election of 9 April 1992 yet another Conservative government was returned, in an election in which only 25% of those who voted in Scotland actually voted for this Conservative government in London, 'Democracy for Scotland' got together with the aim of holding a 'Vigil for a Scottish Parliament' at the foot of Calton Hill in Edinburgh.

Hamish Henderson was one of the first people to come forward to offer support to the group who vowed to stay at Calton Hill until a Scottish parliament was agreed. The vigil started on 10 April 1992 – and soon the portacabin at the foot of Calton Hill, across from St Andrews House, the seat of the Scottish Office, and literally a stone's throw from the Royal High School, earmarked as the seat of a Scottish Parliament since the referendum of 1979, attracted many supporters and became an Edinburgh landmark.

On the hundredth day of the vigil, there was a demonstration at Calton Hill called 'Hands Round Parliament', in which a human chain holding hands together was formed around the old Royal High School at the foot of Calton Hill. On this day 100 people signed a 'Declaration of Calton Hill', a scroll endorsing the Campaign for a Scottish Parliament. Among the first signatories was Hamish Henderson who – being a very distinguished writer – made everyone joyous by his endorsement. Others who signed the 'Declaration of Calton Hill' were Alex Salmond (now the First Minister), Fiona Hyslop (now an MSP) and Tommy Sheridan (now an ex-MSP), to mention but a few.

The group took their message to all corners of Scotland, holding destiny marches and public meetings. From each of these visits a stone was taken back to Edinburgh, where a cairn was built by supporters on Calton Hill. The cairn can still be seen to this day on Calton Hill.

The vigil at the foot of Calton Hill lasted a total of 1979 days, ending after the referendum held on 11 September 1997, in which the people of Scotland voted overwhelmingly for a Scottish Parliament. On 12 September 1997, a party was held at the foot of Calton Hill. It was a cold, blustery night but, sure enough, those who knew Hamish might have guessed that out of his coat would appear a bottle of Stewart's Barley Cream with the comment: "Mighty – that was some shift! I think we deserve a dram."

'Literature must desire to be life, not an idea of life' Hamish Henderson's Vision 'Poetry Becomes People'

Tessa Ransford[1]

The 23-year-old Hamish Henderson was sent to work as an intelligence officer in the North African Campaign early in 1942. (He had to interrogate prisoners and always asked them if they knew any songs!) On setting out, he was reading Yeats, and in particular a poem of Yeats's – 'The Circus Animals Desertion' – with the lines

> Players and painted stage took all my love,
> And not those things that they were emblems of.[2]

Hamish was clear that he was not seeking a literary career, or themes, out of the war experience, rather to be an impartial witness. Indeed, his publisher John Lehmann remarked that it is hard to be impartial when 'in the midst of things', to which Hamish's reply was that it is certainly hard to be impartial *unless* in the midst of things. He wrote the exceptional sequence *Elegies for the Dead in Cyrenaica* – poems which even seventy years on constitute reality rather than being 'about' anything:

So Long

> To the war in Africa that's over – goodnight.
> To the thousands of assorted vehicles, in every stage of
> decomposition littering the desert from here to Tunis –
> goodnight.

---

[1] This chapter is based on a Hamish Henderson Memorial Lecture given jointly with Tom Hubbard at the 2011 Edinburgh People's Festival on 10 August, at the Nelson Hall Community Centre.

[2] W B Yeats, The Poems, London: Dent, 1994, p.394.

To thousands of guns and armoured fighting vehicles
brewed up, blackened and charred
from Alamein to here, from here to Tunis –
        goodnight.

To thousands of crosses of every shape and pattern,
        alone or in little huddles, under which the unlucky bastards lie –
        goodnight.

Horse-shoe curve of the bay
Clean razor-edge of the escarpment,
Tonight it's the sunset only that's blooding you.

Halfaya and Sollum: I think that at long last
        we can promise you a little quiet.
So long. I hope I won't be seeing you.

To the sodding desert – you know what you
        can do with yourself.

To the African deadland – God help you –
        And goodnight.[3]

Hamish was in the midst of things all his life and desired that his poetry be life, become people. What could that mean? The phrase is borrowed from Heinrich Heine's statement that 'Freedom must become people.' Heine's statement in the 1830s that when books are burnt, people will be burnt too is inscribed in the Bebelplatz in Berlin where the Nazis burnt books in the 1930s. The phrase also reminds us of ideas from the Sardinian Communist thinker Antonio Gramsci about culture forming its own 'society' and affecting politics to the extent that it can almost be claimed that 'the politics follows the culture'. If we think about this we can see that it is true. Without a culture of service and subservience there can be no empire, and no mafia, for instance. Without a culture of poetic vision, creative thinking and steady building of infrastructures, there can be no freedom becoming people.

There are individual people and there are groups of people, societies of people, communities of people, nations of people, the world of people. Poetry needs to be 'in the midst of things' in all these circles within circles – for the individual to individuate and live in hope, for the community to have vision, openness and freedom from fear, for nations to operate on

---

[3] Hamish Henderson, *Collected Poems and Songs* (edited by Raymond Ross), Edinburgh: Curly Snake, 200, p.77.

principles of freedom, collaboration and acceptance of diversity rather than fear, prejudice and deterrence.

In Tunis in January this year the people marching in the streets were chanting the verses of a poet, Abu al Qarim Alshabi, who died in his forties a few decades ago. They took courage from this, even as they took courage from the self-immolation of the bullied and harassed fruit seller. For poetry to act as freedom acts in a society, it needs to become anonymous in this way, to belong to everyone, to escape from the boxes into which it is often put as a precautionary principle – kept for academics, mavericks, prizes to a few and the rest ignored – hierarchies of 'best poets' and so on. Gramsci's definition of popular song was:

> ... those written neither by the people, nor for the people, but which the people adopt because they conform to their way of thinking and feeling... the way in which they conceive the world and life... [4]

Gramsci and Henderson knew that folk song must operate in this communal way if it is to be borne on the carrying stream from generation to generation. No amount of oppression can prevent such undercurrents, or simply currents... the flow is all – 'the continuing stream indeed'. The currents, however, need conductors of the energy, to gather and re-diffuse it. Hamish Henderson was such a conductor. Helen Crummy who died recently and who set up and sustained the Craigmillar Festival was another. You will know of others past and present.

> Her vision as organising secretary was that it was about as many people as possible in the community working together to create a better quality of life for Craigmillar – that everybody is creative and has a place in society.... Her book *Let the People Sing!* has been sold and studied for its social insight in many countries... the challenge is to unlock this creative energy and real-life knowledge and use them to regenerate the community and give a purpose for living to the individuals in it. [5]

Psalm 29 in the Bible has the well-known phrase: 'where there is no vision, the people perish'. The German philosopher Martin Heidegger stated that 'poetry is the language of thought'. [6] If poetry becomes

---

[4] Antonio Gramsci, *Selections from Cultural Writings* (edited by David Forgacs and Geoffrey Nowell-Smith), London: Lawrence & Wishart, 1985, p.195.

[5] from Helen Crummy's obituary: Obituaries, *The Herald*, 15 July 2011.

[6] Martin Heidegger, *Poetry, Language, Thought* (translated by Alfred Hofstadter), Harper Prennial, 1975.

people it means that people – the people, communities, societies – have visions, setting them free from fear, and that they are creatively thinking, making connections Other modes of thinking – analysing, rationalising, calculating, plotting, manoeuvring – are not poetry. They can serve the creative thinking which is poetry, but without the vision they can lead to prejudice, oppression, violence, corruption, war.

For a people to think creatively, with vision, the language needs to be used the way poetry uses it, for image, feeling, archetypes, combined with precision, detail, the particular, making 'figures of thought.' Poets 'in the midst of things' are the vision-makers or vision messengers, the witnesses and recorders, the prophets and interpreters.

> Without 'people' there is no poetry –
> Without poetry there is no vision –
> Vision allows freedom from fear
> so poetry/freedom become people

The Scottish Poetry Library became a community, a library as a milieu, a base camp, without hierarchies or selectivity, going out, welcoming in, celebrating diversity and inclusiveness

> When we were children
> time ran errands for us. Later we tried
> to launch our craft on it; it was a grown-up
> counting ten while the children ran to hide.
> Or lay isolated, a ship in a bottle,
> straining in stillness
> against the stone pull of an immeasurable tide.
>
> Through wash of rubble
> this Time defeats me. And the headland's spike
> is crumbling stump. I turn to
> a burnt-out croft behind a ragged dyke.
> From time past a whisper of battle.
> O child, child, hurry.
> For life our mortal blow quickly we'll strike.[7]

The mortal blow we each must hurry to strike is 'on behalf of life' and against fear. As can be seen in 'The Flyting o Life and Daith', there is a dialectic of the rhythm in which we are required unambiguously, heroically, to struggle on the side of life at all times:

---

[7] Hamish Henderson, Collected Poems and Songs, pp.26-27.

Quo life, the warld is mine.
An open grave is a furrow syne.
Ye'll no keep my seed frae fa'in in.
Quo life the warld s mine.[8]

Henderson's concept of the life that contends with death is one of the substantiality of life, its toil, sweat, tears and laughter. And it is to that life to which he wants his works of 'literature' to approximate. Hamish wrote "Love operates faster and surer than time or space or both" and "love cannot operate on your behalf as long as your own sickly fear will not permit love to operate on your behalf."

Henderson was fully aware of the entertainment type of folksy 'come all-ye' song of Irish origin, which overacts and coaxes its audience in an almost pantomime fashion with topicality and knowing jokes. He understood the poet MacGonagall as being in this tradition, and therefore not so much a poor poet as a valid, poetic version of popular entertainment. This is in contrast to the great ballads in their 'sensuous austerity', where the audience is mentally and emotionally at one with the singer and does not need to be wooed. However, the inclusive aspect of the 'come all-ye' tradition was not something Henderson deplored; on the contrary. For poetry and song to 'become people, in the sense of 'freedom becomes people' it must connect at a deep level to human communities and movements, nationally and internationally, passed from singer to singer with varying versions and becoming part of an anonymous treasure in due course, attributable only to this or that singer's version, rather than to an individual 'author'.

Henderson lived in an orphanage while attending Dulwich College after his mother died. He was involved in arranging a public reading at the school of James Elroy Flecker's verse play *Hassan*. There we find a remarkable paeon to the importance of poetry at the heart of culture spoken by the Caliph of Baghdad to Hassan, the sweet-maker.

> In poems and in tales alone shall live the eternal memory of this city when I am dust and thou art dust, when all Baghdad is broken to the ground. If there shall ever arise a nation whose people have forgotten poetry or whose poets have forgotten the people, though they send their ships round Taprobane and their armies across the hills of Hindustan, though their cities be greater than Babylon of old, though they mine a league into the earth or mount to the stars on wings – what of them?

---

[8] *Ibid.*, p.144.

And Hassan replies, 'they will be a dark patch upon the world.[9]'

That 'dark patch upon the world' was what Henderson had fought against in the war against Fascism and in the barren desert landscape itself, but which he had also sensed in the depopulated glens of Scotland and the poverty-stricken city slums. He had also witnessed many brave deeds among the partisans in Italy, notably Corbara, "yon wuddifu callant", for whom he wrote a ballad.[10]

The crux of the matter was for poets not to forget the people or to allow the conditions to prevail when the people forget poetry. It is a huge burden of responsibility:

> How shall I answer those who ask?
> Now, now: before another silence[11]

The founding of the People's Festivals in Edinburgh issued from these beliefs. Unfortunately, despite their success, they were banned by the Labour Party in 1952, perhaps from fear of nationalism and communism. (A Labour Council in Edinburgh similarly closed down the 'Women Live' festivals in 1983 after two successful years.)

Henderson had great ideas for international peace and equality, which he tried to put into practice in Scotland, almost as a crucible of experiment. There were high hopes after the war, before petty factions and international positioning took over. He could have lived in Cambridge or London, or Ireland (where he taught in the WEA for a few years) or Cornwall or America, and he could have made his literary name anywhere (though he was denied entry to Italy because of an 'exclusion order' imposed in 1950 when was translating Gramsci). Hamish could have lived elsewhere in Europe, but he chose to live and work in Scotland, believing in its latent shamanic strength, the deep-seated creative gifts among the people, its fund of archetypal wisdom.

Through his own poetry and song, the School of Scottish Studies, the folk song and folk story revival, through teaching, connecting people and ideas, singing, campaigning – despite the layers of hypocrisy among the

---

[9] James Elroy Flecker, *Hassan: A Play in Five Acts*, London: William Heinemann, 1923.

[10] Hamish Henderson, 'The Ballad o Corbara', *Collected Poems and Songs*, pp.86-92.

[11] Henderson's translation of Salvatore Quasimodo's 'Colour of Rain and Iron', *Collected Poems and Songs*, p.134. See also Tessa Ransford: 'Encompass the Crossed Sword-Blades: Hamish Henderson's Poetry', in *Borne on the Carrying Stream: The Legacy of Hamish Henderson* (edited by Eberhard Bort), Ochtertyre: Grace Note Publications, 2010, pp.137-60.

main power players which kept Scotland dependent, drained of talent and divided – Hamish's prophetic, almost 'blind' vision of a spiritually-bonded people with a courageous history and an inclusive, communitarian, humanitarian sense of what it could and should be as a country, in itself and internationally, is alive and among us to inspire and uphold us in the now of our everyday present.

'All Art is a Collaboration'

Tom Hubbard[1]

In the Preface to his best known play, *The Playboy of the Western World* (1907), the Irish playwright J M Synge states: "All art is a collaboration."[2] Taking my cue from that quote, I would go so far as to say that the most profound art derives from folk tradition – Hamish Henderson knew that instinctively. Many of the great works of modern art, literature and music could not have come about without a synthesis of avant-garde experimentation and of the collective culture of a particular people from a particular place. In music, I would point to, as examples, Béla Bartók in Hungary or Georges Enescu in Romania, who were precursors of Hamish. Through the vicissitudes of their countries' experiences of fascism, Stalinism and now mafiosi capitalism, Bartók's and Enescu's work can still enrich us at a very deep spiritual level and in turn galvanise us to challenge that 'dark patch upon the world' quoted by Tessa Ransford. It reminds us not only of what we are struggling *against*, but also of what we're struggling *for*.

Sure, these composers I have just mentioned were what we would call 'art' or 'classical' musicians, often writing for large numbers of players. On the face of it, all very different from a ceilidh or what we *generally* understand as being 'folk'. But the underlying ethos is the same, and Hamish himself was concerned to bring 'art' and 'folk' idioms together, to their mutual enrichment. For him, it was not either/or.

---

[1] This chapter is based on a Hamish Henderson Memorial Lecture given jointly with Tessa Ransford at the 2011 Edinburgh People's Festival on 10 August, at the Nelson Halls Community Centre.

[2] John M Synge, *The Playboy of the Western World and Riders to the Sea*, London: Routledge, new ed., 1979, p.11.

Borne on the Carrying Stream, the book on Hamish Henderson legacy published in 2010,[3] takes its title from a poem, 'Under the Earth I Go' by Hamish Henderson. It is about how poetry and song, and the energies which create them, continue and also grow and change through succeeding generations:

> Like the potent
> Sap in these branches, once bare, and now
> brimming
> With routh of green leavery
> Remake it, and renew.
>
> ...
>
> Tomorrow, songs
> Will flow free again, and new voices
> Be borne on the carrying stream[4]

The J M Synge quote – "all art is a collaboration" – reminds us too that there is really no such thing as originality. There are really no new stories, no new poems, only current but necessary variations on the ones that have gone before. Once we realise that, the idea of races for literary prizes, promotions in the bookbarns of the chainstores and celebrity authors becomes even more risible.

The Scottish Poetry Library – let us call it the SPL (though I believe that acronym belongs to another organisation whose name escapes me momentarily) – the SPL was a collaboration. Tessa Ransford and I were part of an ever-metamorphosing team that included our committee (that was our gaffer), our helpers, our readers, and of course the poets themselves whose books and recordings were on the shelves. We are not involved in the SPL now, and we continue our work through various other channels and contexts. But what we achieved at the SPL is in a sense unfinished business, and that has to be taken up by younger folk both as individuals and in solidarity with each other – in solidarity with the culture that has nurtured them, and which in turn they need to continue to nurture, in ways which none of us can predict, in ways which none of us *should* predict. That is the nature of the 'carrying stream'.

Actually, the 'carrying stream' image is a more poetic, imaginative way of saying 'unfinished business'. At the SPL, Tessa and I and our team established a very physical presence for poetry in the form of printed books and magazines, there on the shelves for folk to borrow and take

---

[3] Eberhard Bort (ed.), *Borne on the Carrying Stream: The Legacy of Hamish Henderson*, Ochtertyre: Grace Note Publications, 2010.

[4] Hamish Henderson, *Collected Poems and Songs* (edited by Raymond Ross), Edinburgh: Curly Snake, 2000, p.154-55.

home. And we also had recordings. The technology has moved on, and there is now a plethora of ways in which poetry can get out there. Though, I have to say, I miss the magazines, of which there are so few these days; they were places of debate and glorious vituperation. Now, it is all gone awfy bland and passionless.

My own suggestion for taking that 'unfinished business', the 'carrying stream', further is to think of poetry less as a form of literature, and more as a form of theatre – poetry blending its strengths, along with all the other forms that make up theatre, such as music, visual art (theatre's a kind of sculpture in motion, after all), sets, props, dance, gesture, facial expression, body language in other words, costume, lighting – you name it. Poetry itself becomes part of a team, not some wee comfort zone entire of itself.

Tessa and I have had some argument about this, and I want to answer an objection she has made to me about 'performance poetry', a genre about which she has doubts. I do not mean 'performance poetry' at all, as that is something which can become a comfort zone, too. The phrase 'performance poetry' implies that only a particular kind of poetry can be performed, that a particular kind of poetry is specifically written to have an immediate and in my view often very superficial impact. This can lead to a smug, self-conscious, look-at-me atmosphere akin to the more predictable forms of stand-up: performer and audience hugging themselves and each other with knowing grins. Pretty unchallenging and cosy. In answer to that, I would argue that surely *all* good poetry is performable, even complex poetry, whether or not it is composed with performance in mind – what I would suggest is that it needs theatrical skill, theatrical resources, to reveal it at full strength.

So, you may ask, what kind of theatre? Last April, in Connecticut, I was in the audience at a production of *A Dream Play* by the Swedish dramatist August Strindberg. I was bowled over by the company's use of puppets, including gigantic heads. Gigantic heads can mean many things – oppressive busts of political bigwigs, mysterious images as on Easter Island, they can be variously symbolic and/or satirical.

You might think, what has this got to do with Hamish Henderson, who was concerned after all with poetry and music and was not a man of the theatre as such. But he was concerned with *performance*, and that is clearly a strong common factor. Folk theatre in his beloved Italy was based on *commedia dell' arte*, with its masks and patchy costumes. Hamish was also a keen student of German culture, and he could have hardly been unaware of the street puppetry that had been around in Germany for centuries – such as the Faust and the Devil puppet plays in the old town squares of Frankfurt.

Around the time, last spring, that I was responding to that puppetry element in a theatre-piece in Connecticut, my head was still full of the content of this book on Hamish, not just the ideas in my own essay[5] but what had been said by other contributors. It is a tribute to the wider influence of Hamish that someone can feel drawn to a folk art in which he had no direct involvement. But, I repeat, that is the nature of the carrying stream, you cannot and should not predict where it might flow.

However, my interest in all this goes a lot further back; it is Hamish's vision that gives me the confidence to revive that interest. In years past, in Poland and elsewhere, I had learned about theatre which uses puppets, masks, i.e. which uses objects and does not just rely on 'human' actors. Though with masks and certain other objects worn by a flesh and blood performer, you can have an 'actor' which is half-object, half-human, and that can have a powerful impact on stage. I had been aware of all this already, twenty years or so ago. But my more recent experience in Connecticut made me want to learn more, much more, about the power of puppetry. I spoke to the folk who made and manipulated the puppets – they were called the BREAD AND PUPPET THEATRE COMPANY, based in Vermont, and had been founded by a German puppeteer and community activist called Peter Schumann. Their political activity included a campaign on behalf of a US army private who had been getting the run-around from his superiors in the military, judicial and political hierarchies.

It turned out that our part-time Professor of Puppetry on the campus had been with the Bread & Puppet Theatre Co. for many years. John Bell is an international expert on the art of puppetry and runs his programmes in Connecticut on a shoestring. The puppet museum is brilliant and is housed in a shack – the university tried to close it down until there was an outcry. John is also active in the Boston area, with his involvement in street theatre there – it is all great fun and challenges the passive consumer entertainment culture that we mistakenly call 'popular' ('popular' surely should mean by and of the people, not just for the people). John gave me this HONK! badge – it is to do with street musicians in pageants through the streets of Cambridge, Massachusetts.

I am convinced that one possible future for poetry, if it can hitch its wagon to theatre, is to get together with the guys who are doing puppetry. Puppets, because they are not flesh-and-blood human actors, implicitly question the 'star' system – they distance the spectator from all that. You cannot make a celeb out of a puppet (though you'll probably cite Miss Piggy and Kermit the Frog against me). It is all akin to Bertolt Brecht's idea of theatre: you concentrate on what is going on in a piece, you enjoy it but you also *think* about it, instead of drooling dorkily over

---

[5] Tom Hubbard, 'Hamish Henderson and Béla Bartók: Bridgeable Chasms', In E Bort (ed.), *Borne on the Carrying Stream*, pp.114-22.

such and such a Hollywood bigbucks megastar.

In France, recently, I checked out the puppet theatres there – in Lyon they have the great tradition of GUIGNOL. This is rooted in nineteenth-century working-class culture: the Guignol puppets take the piss out of the high-heidyins, and the scripts are a gloriously vulgar, rough and tumble kind of poetry. Apparently if you want to research that stuff thoroughly, you have to go to the police records of the time – Guignol puppet theatre had to contend with censorship and official heavy-breathing generally. Guignol's present-day activists will say, OK, it maybe seems old-fashioned entertainment in an age of video games, but the folk still come in droves to the open-air shows.

I think myself that a combination of poetry and puppetry could prove cool and funky to the generations coming up. (My 21-year-old art graduate daughter will curl up into a corner if she finds me using the words cool and funky.) I can only *suggest* that bringing poetry and puppetry together is something that emerging poets and puppeteers might consider looking into; I could not and would not attempt to *prescribe* the way it might go, if it happened. Nobody is going to listen to me if I come over all patriarchal gravitas, complacently croaking in my private morass of pompous old fartitude.

I have been privileged to work abroad and to learn about these alternative modes of expression on the spot, as it were. But being so privileged makes me feel all the more obliged to pass on my experiences to others who might make creative use of them. In France, too, and in Belgium, I have explored the culture of *bandes dessinées*, our equivalent being graphic novels – if you like, the kind of comic strips that are serious without being solemn. Again, maybe poets could consider publishing in that form and so get across to a wider (and younger) audience. It can be seriously lyrical, seriously subversive, seriously funny and even seriously serious. And for all I know, maybe much of what I have been blethering on about is happening already. If it is, it is probably my fault that I did not know about it, and if anyone can put me right on that, I would be muckle obliged to them.

Let me conclude with this, from Peter Schumann:

> But we, puppeteers of the world, should break away, should move off, as the German puppeteer Hölderlin said: understand the freedom to rise; or as the rooster said to the donkey in the Bremen town musicians: come along, something better than Death we find anywhere.[6]

---

[6] Peter Schumann, *The Old Art of Puppetry in the New World Order: A Lecture with Fiddle,* St Johnsbury, Vermont: Troll Press, 1993.

Working on the Hamish Henderson Papers

Steve Byrne

Since Hamish Henderson died in March 2002, the fate of his personal papers has been in a state of continuing uncertainty. They consist of around 30 cardboard boxes, plus several old leather suitcases, containing a lifetime's correspondence with a wealth of notable figures from the fields of politics, folklore and folksong, academia and poetry, alongside diaries going as far back as the 1930s and, perhaps of most interest, from during the Second World War. These often feature drafts of Hamish's poems and songs, amongst an absolute myriad of notes, snippets, comments, observations, items collected from soldiers (from all sides) at the front and letter drafts, alongside a wealth of ephemera from events and organisations with which Hamish had contact throughout his life.

In the years following his death, both Hamish's extensive library and personal papers were offered for sale to a number of institutions. The books themselves were not particularly rare from a librarian's point of view, but the collection itself was an insight into the mind of a voracious bibliophile. In the end, the books along with a small number of manuscript items, a handful of letters and photographs were catalogued and sold by the bookseller Carmen Wright.[1]

For a multitude of reasons, relating in some cases to competing priorities at public institutions (e.g. the significant demands on the National Library of Scotland in acquiring the John Murray Archive in 2005), and in other cases to personalities and poor communication, the main collection of Hamish's papers remains unsold, despite a number of initial surveys undertaken by interested parties over the years.

---

[1] In September 2011, Carmen returned a portion of unsold material to the Henderson family to be added to the archive.

The purpose of this article is to highlight the current campaign through the setting up of the *Hamish Henderson Archive Trust* to make some positive progress on the fate of the material, consider its contents and historical value, and look towards its future. It is useful, however, to outline the discussions and negotiations in which I and others have been engaged in recent years, in order to set the context for where we are now.

Recent Progress

I first became involved in this process in 2008 via Dr Fred Freeman, maestro of the *Complete Songs of Robert Burns*, producer of the Greentrax Hamish tribute CD, *A' the Bairns o Adam*, and a great friend of the Hendersons, who himself had done a power of work in trying to find a suitable home for the papers. With my local authority arts background (as Traditional Arts Officer for the City of Edinburgh Council for five years 2002-2007), I offered to bring my experience of fundraising and funding applications to bear on proceedings, as well as perhaps my more objective standpoint to negotiations, as someone who never knew Hamish personally, with the potential for a mediating role.

After a number of fruitless attempts up until summer 2009 to find out the state of play with the public bodies who had previously been in touch with the family, we were able to secure a meeting in November 2009 with the then Culture Minister Michael Russell MSP, prior to his giving the Hamish Henderson Memorial Lecture at the City Chambers as part of that year's Carrying Stream Festival. Myself, Fred Freeman and Paddy Bort (organiser of the festival and chair of Edinburgh Folk Club) attended, and Mr Russell apologised to us for the lack of response to date from public bodies under his remit and assured us matters would be taken forward in a more constructive manner. However, the change of minister barely three weeks later meant that, frustratingly, progress stalled yet again.

At this point there was a palpable sense of disappointment and demoralisation at what seemed a cumulative apparent lack of interest, compounded by years of dead ends and rather lackadaisical responses, initially to the family directly, and now to the small group of folk trying to help reset negotiations. Inevitably, thoughts wandered to the perennial difficulty in pigeon-holing Hamish, no bad thing of course, given his wide field of interest, but in some ways this seemed to translate, rightly or wrongly, into ambivalence towards his legacy at the national level.

Whatever was going to happen, we needed to form a partnership with a professional institution in order to move the process forward and make a joint bid for funding. This was also crucial in order to access various funds that exist mainly for public institutions, such as the Friends of the

National Libraries, the National Heritage Memorial Fund, and the National Acquisitions Fund. Wearied by lack of progress with national bodies, we hit upon the idea of approaching Edinburgh City Archives, inspired by the curatorship and permanent loan of the Charles Parker Archive at Birmingham City Council.

The City Archives were very receptive and enthusiastic, and in early 2010 discussions moved towards the idea of submitting a bid to the Heritage Lottery Fund (HLF). The process is normally instigated via a preliminary outline application, which then levers a meeting with HLF to discuss the details and suitability of projects for a full multi-stage bid to their Heritage scheme. We submitted the outline application in July 2010, and arranged to meet with HLF in September 2010. It became quickly apparent, however, that in order to gain funding from HLF, we would have to add on a large educational element to the project which, while not averse to in principle, we were simply not in a position to do at that point, with no official 'Hamish Trust' in existence and no 'staff' to undertake the immense amount of work involved in designing, applying for and delivering such a project. We had gained a broadly similar impression from discussions with the Scottish Poetry Library about their own project on the papers of Edwin Morgan funded by HLF, so it was not entirely unexpected. Unfortunately the HLF officer had also never heard of Hamish, so we were somewhat on the back foot to begin with.

It was our impression that Edinburgh City Archives were in a fairly similar position to the informal group of emerging Trustees, namely very keen, with warm willingness to take the material on, but perhaps with limited capacity in terms of funds or staffing to engage concertedly in driving forward an external project alongside their already pressured budget as part of a local authority in the current climate.

So from autumn 2010, we felt we were essentially at square one again, having more or less exhausted most avenues, and ourselves!

Fundraising 2011

Aware that discussions had reached yet another stalemate, by spring 2011 it seemed time for a constructive new approach. I took the view that some kind of tangible work needed to be done on the papers to actually quantify and qualify this rather vague concept of a 'Henderson Archive', one that had grown and been spoken about at great length over the years. Ultimately, it seemed that the papers needed to be put in a more accessible, *assessable* form and, yes, to make the papers more saleable to whoever might be in a position to consider acquiring them. It had crossed my mind that the rather jumbled state of the papers might have been off-putting to potential buyers, so a sense of order could only be helpful.

Knowing also that my own freelance contract was coming to an end in June 2011, and that I would have time to concentrate on pushing things forward in July, I resolved to 'go public' with Kätzel Henderson's blessing and begin a fundraising campaign to actively undertake work on the papers, so that at least something concrete was being done amidst the effective stalemate. Essentially, what was required was an inventory of the papers – not a catalogue, as that would take too long and require too much resourcing at this stage, but a basic listing of the items therein, so that a real sense of the weight of importance of the material could be gained and viewed objectively by potential acquirers, valuers and the like.

The long-mooted Hamish Henderson Archive Trust was officially formed in June 2011, with Trustees including myself, Dr Fred Freeman, Prof. Frank Bechhofer, who proposed Hamish's honorary doctorate at the University of Edinburgh, Eberhard 'Paddy' Bort of Edinburgh Folk Club and the Carrying Stream Festival, and Chris Wright, a former colleague of mine at the *Tobar an Dualchais / Kist o Riches* archive project. My background as an arts officer used to dealing with organisational structures, charity governance and obligations and duties of trustees/office bearers was brought to bear on proceedings, using the guidance of the Scottish Council for Voluntary Organisations (SCVO) to compose our Trust Deed. The Trust's purpose was declared as follows:

> The advancement of the education of the public in the poetry, traditional culture and folklore of Scotland, particularly concerning the life and works of the poet, foiklorist, and songwriter Dr Hamish Henderson (1919-2002), major contributor to the School of Scottish Studies at the University of Edinburgh, through securing Dr Henderson's personal archives for the nation, and conserving, digitising and publishing them, to increase the public's interest in and awareness of Scottish poetry, traditional music, song and storytelling by making the material publicly available for research purposes primarily in the fields of ethnology, folklore, literature, politics and history.

I knew that there was an established group of interested individuals out there via the Hamish Henderson Facebook page that I had set up a couple of years previously; and through regular arts newsletters that I receive, I was aware of the relatively new concept of crowdfunding, based on crowdsourcing, namely asking for small amounts of money from many individuals or supporters towards arts projects. Putting two and two together, with some research into the various methods, and seeing that my pal Fil Campbell, the Fermanagh singer, had successfully used it, I settled on Sponsume.com (other crowdfunding sites are available!).

Jack Foster, local session singer, soundman for Edinburgh Folk Club, and pioneer of the much-missed *Garden Sessions* folk website and podcasts – had caught our attention with some of his online videos in the run-up to the last Scottish election, and we asked him to produce a video for the campaign at Sponsume, which he duly did with consummate skill.

Setting a modest target of £2,000, with a campaign length of 40 days, I settled in for the long haul. Within 48 hours, however, thanks largely to the power of social networks, we had already trumped our target. By the end of the campaign in July, we had raised nearly £6,000 from both online and offline donations, to be used mainly towards the inventory process, and funds are still trickling in.

In August 2011, we received the good news that we had been awarded a further £3,000 from the Barry Amiel and Norman Melburn Trust, which supports projects dealing with socialist history. Given Hamish's longstanding links with the political left, this was an easy fit.

Work begins

In July 2011, we were in a position to begin work on the papers themselves, and the Trustees agreed to appoint myself and Chris Wright to undertake the inventory work, as folklore specialists and researchers used to working with archive material, albeit primarily sound archives, with our knowledge of similar databases and cataloguing systems to that which the project would require, having both worked for *Tobar an Dualchais / Kist o Riches*, and myself as a graduate of the School of Scottish Studies. We also sought advice from Kirsty Stewart of the National Archives of Scotland, currently seconded onto the Carmichael Watson project (dealing with the papers of Gaelic folklorist Alexander Carmichael, 1832-1912),[2] going on a site visit there to view the holdings and discuss materials and working practices.

We looked at a number of options for locations to undertake the inventory work, but given various concerns about regularity of access in what was intended to be a compressed, intensive period of work, the decision was soon taken to work on the papers *in situ* in Mrs Henderson's flat in the southside of Edinburgh. We cleared the spare room and, with a visit to IKEA's office department plus a helpful donation of a filing cabinet through the HH Archive Trust's Facebook page, we kitted the room out into a simple, functional workspace.

With the advice we had received, we opted to use professional archival materials of the best quality we could reasonably afford, engaging

² www.carmichaelwatson.lib.ed.ac.uk

Preservation Equipment Limited (PEL), a Norfolk-based company regularly used by libraries and archives.

We made an initial inventory of each box or case, a physical description, and approximate contents, how full each box was, and photographed the top items to allow for identification later when selecting the next box to work on. The process was greatly aided by Kätzel Henderson's own considerable efforts in going through the material herself some years previously to label the boxes according to approximate kinds of material, e.g. letters, manuscripts, diaries, although the sorting was, by Mrs Henderson's own admission, somewhat limited by her time and knowledge.

Starting primarily with the boxes labelled 'letters', we separated the items out into various types:

- Correspondence (in alphabetical order)
- Grouped letters relating to a particular subject, e.g. the 'NOBE' (Hamish's refusal of an honour from the Thatcher government)
- Ephemera – consisting of newspaper cuttings, concert tickets, membership cards (e.g. TMSA, CND), event posters, magazines, contracts
- Items sent to Hamish, including poems, articles, song lyrics, sheet music, drawings and photographs – sometimes without attribution
- Anything identifiably in Hamish's own hand that is not a letter, whether written or in print
- Anything identifiably related to Hamish's poetry
- The diaries (already separately stored)
- Fieldwork notes
- Transcriptions, mostly of folk tales
- School of Scottish Studies internal material, including staff bulletins, meeting notes, course info, circulars
- Family items, e.g. letters or cards from Hamish's daughters, of less relevance to the archive, which will be retained by the family.

Initially, the letters were sorted into broad alphabetic groupings (A-E, F-J and so on), and then sorted out further into individual letters of the alphabet. These were then put in alphabetical order, and placed into foolscap files into two filing cabinets.

The bulk of the work in summer and autumn 2011 consisted of attributing and alphabetising the correspondence before adding it into a computerised inventory list. At the time of writing, we conservatively estimate there to be in excess of 8,000 letters, although that figure is likely to rise.

What's in the archive – and what's not

What is not surprising of course, is the amount of material from fieldwork informants – the Stewarts of Blair, John MacDonald of Pitgaveny (a prolific and often comical correspondent with Hamish over several decades, who often included cartoonish drawings), the Stewarts of Fetterangus, Jane Turriff, the Sutherland Stewarts, Jimmie MacBeath, Jeannie Robertson, Lizzie Higgins and family. The benefit of our *Tobar an Dualchais / Kist o Riches* knowledge stood Chris and I in good stead for being able to identify quite a number of the correspondents who may have otherwise gone unknown, and it was very satisfying to see letters which helped fill in some of the gaps on tapes that we had both catalogued.

Some of the correspondence is quite enlightening, demonstrating the difficulty some informants had with their emerging celebrity status, along with ongoing money issues. What is apparent is just how generous Hamish was towards many of the people he recorded, helping them out in times of need. Perhaps more amusingly, there are several fieldwork expense lists which, in the early days of collecting, explicitly outlined the bottles of beer and whisky bought for the likes of Jimmie MacBeath, but after a year or two, turned to more non-specific terms like 'sustenance' or 'refreshment' – clearly Hamish had been *telt*! The original receipt from a bar in Causewayend in Aberdeen, presumably for the first trip to record Jeannie Robertson, is also in there.

What became apparent, however, was that an amount of material was in fact sold by Hamish himself during his lifetime, most likely to alleviate personal financial difficulties, made easier by what seems in hindsight a handful of benevolent librarians at Edinburgh University Library (EUL) and the National Library. This included letters from Hugh MacDiarmid, Sorley MacLean, Robert Garioch, Ewan MacColl and some from Jeannie Robertson. We have yet to establish a full list of all the items Hamish sold, but we have most of the correspondence from EUL and NLS and intend to compare it with their acquisitions lists at some point in the near future. At the time of writing – in mid October 2011 – we have, however, been unable to trace the status or location of the EUL material via their catalogue system.

There are many interesting sets of correspondence with a whole host of individuals, partly listed in the appendix to this article. Many of these relationships are covered in Tim Neat's biographies, but they are really brought to life by seeing the words on the page, often crackling and bristling with banter.

Some of the more unusual letters are from the pop and rock world, with people like Pete Brown, the performance poet who wrote the lyrics for several songs by *Cream* (yes, Eric Clapton, Jack Bruce, Ginger Baker), Sir George Martin, the Beatles' producer, writing about Jeannie Robertson recording for EMI, and Lonnie Donegan's manager Peter Buchanan, who co-authored 'My Old Man's a Dustman'!

From the world of politics, there are letters from former Prime Minister Gordon Brown and the late Robin Cook MP (from their days in student politics), from Jim Sillars, seeking support and funds for the setting up of the Scottish Labour Party in 1976 and, perhaps surprisingly for some, confirmation from the Labour Party in the late 1990s that Hamish joined the party around the time Tony Blair came into government.

Letters on political causes appear from the ANC, thanking Hamish for his song 'Rivonia' (aka 'Free Mandela'), and the USSR Embassy, regarding the case of Raoul Wallenberg. There are also replies from the US Embassy in London to Hamish's letters of support for Paul Robeson, in the wake of the latter's persecution by the House Committee on Un-American Activities in 1956, (reminiscent of other letters in support of Pete Seeger during his similar ordeal), and Hamish's request for clemency in the case of executed American communists Julius and Ethel Rosenberg.

Hamish also had an extended battle by letter with the Mechanical Copyright Protection Society for many years, regarding his authorship of songs being recorded by various artists for which he was not receiving royalties, in some cases even engaging lawyers across the pond to take on American artists who had failed to credit him.

There are also collections of bawdy songs (a favourite pastime of Hamish's), a number of items relating to the Aberdeenshire fiddler J.F. Dickie, including what seem to be transcriptions of songs from his mother and an envelope bearing the scrawl of none other than James Scott Skinner, plus a valuable group of material relating to Gavin Greig, presumably given to Hamish by the late Arthur Argo, Greig's great-grandson, including some of Greig's own notebooks.

All in all, Hamish's broad connections are evident across many sectors of society, political and cultural. In the written, 'snail mail' format, one also gets a real sense of the different pace of life and methods of communicating over extended periods of time, the additional effort involved, and the networks Hamish built up. He had a strong Irish connection with folklorists and poets, and a worldwide academic fraternity, including scholars from the USA, Switzerland and Germany. As our work continued, I coined the phrase 'human Google' to refer to

Archive filing

Diary Box

Letters and old Songs

Songs from WWII, Italy.

Hamish and the nature of the many enquiries he would receive from members of the public, often via the School of Scottish Studies. He seems to have made every effort to reply, even if it took him many months, to whatever kind of enquiry came his way.

Issues and problems, now and in the future

The main difficulty with a collection such as this is that it has had very minimal sorting to date. The papers were mixed up, folded, torn, with some needing careful handling, pages were missing, some letters had no final page, thereby rendering the sender a mystery, and so forth. Part of the reason for the condition of some items seems clearly to have been down to Hamish himself who readily re-used the back of letters and other scraps of paper to make notes and write draft replies upon.

At some stage, attempts had been made to sort the letters, in some cases this seems to have been Hamish himself, perhaps aided by his assistants. Several of the boxes looked as if they were in the same state as when Hamish's office at the School of Scottish Studies was decanted into archive boxes. With the wide variety in paper and ink quality, with some standing the test of time better than others, along with, in truth, rather ineffectual storage over the years, the material was in need of careful handling and preserving.

Of course, as one might expect, there were difficulties with names, legibility of writing, and similarities of signatures and handwriting. We had any number of Toms – Scott, Nairn, Munnelly, Law, Kines, Smith – and a number of Johns – Press, Willett, Brookes – and a few Alans, Michaels, Judys, Robins and Sandys.....! As time went along, this became easier, and we kept as many notes as possible, in some cases copying or photographing the letters to reference details of handwriting or signature, or in other cases engaging my photographic memory and curious knack for remembering addresses! We also set up a whiteboard with names, surnames, locations and other clues, turning it somewhat into an incident room reminiscent of Crimewatch – CSI Marchmont anyone?!

Thankfully, a small amount of the correspondence extracted from Hamish's office at the School was still in alphabetised foolscap files, which helped give clues in the case of letters without surnames or clear attributions. Many of the letters lacked dates, or in some cases gave just a day and a month, but no year. Clues often had to be found through adjacent letters from the same correspondent, addresses, postmarks, or using Tim Neat's invaluable biographies, as well as the diaries, essay collections, and of course the immense power of *Google*.

Kätzel Henderson put in a great deal of time and effort herself over the years into sorting out the letters by correspondent and approximate decade, and was able to enlighten us on many occasions where a letter remained unidentified. Additionally, some of the sorting done by Tim Neat when researching the biographies was evident, although the material was only partially sorted in places and, as a whole, was not in a particularly straightforward order for our purposes.

There is a mixture of tongues amongst the papers, in the war diaries especially – from page to page in Italian, German, French, Gaelic, as well as Scots and English – and the full cataloguing and research process further down the line will need to take this into account. Thankfully, I am fluent in German and Chris is in French, and I can make a fair stab at reading Italian, so we were able to make basic identification and sorting of most of these items for the purposes of the inventory.

Hamish also often copied out poems he liked, so extracting the Hamish hand will be a difficult task for future researchers. There are a large number of scraps and letters with Hamish's writing on the back, including drafts of replies and snippets of lyric or poetry.

Whoever takes on the archive in the long term will need to engage researchers and cataloguers with an appreciation of the wide swathe of contacts and walks of life with which Hamish interacted. There is a concern at the Trust regarding the value of fieldwork informants whose letters form a significant portion of the papers. To those of us with the benefit of working closely with *Tobar an Dualchais / Kist o Riches*, these names are instantly recognisable, but since they are not necessarily household names to more mainstream researchers, care needs to be taken to ensure the ethnological aspect of the material is not sidelined amongst the headline names of poets and politicians.

The large amount of ephemera and other non-correspondence has been separated out, but itself needs sorting in altogether different manner, which again is a future concern. All in all, the 'miscellaneous' material takes up perhaps 40-50% of the total volume, and amongst it are posters and tickets relating to events that are again recognisable to those familiar with the School's sound archive, such as the Linburn Ceilidh (1959) or the Scott Conference (1971), but may mean next to nothing in a more mainstream setting.

Anything that is identifiably in Hamish's own hand, whether written or in print, we have kept separate, and again this needs to be dealt with in its own way, not least because Hamish also had a shorthand of his own which needs analysed and decoded! Often he would begin a draft with 'L à [name or initials]' – presumably French *lettre à / letter to*. Whenever he had replied to a letter he received, Hamish would mark it 'Axod' in the top corner.

The Way Ahead

As of October 2011, the correspondence is now all alphabetised for the first time ever. It is currently in the process of being assigned inventory numbers and stored in a computer database. Items have been unfolded, reassembled, reunited, with the more fragile items safely stored in archival quality acid-free plastic sleeves. By the end of 2011, we should have all the correspondence in a database, allowing the most complete view of the contents of Hamish's papers that there has ever been. With the material now in a more organised, accessible and *assessable* condition, with more clarity on its component parts, in time the vague idea of a Hamish Henderson Archive should begin to solidify.

The momentum is now there to take the project forward to a positive conclusion, with the strength of feeling now amongst our supporters and donors, through the fundraising campaign, as well as the beginnings of a media campaign. The project has been highlighted by Jim Gilchrist in *The Scotsman*,[3] we will be discussing the project on the Mike Harding BBC Radio 2 show at some point in the future and we are awaiting receipt of letters of support from luminaries from across the spectrum, including

---

[3] Jim Gilchrist, 'Crowdsourcing for Hamish Henderson's papers boosts hope of overdue tidy-up', *The Scotsman*, 28 June 2011.

Pete Seeger himself. The pressure is on national institutions to make a move and meet the public demand.

There are those who have queried why the papers are not simply donated. As part of one process of negotiation, the papers were valued in 2004 at £92,000. The reality is, as is broadly known, Hamish was a shambles with money and often generous to a fault. He was also cruelly defrauded of many thousands of pounds by one of his former assistants towards the end of his life. It is the Trust's view that Hamish's family should see some of the benefit of his life's work. The family are also very keen that the material remains in Scotland, which they believe would also have been Hamish's wish, and this is probably why the material has never appeared on the open market.

It is also a very normal arrangement for papers of a notable public figure to be sold to institutions by either the person themselves during their lifetime (and in Hamish's case there is a precedent for this), or by the deceased's estate. Consider the Sassoon papers, bought by Cambridge University for £1.25m in 2009, with a grant of £550,000 from the National Heritage Memorial Fund (NHMF), the acquisition of the Harold Pinter archive by the British Library for £1.1m in 2007, again with a grant from the NHMF of £216,000, the JG Ballard papers, acquired by the British Library in 2010 for £350,000 via the Acceptance in Lieu Scheme[4], the archive of Sir Alan Ayckbourn, bought by the University of York for £240,000 or, earlier this year, the papers of Alan Turing, secured again with NHMF funds totalling £213,000.

In many cases, these kinds of archives are 'bought for the nation' to avoid them being sold abroad. Regarding the Sassoon papers, in a *Guardian* article the former poet laureate Andrew Motion said the news that the archive seemed likely to stay in Britain should be celebrated:

> It's perfectly true that US libraries do an extremely good job of looking after archives, and to say they should be kept here does not imply that they would not be looked after in the US, in fact they are rather brilliant.
>
> But I think there is something quite primitive about the connection between the writer and the country they write in. Philip Larkin talked about the meaningful and the magical when it came to archives and this is both meaningful and magical.[5]

---

[4] This is a scheme whereby cultural works can be gifted to the nation in lieu of inheritance tax liability.

[5] 'Siegfried Sassoon archive likely to stay in UK after £550,000 award', *The Guardian*, 4 November 2009, www.guardian.co.uk/books/2009/nov/04/siegfried-sassoon-archive-award-cambridge>, accessed 14 Oct 2011.

Why should we not think the same way about Hamish? In comparison to the amounts quoted above, the valuation on Hamish's papers seems fairly modest, even minus some of the big-name correspondents. Hamish may not have been a Nobel Laureate or a celebrated Great War poet taught in most schools, but away from those headline accolades, let us add up the sum of Hamish's parts. In the 1930s, he worked with the Quakers to help Jews escape from Nazi Germany. As an intelligence officer in the Second World War, he oversaw the radio broadcast of the surrender of Italy given by Marshal Graziani. For his war poetry, he won the Somerset Maugham Prize for Literature in 1949, aged barely 30. He remained in regular contact with other war poets such as Victor Selwyn and the Salamander Oasis Trust throughout his life. He made the first translation of Gramsci's prison letters in the late 1940s. Upon returning to Scotland after the war, he championed the folk culture of a country, helping establish a major folklore institution along the way, sparking off the public consciousness with the first Edinburgh People's Festival Ceilidh in 1951. From the 1960s on, he was an anti-apartheid campaigner who wrote one of the first songs in support of Mandela and the Rivonia group. As a songwriter, his songs were acknowledged and sung and remade by Pete Seeger and Bob Dylan and taken on by the folk community at large. In the 1980s, the seasoned CND peace campaigner refused an OBE from the Thatcher government. Add to all that the MacDiarmid flytings, the championing of the Travellers, the synthesis of Highland and Lowland, the Scots and Gaelic languages, and you still have not arrived at a comprehensive list.

It must be remembered that the papers are not just about Hamish, but also the hundreds of individuals and organisations with whom he interacted, painting such a broad picture across many disciplines. They are a poetical, political and ethnological history not just of Scotland, but the wider UK and Ireland in the twentieth century, a time of post-war political and cultural upheaval.

The time for ambivalence is over. As I said in the conclusion to the fundraising video back in June, Hamish's contemporaries have long had their papers committed to the national record, and it is now an embarrassment that a culturally unique figure like Hamish, champion of our folk culture, has had to wait so long. It is time to give Hamish his rightful place in our national archives and secure these vitally important papers for Scotland. The Hamish Henderson Archive Trust will work tirelessly to make this happen.

Contributions towards the work of the Hamish Henderson Archive Trust can be made online at www.hendersontrust.org . Cheque donations can be sent by post to 155/2 Broughton Road, EH7 4JJ, made payable to 'Hamish Henderson Archive Trust'.

Appendix – list of correspondents

Hamish's letters cover a sixty-year period from the late 1930s to the early 2000s, with correspondents including many prominent figures in the political and cultural life of twentieth-century Scotland and further afield. The following list, whilst containing around 150 individuals and organisations, is not exhaustive:

Folksong & Folklore

Annie Arnott
Moses Asch
Margaret Bennett
Dominic Behan
Morris Blythman
Katharine Briggs
Mary Brooksbank
Alan Bruford
Norman Buchan
Francis Collinson
Peter Cooke
William Donaldson
Richard Dorson
Sheila Douglas
Jock Duncan
Helen Hartness Flanders
Maurice Fleming
Edith Fowke
Howard Glasser
Kenneth Goldstein
Herschel Gower
Len Graham
Roy Guest
Peter Hall
Robin Hall
Dave Harker
Lizzie Higgins
Serge Hovey

Maud Karpeles
Alexander Keith
Peter Kennedy
Norman Kennedy
Gershon Legman
Dick Leith
Albert L. Lloyd
Alan Lomax
Max Lüthi
Emily Lyle
Caroline Macafee
Ewan MacColl
Jimmy MacBeath
Cathal McConnell
John MacDonald
('Molecatcher')
Matt McGinn
Jimmie MacGregor
John MacInnes
Calum MacLean
Flora MacNeill
Willie Mathieson
Willie Mitchell
William & Norah
Montgomerie
John Moulden
Tom Munnelly
Seán O'Boyle
Peter & Iona Opie
Seán O'Riada

Roy Palmer
James Porter
Jean Redpath
Roger deVeer
Renwick
Jean Ritchie
Jeannie Robertson
Ian Russell
Willie Scott
Peggy Seeger
Pete Seeger
Peter Shepheard
Leslie Shepherd
Murray Shoolbraid
Ellen Stekert
Belle Stewart
Davie Stewart
Essie Stewart
Sheila Stewart
John Strachan
Jane Turriff
Betsy Whyte
Duncan Williamson
Linda Williamson

Poetry

J.K. Annand
John E. Brookes
Pete Brown

Andy Croft
Helen B. Cruick-
shank
Ian Hamilton Finlay
G.S. Fraser
Robert Garioch
Viv Griffiths
Douglas Hall
Donald Hall
T.S. Law
George Campbell
Hay
Nicholas Johnson
Maurice Lindsay
Norman MacCaig
Hugh MacDiarmid
Sorley MacLean
Louis MacNeice
Naomi Mitchison
Edwin Morgan
Edwin Muir
Tom Pickard
Tom Scott
Victor Selwyn
Sydney Goodsir
Smith
Douglas Young

Politics

Gordon Brown
Oliver Brown
Janey Buchan
Norman Buchan
Ken Coates
Robin Cook
Lawrence Daly
Tom Driberg
Nan Milton
Pino Mereu
Tom Nairn
John Reid

Literature

David Daiches
Alasdair Gray
Lorn MacIntyre
Alexander McCall Smith
Willa Muir
John Press
Philip Toynbee
John Willett

Other

Kenneth Alexander (Economist)
Campbell Christie (ex-STUC Secretary)
Lionel Daiches (lawyer)
Alec Finlay (publisher)
Victor Kiernan (Marxist historian)
John Lehmann (publisher)
Sir George Martin (record producer)
Jonathan Miller (author, broadcaster)
John McGrath (playwright)
Sean O'Casey (playwright)
Ronald Stevenson (composer)
Norman Stone (historian)
E.P. Thomson (Marxist historian)

Organisations

ANC	TMSA
BBC	Topic
Decca	
EFDSS	
EMI	
Foreign Languages Press (China)	
MCPS	
PRS	
Scotland-USSR Friendship Society	

Coda

The 1951 Edinburgh People's Festival Ceilidh

Ewan McVicar

Alan Lomax was collecting in Edinburgh in August 1951, and luckily was on hand to document the legendary Edinburgh People's Festival Ceilidh. This lively, rollicking, and moving concert he was able to preserve for Scotland was so important because it alerted astonished city folk to the living continuing richness of Scotland's traditional song heritage. It was a key event that heralded, generated, and vitalised the Scottish Folk Revival of the 1950s and 1960s, featuring some of the leading lights of the traditional music scene – and the poet, songwriter, and folklorist Hamish Henderson as master of ceremonies.

A Cultural Explosion

Norman Buchan: *As I went into the Oddfellows Hall the bloody place was packed, feet were going, and it was Jimmy MacBeath singing 'The Gallant Forty-Twa.' Hamish had assembled these people. Jessie Murray sang 'Skippin' Barfit Through The Heather'; ... Flora MacNeil was singing 'The Silver Whistle [Có Sheinneas An Fhideag Airgid]' - beautiful! I'd never heard anything like this. John Strachan was singing about forty verses of a ballad... An amazing night for people who'd never heard them before! It swept me off my feet completely.*[1]

Hamish Henderson: *What made this inaugural People's Festival ceilidh so important was the fact that this was the first time such a masterly group of authentic traditional musicians and ballad-singers from rural Scotland had sung together to a city audience; the result was a veritable cultural explosion, for a number of the 'folk' virtuosi of the future were present in the audience.*[2]

---

[1] Norman Buchan, *Tocher* No. 43.
[2] Hamish Henderson, *Alias MacAlias*.

Neil McCallum: *The beauty of the evening was probably due to the fact that the Gaelic and Lallans singers were operating in the true folk tradition, singing music that was unscored and also, if I may use the word, untitivated. Though the ceilidh was public it remained intimate owing to the smallness of the hall.*[3]

The official Edinburgh Festival began in 1947, and Theatre Workshop was there to help initiate the Fringe.

Colin Fox: *The 1945 Labour government, radical in much of its social planning, created the Edinburgh International Festival by enlisting what Hamish Henderson called, "The Edimbourgeoisie... the city's arty elite and effete middle class, to organise the party and draw up the invitations. They remain firmly in charge to this day, self-elected critics and guardians of taste and morality."*[4]

The People's Festival

In 1951 the Edinburgh Labour Festival Committee was established to organise a People's Festival. The aims were "to initiate action designed to bring the Edinburgh Festival closer to the people, to serve the cause of international understanding and goodwill." Committee participants included the Trade Unions' Council, the Miners' Union, the Labour party and the Communist Party. Cultural groups, independent arts organisations and individual arts activists became involved. Theatre companies were invited to participate. As Henderson wrote: "The idea began to be canvassed of a native popular festival, based on the Scottish working-class movement which would undertake the sort of cultural activity which the 'big' Festival seemed likely to ignore."[4]

Janey Buchan (later Labour MEP for Glasgow) and Norman Buchan, at that time a schoolteacher of English, later organiser of the 1953 People's Festival, then Labour MP and Shadow Minister for the Arts, were heavily involved. Janey said in the 1994 Radio Scotland McGregor's Folk programme:

> I was the person who took the minutes. I used to come out of my work [in Glasgow], nip up to Queen Street station, get on the train— it took an hour and a half, Glasgow to Edinburgh. If I got on the right train I would get into Edinburgh just in time to get to the beginning of the meeting.

---

[3] Letter to the *Scotsman* newspaper from Edinburgh critic and novelist Neil McCallum, June 9, 1951.

[4] Hamish Henderson, *Alias MacAlias*, p. 9.

We had to look for spare beds, we had to look for halls. Of course marvellous people came to our assistance in Edinburgh, especially in the CP [Communist Party]. You would just call up and people would come up with spare beds. You look back and wonder how did you summon up the physical energy to do what we did? We didn't have a car among the lot of us, we did it all on tram and bus, and on our two feet.

The 1951 Festival organiser, Martin Milligan, reported in the March 1952 *Communist Review*:

Although the committee was formed only at the beginning of May, August 26th to September 1st was also Edinburgh's first "People's Festival Week." The committee had taken a hall in central Edinburgh for the week, and there presented daily in the evenings plays, concerts and film shows, supplemented by a programme of morning and afternoon lectures on arts and the people—sixteen complete events in all—all contributed by working-class people, or by people closely associated with the labour movement.

The Conservative press was alert to the threat. On August 8, 1951, the column *A Scotsman's Log* in the Scotsman newspaper sneered at the employment of the term "people," and especially at the assumed support for the Festival from trades unions.

The week of events was a great success. Poetry readings, arts exhibitions, and plays. Barrhead Co-Op Junior Choir and soloists. Glasgow Unity Theatre performing Scottish miner Joe Corrie's play *In Time Of Strife*. Theatre Workshop brought MacColl's play *Uranium 235*: "A modern morality play for the atomic era." Theatre Workshop was so popular it stayed on till 15th September, performing MacColl's ballad opera *Johnny Noble* as well as *Uranium 235*, which was later described on TW posters as "the sensational success of the '51 Edinburgh Festival."

Although the People's Festival was planned as a counterweight to the International Festival's inattention to Scots culture, there was in fact Scottish music in the official 1951 Festival. The Scotsman newspaper featured days of continuing debate about the chaos of the Pipers' March down Princes Street that had initiated the Festival. In the Freemason's Hall there were two evenings of the music of Scotland. Performers included two who had already been recorded by Lomax – Jimmy Shand playing accordion, and John Mearns singing Bothy Ballads "with endearing gusto."[5]

---

[5] *Scotsman review*, 1951.

Henderson credits the renowned innovative theatre director Joan Littlewood with some of the impetus for the People's Festival, and in *Joan's Book* she gives a vivid and exciting account of various People's Festival events, but sadly none of her dates or descriptions tally with other accounts, or newspaper reports of the time. She has perhaps conflated and over-dramatised various Edinburgh Festival-time events.

The Ceilidh

The People's Festival Ceilidh arose from a need to support financially Theatre Workshop's visit. Poet and arch stirrer of the cultural pot Hugh MacDiarmid wrote to Henderson on July 12, 1951:

> Will you still be in Edinburgh when Theatre Workshop are there? I hope so. I'll be through then too. Since the short season they have in Edinburgh will not leave them with any dough after defraying their expenses it has been requested that they also have a number of ceilidhs and if you are on the spot you might help to organise these... Alan Lomax will take part and I understand Flora MacNeil and Calum Johnstone [sic] have also agreed.

Hamish Henderson says when this letter came he had already been put in charge of the Ceilidh. In the Festival programme he wrote:

> In Scotland... there is still an incomparable treasure of folk song and folk music... The main purpose of this Ceilidh will be to present Scottish folk song as it should be sung. The singers will all without exception be men and women who have learned these splendid songs by word of mouth in their own childhood, and who give them in the traditional manner. This fact alone will make the People's Festival Ceilidh an absolutely unique thing in the cultural history of Edinburgh.

And so it proved to be.

Friday night in the Oddfellows Hall arrived. Theatre Workshop's stage lights troubled the singers. There was a calm enough beginning. John Burgess says that a few douce Edinburgh dames walked out early on. The poster "looked conservative" but their prim sensibilities were soon threatened by the honest gruff voice of Jimmy MacBeath. The atmosphere became so supercharged that the listener now half expects sparks to shoot out of the speakers, the applause and cheering was so loud and prolonged that Lomax turned off his recorder between songs to conserve tape, thereby losing the start of some pieces.

Three elements were combined – Gaelic song, piping, and North-East Scots song. Three older performers aged 57 to 76, three younger ones aged 16 to 21.

Hamish Henderson: *It was generally agreed by critics and punters alike that the most notable event, and the one most likely to bear fruit in the future, was the ceilidh: this was an amazing, indeed epoch-making folk-song concert which brought together some of the 'greats' of the traditional folk-scene: outstanding tradition-bearers from the Gaelic-speaking Hebrides, and ballad-singers from Aberdeenshire, heartland of the great Scots ballad tradition.*

The Barra singers Flora MacNeil and Calum Johnston presented Hebridean folk-song, stripped of its Kennedy Fraser mummy-wrappings. Jimmy MacBeath sang 'Come A' Ye Tramps and Hawkers' for the first time on any stage (as opposed to the reeling road, or the booths of Porter Fair). John Burgess, master piper, played us marches, jigs, strathspeys and reels with all the expertise of Auld Nick at Kirk Alloway. John Strachan, the Fyvie farmer, and Jessie Murray, the Buckie fishwife, sang versions of classic ballads such as 'Johnnie o' Breadisley' (Child 114) and 'Lord Thomas and Fair Ellen' (Child 73) which convinced even the most sceptical that a noble oral tradition was still with us.[7]

Janey Buchan: *When John Strachan, who was himself a wealthy farmer, sang two lines and said, "The fermer I am wi the noo, He's wealthy but he's mean," that summed up every employer people like me ever had in their life. But he could sing that and maybe not see the irony of himself singing it.*[6]

Hamish Henderson: *After the 'official' ceilidh had finished, we carried on in St Columba's Church hall in Johnstone Terrace, and there Jimmy excelled himself. Ewan MacColl and Isla Cameron joined us to sing "Eppie Morrie" and "Can Ye Sew Cushions?," the Theatre Workshop show having finished, and the sight of Ewan's face, when he first received the full impact of Jimmy's personality and performance, remains vividly in my memory.... Then the pipes sounded again, and the dancing started.*
    Hugh MacDiarmid honoured us with his presence; part of "A Drunk Man Looks at the Thistle" were spoken during the evening, and at the end of a second or 'unofficial' part of the show he was so moved that he publicly embraced old John Strachan after the singing of "Goodnight and joy be wi' ye a."

---

[6] Janey Buchan, Radio Scotland, 1994.

Later that night – or was it that morning – Jimmy MacBeath stopped in York Place, shook himself loose from the friends who were supporting him home, and lifting his mottled face to the moon, sang "The Bleacher Lassie O' Kelvinhaugh." All over Auld Reekie the ceilidh was continuing. In a sense, it is continuing still.[7]

Reactions to Ceilidh

There were few reviews of the event. Henderson wrote in a 1951 letter:

> *The People's Festival Committee has asked me to arrange another ceilidh to be held in December.*
> *P S Honor Arundel gave the Ceilidh a very good review in the [Daily] Worker. The only thing she found to criticise about the People's Festival Week was that it hadn't devoted an evening to the works of 'that veteran fighter for Scottish independence, Hugh MacDiarmid.'*[8]

Martin Milligan took a passing swipe at American culture:

> *Such an event as the 'Ceilidh' on the Friday evening helped to give living substance to phrases about our national cultural heritage. For this programme of Scots and Gaelic folk-song (sung not in concert-hall style but as it is still sung in those parts of Scotland where folk-singing remains a living cultural tradition, by working people from those districts) began to reveal an, as yet, little-explored treasury of song and singing whose range of beauty, wit and humanity astonished, excited and delighted all. By the end of the evening it had very obviously moved the whole audience with a quality of pleasure and pride that made more intolerable than could many speeches the violence and tawdriness of the imperialist-American films and dance music that clutter up our cinema and radio programmes, etc.*[9]

Norman Buchan's highly influential efforts to support and educate young urban singers were inspired by that night:

> *Looking back, I know that though the evening was devastatingly new to me, it really shouldn't have been. Although I grew up in the Orkney islands, my folk came from the North-East coast. The Revival didn't really start that night at the Festival Ceilidh. Things were going on, it's just that we didn't know about it. There were still ballad*

---

[7] Henderson, *Alias MacAlias*, p. 9.
[8] Henderson, *The Armstrong Nose*, p. 56.
[9] *Communist Review*, 1952.

*singers going around, there were still professional entertainers like
G. S. Morris and John Mearns singing bothy ballads. They were even
beginning to appear on records. But no-one said to us, "Look, these
things matter. They matter for you in the cities. You should listen to
this and learn."*[10]

The People's Festival 1952 and after

The Festival was judged a resounding artistic and cultural success, if
not a financial one. Martin Milligan commented that the Committee
suffered "a fairly serious financial loss." The financial report on the 1951
festival read "Total expenditure £400, total income £350." Milligan's
comments show the politically committed motivation that drove aspects
of the People's Festival: "The leading role the Communist Party can play in
the defence and development of British culture was made evident at the
conference by the quality of the contributions by its spokesmen there."

Seventeen organisations had backed the first Festival. The 1952 Festival
had the backing of fifty organisations, and was a triumph. As Colin Fox
wrote:

> *The 1952 Festival ran for three weeks. There was a People's Art
> Exhibition and The Edinburgh Evening News carried daily reports
> of the People's Festival events. Ewan MacColl wrote a new play
> called "The Travellers." There was a special celebration of Hugh
> MacDiarmid's 60th birthday. An impressive programme of lectures,
> films, dances and concerts was held. Willie Gallacher, the former
> Communist MP for West Fife, spoke on the 'American Threat to
> British Culture.' The Ceilidh in the Oddfellows Hall was again the
> grand finale and introduced performers from the Western Isles and
> guests from the West Indies.*[11]

However, the involvement of the Communist Party in those days of the
gathering ice storm that became the Cold War caused unease to the
Labour party members involved in the Festival.

Colin Fox: *But just as there seemed no stopping its advance, the EPF
became a victim of McCarthyism. [In December 1952] The Scottish
Trades Union Congress proscribed the Festival as a "Communist Front."
This was a shattering blow to the many people involved in its success
and although the 1953 festival was bigger than the first, it had declined.*

---

[10] Radio Scotland, 1994.
[11] Colin Fox, *Socialist Voice* 32, 2001.

There were many highlights and the organisers spoke bravely. But it was bravado.[12]

The Ceilidh was a central event each year. The 1953 programme said, "This has become such a well-loved and accustomed feature of our Festival that it needs little introduction. We are negotiating to obtain the biggest possible hall in Edinburgh for the event in order to ensure that no-one need be disappointed." But the 1954 People's Festival was the last.

The Recording

This recording is of course not the whole concert. The event began with piper John Burgess; then John Strachan sang 'The Guise O Tough.' Through the limitations of tape-recording a live event, several songs were truncated. The mounting excitement of the audience was such that much applause and cheering has been edited out. There was a long vote of thanks in Gaelic and English.

Some songs performed in the ceilidh but not included here can be heard sung by John Strachan and Jimmy MacBeath on their albums in the *Alan Lomax Collection: Portrait* series. A *Portrait* album of Flora MacNeil is also planned.

A particular richness of the recording is the preservation of Hamish Henderson's legendary manner of presenting song and music – warm and inclusive, enthusiastic yet wry, knowledgeable but not always fully accurate, delighted at what he had found to share with others.

Ewan MacColl: *Hamish's extempore performances were, as far as I am concerned, one of the most memorable aspects of those early People's Festivals (forerunners of the Fringe). By day one encountered him on the streets and squares of Edinburgh, generally accompanied by one or two of his discoveries, Jimmy MacBeath, Frank Steele, or Jeannie Robertson, or he would be bent over a hypnotised acquaintance lilting his latest 'find.' At night he could be found presiding over the ceilidh which generally began at 11pm and finished at two or three in the morning. There must be hundreds of Edinburgh folk who heard their first traditional song at those splendid affairs.*[13]

Morag NicLeod, who provided the transcriptions, translations and notes for the Gaelic songs in the recording, considers that

> *Calum Johnston, Flora MacNeil and the organisers of the People's*

---

[12] Fox, *Frontline* 5.
[13] Ewan MacColl, *Tocher* 43.

Ceilidhs may be credited with bringing a sample of the best Gaelic songs to the attention of non-Gaelic-speaking audiences in Edinburgh – and to some Gaelic-speakers as well, who may not have been aware of the richness of the tradition. Calum and Flora were both from Barra and had a tremendous repertoire of a variety of types of song.

The quality of the North-East Scots songs and singers is also astonishingly high. It is a pity Jessie Murray has a troublesome cough, and John Strachan is not in his best voice – his *Songs of Aberdeenshire* album [Rounder CD 1835] shows him in much better fettle. Traditional Scots songs draw on a surprisingly small stock of tunes. The primacy of lyric over tune, and the way that individuality of performance style disguises similarities between airs, is neatly demonstrated here. Four of the Scots songs on this CD employ tunes that are so close to each other they are first cousins. The eight volumes of the *Greig-Duncan Folk Song Collection* give multiple variations of text and tune for most of the North-East songs sung at the Ceilidh.

The Performers

Mrs Budge
Attempts to identify or trace this Lowlands young woman, a friend of Hamish Henderson, have been fruitless. There are 26 Budges in the current Edinburgh telephone directory.

John Burgess

He lived in Easter Ross in Northern Scotland. "John D Burgess is a phenomenon in the world of piping. At the age of four he began to take an interest in playing... His rise was meteoric. From an infant prodigy he became the boy genius..." In 1950, in his first appearance aged 16, he won Gold Medals for his playing in piobaireachd competitions in Oban and Inverness, "An achievement never before dreamed of and never likely to be equalled." [Seamus MacNeill, 1976 record sleeve]
"The main things that set Burgess apart from his peers are his stunning technique, and the brisk speed that he takes a lot of the tunes at, even to this day. A successful competitor ... but mainly known as a 'showman' piper, a great player, but also a great storyteller and character." [Dougie Pincock, by letter, 2002]

Hamish Henderson

Perthshire-born, Edinburgh-based Hamish Henderson, who was a collector of song and story, a discoverer of many key tradition bearers, a poet, songwriter, and towering figure in the Scottish folk revival was Alan Lomax's guide and companion in Edinburgh and on his collecting trips in North-East Scotland.

Calum Johnston

Born 1891 on the Outer Hebridean isle of Barra, he worked as a draughtsman in Edinburgh, retired to Barra. He died suddenly in 1973 while piping the coffin of novelist Sir Compton Mackenzie to its grave in violent weather. Calum and his sister Annie "represented ... the cultured and educated Gaelic-speaking Highlander who could move in any society, but who has never forgotten or despised the Gaelic oral tradition which had been the ambience of his childhood." [John Lorne Campbell]

Jimmy MacBeath

Born in the Buchan fishing village of Portsoy 1895, died 1972. For most of his life Jimmy footslogged the roads of Scotland and beyond, earning pennies from street singing and shillings from casual labour, living in "model" public lodging houses.

> *Jimmy was much affected by the reception he got* [at the 1951 Ceilidh], *and at the end of the show he informed the audience that this was his 'swan-song', the culmination and the conclusion of his singing career: for reasons of ill-health and age he would never be able to sing at a similar function again. (He was to visit Edinburgh and sing at my ceilidhs for close on another twenty years.)* [Hamish Henderson][14]

In the 1960s Jimmy began to be recorded commercially and to sing in folk clubs and festivals. Alan Lomax described Jimmy as "a quick-footed, sporty little character, with the gravel voice and the urbane assurance that would make him right at home on Skid Row anywhere in the world." In November 1953 Lomax recorded several hours of Jimmy singing and talking. Much of this has been issued on the albums *Jimmy MacBeath: Tramps & Hawkers* [Rounder CD 1834] and *Two Gentlemen Of The Road* [Rounder CD 1793] with John Strachan.

---

[14] Henderson, *Alias MacAlias*.

Flora MacNeil

Born on the isle of Barra at the southern end of the Outer Hebrides. When she moved to work in Edinburgh in 1947, "she was already a most accomplished traditional singer, with a repertoire more varied and more extensive than anyone else of her age." Through her "own distinctive interpretations" and "highly assured technique" she became "one of the leading figures in the post-war revival of traditional Gaelic song." [Dr John MacInnes] "It was in Edinburgh one June night in the house of Sorley MacLean, a poet, that Scotland really took hold of me. A blue-eyed girl from the Hebrides was singing." This was Flora singing 'Cairistiona.' [Lomax, 1957 BBC Radio]

Jessie Murray

A fishwife living in the North-East port of Buckie, Jessie would have trudged from door to door, 'a little lady' dressed all in black wearing a black shawl, a basket of fish or shellfish on her back. She was a fisherman's widow aged at least 70 in 1951, and died in the 1950s. "I always remember Jessie Murray, and she came forward and gave a little curtsey to the audience. And she sang 'Skippin Barfit Through The Heather,' and of course these were songs you had never heard, and clearly the whole audience had never heard either." [Janie Buchan, Radio Scotland 1994]

John Strachan

Born 1875 on the Aberdeenshire farm of Crichie near Fyvie and died in 1958 on the same farm. A wealthy farmer, he "took a kindly paternalistic interest in the welfare of his fee'd men," and was a highly knowledgeable champion of the songs of farm life and old ballads. "John Strachan says he's a farmer. Really he's a poet, and chronicler—with all the best bits of Buchan stored in his head." [Lomax, 1951 BBC Radio]

John Strachan's *Portrait* CD shows the richness of his versions of songs, which led the American collector James Madison Carpenter in 1930 to invite John to visit Harvard College, but to his regret John did not go. "I wis pretty busy, I'd a lot o' farmin to do." [Henderson, *Alias MacAlias*]

Blanche Wood

"Brown-haired and bonny Blanche Wood. Hers was the clear bell-like voice one hears so often in the North." [Lomax, 1957 BBC Radio] Blanche is a K-Nocker, of the small fishing village of Portknockie, five miles east of the port of Buckie. In 1951 she was 18, and in the ceilidh sang songs her aunt Jessie Murray had taught her. Blanche's father was a fisherman, and named a new boat for her, The Girl Blanche, launched by Blanche herself at age 15. Blanche married Robert Allen, who sawed the keels for fishing boats, but by 1961 the boatyards had shut and they moved to Edinburgh, where they still live. Blanche and her sister formed a singing double act which toured working men's clubs in Scotland and England, singing 'more modern songs.'

Track List

01. **THE HAIRST O RETTIE** John Strachan
02. **SKIPPIN BARFIT THROUGH THE HEATHER** Jessie Murray
03. **THE TAY BRIDGE DISASTER** Hamish Henderson
04. **THE GALLANT FORTY TWA** Jimmy MacBeath
05. **BLUE BONNETS OVER THE BORDER** John Burgess
06. **GREAT MY JOY** Hamish Henderson
07. **ORAN EILE DON PHRIONNSA** Calum Johnson
08. **MO RUN GEAL OG** Flora MacNeil
09. **FAILTE RUDHA BHATAIRNIS** John Burgess
10. **THE BONNY LASS O FYVIE** John Strachan
11. **MORMOND BRAES** John Strachan
12. **NOT JUST ELDERLY PEOPLE** Hamish Henderson
13. **I'M A YOUNG BONNIE LASSIE** Blanche Wood
14. **THE ALE HOOSE** Jessie Murray
15. **[THE BIG STUFF]** Hamish Henderson
16. **BARBARA ALLEN (Child #84)** Jessie Murray
17. **JOHNNIE O BRAIDISLIE (Child #114)** John Strachan
18. **LORD THOMAS AND FAIR ELLEN (Child #73)** Jessie Murray
19. **TEA AND CAKES** Hamish Henderson
20. **TOO GOOD TO STOP AT TEN O'CLOCK** Hamish Henderson
21. **DONALD MACLEAN/THE IRISH WASHERWOMAN** John Burgess
22. **ERIN GO BRAGH** John Strachan
23. **PORTNOCKIE ROAD** Blanche Wood
24. **THE REID ROAD** Blanche Wood
25. **THE MOSS O BURRELDALE** Jimmy MacBeath
26. **CO SIOD THALL AIR SRAID NA H-EALA** Flora MacNeil
27. **MO NIGHEAN DONN BHÒIDHEACH** Flora MacNeil
28. **FUIRICH AN DIUGH GUS AM MAIREACH** Calum Johnston
29. **I DON'T THINK WE SHOULD SING ANY MORE** John Strachan
    and Hamish Henderson
30. **JIMMY RAEBURN** Jessie Murray
31. **A GREAT SONG AT THAT** Hamish Henderson
32. **ORAN DO MHACLEOID DHUNBHEAGAIN** Calum Johnston

33. **HAMISH ONCE WROTE A SONG** Mrs Budge
34. **THE JOHN MACLEAN MARCH** Mrs Budge and Hamish Henderson
35. **SCOTS, WHA HAE** Hamish Henderson with People's Festival
Ceilidh singers and audience

01. THE HAIRST O RETTIE
Sung by John Strachan

The song celebrates how the arrival around 1890 of a "back delivery" mechanical reaper dramatically shortened harvesting time, and did away with the three person teams of hand scythe reaper, gatherer and bander. The song was written by William Park, blacksmith at the huge farm of Rettie near the North-East port of Banff. Willie Rae was not the farm owner, but the grieve [head-workman]. John Strachan considered this song "the best bothy ballad that ever existed." John's 'five on the throne' began with Victoria, and he lived to see a sixth monarch, Elizabeth, who is Second of England but First of Great Britain.

Hamish Henderson (spoken): *The next song is 'The Hairst o Rettie.' It's got a fine satirical touch at the beginning, because the, the author of it wrote, "I hae seen the Hairst o Rettie, an twa three on the throne." And John asked me to say that he's seen five on the throne now, and the People's Festival Ceilidh into the bargain.*

John Strachan (spoken): *Oh, me ah wid like tae see instead o this blasted lamps, looking* [15] *[...]. Can ye nae pit them oot? Oh, I nay like o this ava.*

(Sings) I hae seen the hairst o Rettie,
Aye and twa, three on the throne,
Ah've heard for sax or seven weeks
The hairsters girn and groan [complain],
But a covie [cove-man] Wullie Rae
In a monthie an a day,
Gart aa the jolly hairster lads
Gae singin doon the brae [hillside].

A monthie and a day, me lads,
The like was never seen,
It beats tae sticks the faistest strips
O Victory's new machine.
A Speedwell now brings up the rear,

---
[15] John is complaining about the brightness of the theatrical lighting. It was lowered for the second half.

A Victory clears the way,
And twenty acres daily yields
Nor stands to Wullie Rae.
He drives them roon and roon the field
At sic an awfu rate,

He steers them cannie oot an in
At mony's the kittle gate [awkward field gate].
He wiles [beguiles] them safely ower the clods
Frae mony's the hidden hole,
For ye'll come wi nae mishanter [mischance]
If you leave him wi the pole.

He sharps their teeth to gar them bite
And taps them on the jaws,
And when he finds them dully like
He brawly [very well] kens the cause.
A boltie here, a pinnie there,
A little oot o tune.
He shortly stops their wild career
And brings the slooshit [reprobate] doon.

He whittles aff at corners
An maks crookit bitties straucht [straight],
An sees that man and beast alike
Are equal in the dracht [loading].
And aa the sheaves are lyin stracht
And neen o them agley [awry],
For he'll coont [count] wi ony dominie [schoolmaster]
Fae the Deveron tae the Spey.

He's no made up o mony words
Nor kent [known] to puff and lee,
But just as keen a little chap
As ever ye did see.
If ye be in search o hairst work
Upon a market day,
Take my advice, be there in time
And look for Wullie Rae.

Noo we hae gotten't in aboot [got the harvest in]
And a wir thingies ticht [all our possessions safely tidied away],
We gaither roond the festive board

To spend a jolly nicht,
Wi Scottish sang an mutton broth
To drive all cares away,
We'll drink success to Rettie
And adieu to Wullie Rae.

Come all ye jolly Rettie chaps
A ringin cheer tae aa.
A band o better workin chaps
A gaffer never saw.
Sae eager aye tae play their pairt
And ready for the brae.
It was you that made the boatie row
An 'twas steert by Wullie Rae.

02. SKIPPIN BARFIT THROUGH THE HEATHER
Sung by Jessie Murray

The title is striking, though to tread barefoot on hard jagged heather stalks would make one jump rather than skip – even a lass who went barefoot all summer long. Although Hamish Henderson said in 1951 the song "had not been heard by many," versions of it were collected by Lomax from Jimmy MacBeath[16] and Jeannie Robertson. The latter's version, titled 'The Queen Among The Heather,' provided the title for her album in the Alan Lomax Collection's *Portrait* series [Rounder CD 1720]. The song remains achingly popular among North-East women singers, and the variety of versions there are of this song illustrate well the changes wrought by the oral process. Other titles include 'Up a Wide and Lonely Glen' and 'As I Came O'er the Craig o Kyle.' Robert Burns knew it as 'O'er The Muir Among the Heather.'

Hamish Henderson (spoken): *Our next singer comes from Buckie, or rather from Portknockie, up on the Banffshire coast, Mrs Jessie Murray. And she's going to sing a lovely old folk song that I don't think as yet has been heard by many people at all: 'Skippin Barfit Through the Heather.'*

Jessie Murray:
As I wis waakin doon yon hill,
It was then a summer evening.
It was there ah spied a bonnie lass,
Skippin barfit throu the heather.

---

[16] Jimmy's version can be heard on the *Two Gentlemen Of The Road* [Rounder CD 1793].

Eh, bit she was neatly dressed,
She neither needed hat nor feather.
She was the queen amang them aa,

Skippin barfit throu the heather.
"Will ye come wi me my bonnie lass?
Will ye come wi me and leave the heather?
It's sylkes and saitins thee will wear,
If ye come wi me and leave the heather."

She wore a goon o bonnie blue,
Her petticoats were a phaisan colour, [pheasant]
And in between the strips were seen
Shinin bells o bloomin heather.

"Oh, young man, your offer's good,
But sae weel I ken you will deceive me.
But gin ye take my heart awa,
Better that I had never seen ye."

Oh, bit she was neatly dressed,
She neither needed hat nor feather.
She was the queen amang them aa,
Skippin barfit throu the heather

03. THE TAY BRIDGE DISASTER [Introduction]

At 7.15pm on the stormy night of 28th December 1879 the railway bridge over the firth of Tay from Fife to Dundee, opened only 19 months before, collapsed and 75 train passengers drowned.

As interviews on Jimmy MacBeath's *Tramps and Hawkers* and MacBeath and John Strachan's *Two Gentlemen of the Road* show, Jimmy had been tramping the roads and singing in the streets since he was a teenager, 40 years earlier, although he also worked in Canada and served in France in World War I. But though he had done various labouring and farm work, he was never a metal-working "tinker," nor born of traveller stock.

Hamish Henderson (spoken): *She was born at the very hour and*
minute, she tells me, of the Tay Bridge Disaster, and so, as she came
over the Tay Bridge, as she came over the Tay Bridge today, she got
a fleeting feeling she mightn't see the ceilidh. But here she is now,
and we'll have another fine song from her in a minute. But our next
candidate is a man who knows the roads of Scotland very well, Jimmy

*MacBeath. For fifteen years now he's been going up and down the
roads of Scotland, chiefly in Buchan and the North-East, singing at fairs
and weddings and wakes.*

04. THE GALLANT FORTY TWA
Sung by Jimmy MacBeath

The 42nd Highland Regiment, also known as the Black Watch, from the
dark Government tartan they wore, were formed in 1739 to keep dissident
Highland clans in order. This lighthearted theatrical song, with its listing
of Scots regiments, shows Jimmy had an equally warm and winning way
with comic songs other than those of farm life. On his Rounder *Portrait*
CD Jimmy sings two more verses, about the recruit's large head and
gluttonous appetite. Here they were lost because the tape ran out.

*[It's] noo I am a weaver, an they caa me Jaickie Broon.
I ainst [once] wis a weaver, and ah lived in Maxwell toon.
Noo ah've jinet the sodjers, tae Perth ah'm gaun awa,
Tae jine the Hieland regiment, the gallant Forty-twa.*

Chorus:
*You may taalk aboot your First Royal Scottish Fusiliers,
Your Aiberdeen Mileesha, an your dandy volunteers,
Yer Seaforths in their stickit [stitched] kilts, yer Gordons big and braw.
Gae bring tae me the tartan o the gallant Forty-twa.*

*The very first day on parade wis a lot o raw recruits.
When the sergeant he got on to me for aye lookin at my boots.
He tepped me on the shouder and says, "Lad, you'll come awa,
For I think you're gaun tae mak a mess o the gallant Forty-twa."*

05. BLUE BONNETS OVER THE BORDER
Played by John Burgess

The Blue Bonnets is a pipe standard nowadays, and not many pipers
would be aware that it's a hybrid tune, based on the melody of the song
of the same name, but with first and second parts imported from another,
older tune. [DP]

One authority, Samuel Bayard, thinks that the tune was fashioned in
the 1740's into a quick dance piece in 6/8 from a slow 3/4 time song tune
from about 1710 or earlier called 'O Dear Mother (Minnie) What Shall I
Do?' Sir Walter Scott then wrote a lyric based on an old Cavalier song.
'Blue Bonnets' is a metaphor for the Scots marching men, who are going
"over the border" into England seeking a fight.

Hamish Henderson (spoken): *Well now, I think we'll hear the pipes again. And because we're going to have one or two of the songs of Scotland's history, the folk songs that have come out of the political struggles in the past, we'll ask John Burgess to play 'Blue Bonnets Over the Border'.*

John Burgess plays.

06. GREAT MY JOY [Introduction]

Hamish Henderson (spoken): *One of the great movements [which shook Scotland] two hundred years ago was the Jacobite movement, the last great Stuart rebellion, and in the West of Scotland it brought out many fine songs. The song that you're going to hear now from Calum Johnston is one of the songs of Alexander MacDonald, the Clan Ranald bard, Alasdair mac Mhaighstir Alasdair. And the song that he's going to sing is one called 'A New Song for the Prince.' The words mean, "Early in the morning as I wakened, great my joy, for I hear that he comes to the land of Clan Ranald."*

07. ORAN EILE DON PHRIONNSA (Another Song to the Prince[17])
Sung by Calum Johnston

Alexander MacDonald (c. 1700–1770) the composer of this song, was the son of a clergyman in Ardnamurchan and had an impressive pedigree within the MacDonalds of Clanranald, including being a first cousin of Flora MacDonald. Known as Alasdair mac Mhaighstir Alasdair, he was one of the foremost Gaelic poets, and a great number of his poems are on Jacobite themes. Whether MacDonald himself gave the two published 'Songs to the Prince' that title, we cannot be certain. The strong rhythm and the wide melodic range help to convey the enthusiasm of the bard for the Prince's arrival. Calum Johnston would also be keen to show his own admiration for this poet and for the Highlanders who fought for Charlie. This is apparent in an understated way, however, as good traditional Gaelic singers leave the sounds and the phrasing of the words to express their feelings in a song. [MN]

> *Moch sa mhadainn 's mi dùsgadh*
> *'S mòr mo shunnd 's mo cheòl gàire*
> *Bhon chuala mi 'm prionnsa*
> *Thighinn do dhùthaich Chlann Ràghnaill*
>
> **Sèist:**
> *Hùg ó la ill ó*
> *Hùg ó ró nàillibh*

---

[17] Prince Charles Edward Sobieski Stuart, (1720-88), "Bonny Prince Charlie."

Hùg ó la ill ó
Seinn o ho ró nàillibh.

Bhon chuala mi 'm prionnsa
Thighinn do dhùthaich Chlann Ràghnaill
Gràinne mullaich gach rìgh thu,
Slàn gun till thu Theàrlaich.

'S ann tha 'n fhìorfhuil gun truailleadh
Ann an gruaidh as mòr nàire.

Mar ri barrachd na h-uaisle
'G èirigh suas le deagh nàdar.

'S nan tigeadh tu rithist
Bhiodh gach tighearna nan àite.

'S nan càiricht' an crùn ort,
Bu mhùirneach do chàirdean.

Translation:
[The vocable[18] refrain (*sèist*) follows each verse, and the last couplet of each stanza becomes the first couplet of the next.]

As I awoke early in the morning, great was my joy and merriment
On hearing that the Prince is coming to the land of Clanranald.

On hearing that the Prince is coming to the land of Clanranald.
You are the best of all rulers. May you come back in good health.

The purest of blood without blemish is in that truly modest face.

Along with a surfeit of nobility and good nature.

And if you were to return all the lairds would be at their posts.

And if the crown was placed on you, your friends would be joyful.

08. MO RUN GEAL OG (My Fair Young Love)
Sung by Flora MacNeil
The late Dr John Lorne Campbell of Canna edited *Highland Songs of the Forty-five*, which contains the texts of thirty-two contemporaneous

---

[18] Vocables are syllables which have no lexical meaning used in refrains in Gaelic and Scots (and other languages) for their sound quality.

Jacobite songs, with translations into English. All are by well-known poets. This song is not included.

Flora MacNeil's song is attributed to Christine Ferguson, the wife of William Chisholm of Strathglass, and it is a more personal expression of loss caused by loyalty to the Prince. Her descriptions of her warrior husband do, however, borrow from the conventional phrases used by the better-known poets in their panegyric[19] verse. Although variants of the tune have been recoded by the School of Scottish Studies, Flora has succeeded in making it her song over the years. Her beautiful voice well illustrates the poignancy of the widow's grief and – possibly – resentment. What makes this song different is the personal nature of her reproach, not for the Highland people's loss but her own bereavement.

Hamish Henderson (spoken): *Now, one of the songs that you'll hear now from Flora is a lament, 'The Lament Of William Chisholm of Strathglass.' It's a most beautiful poem. In it the woman reproaches Prince Charlie for the losses that he has caused the Highland people.*

Flora MacNeil:
Och a Theàrlaich òig Stiùbhart,'s e do chùis rinn mo lèireadh;
Thug thu bhuam gach nì bh'agam ann an cogadh nad adhbhar;
Cha chrodh is cha chaoraich tha mi caoidh ach mo chèile
Bhon là dh'fhàgadh mi 'm aonar gun sìon san t-saoghal ach lèine,
Mo rùn geal òg.

Bu tu 'm fear mòr bu mhath cumadh, od mhullach gu d' bhrògan;
Tha do shlios mar an eala,'s blas na meal' air do phògan;
D'fhalt dualach donn lurach mu do mhuineal an òrdugh
'S e gu camlubach cuimir, 's gach aon toirt urram da bhòidhchead,
Mo rùn geal òg.

Bu tu 'm fear slinneanach leathan bu chaoile meadhon 's bu dealbhaich;
Cha bu tàillear gun eòlas dhèanadh còta math geàrr dhut
No dhèanadh dhut triubhas gun bhith cumhang no gann dhut -
Mar ghealbhradan do chasan le d' gheàrr osan mu d'chalpa,
Mo rùn geal òg.
Bu tu iasgair cuain agus caolais, ged bhiodh gaoth ann cha tilleadh;
Nuair a shuidheadh an diùlnach, aig an stiùir fear gun bhiorradh.
Bu bheag eagal no cùram bhitheadh a rùin orra ghillean -

---

[19] A type of verse used on special occasions – births, marriages, deaths and victories in battle – by poets who had obligations to a patron. Metres varied, but the language was formulaic.

Ged a thigeadh i dùmhail, chumadh an diùlnach i tioram,
Mo rùn geal òg.

Och nan och, bu mhì bochdag 's mi ri 'g osnaich an còmhnaidh.
Chaill mi dùil ri thu thilleadh, thuit mo chridhe fo dhòrainn.
Cha tog fidheall no clàrsach, pìob no tàileasg no ceòl mi;
Bhon là leig iad thu 'n tasgaidh, cha dùisg caidreabh duin' òig mi,
Mo rùn geal òg.

Translation:
Alas, young Charles Stewart, it is your cause that has left me desolate.
You took from me everything I had in a war on your behalf. It is not cattle
or sheep that I mourn, but my spouse, since the day I was left alone, with
nothing in the world but my shift, my fair young love.
You were the tall man of good form, from your crown to your shoes. Your
side was like the swan and your kisses tasted of honey. Your curled, brown,
beautiful hair arranged neatly around your neck, ringleted and elegant,
and everyone paid tribute to its beauty, my fair young love.
You were broad-shouldered, slim-waisted, well-formed: it was no unskilled
tailor who could make a doublet for you, or trews that were not too tight
or insufficient for you. Your legs were like the silver salmon with your short
hose about your calf, my fair young love.
You were a fisher of both ocean and narrows; strong winds would not
make you return. When the brave man sat down, there was a fearless
one at the helm. Your lads, my love, did not have any fear or anxiety—
when it turned stormy the brave man would keep her dry, my fair young
love.
Alas and alack! What a wretch I am, ceaselessly sighing. I lost hope of your
return, my heart burst with grief. Neither fiddle not harp will rouse it, nor
pipe nor gaming nor music: now that they have laid you to rest, young
men's company does not arouse me, my fair young love.

09. FAILTE RUDHA BHATAIRNIS
Played by John Burgess
This is the air of a fairly modern Gaelic song, composed by John Ferguson
from Vaternish. Oddly, the tune title in translation means 'Welcome to Rhu
Vaternish,' while the English name of the tune is 'Leaving Rhu Vaternish.'
"Failte" is "Welcome," "Leaving" would be "Fagail." Rhu Vaternish is
Vaternish Point, the northmost part of the peninsula of Vaternish, in the
north-east of the Inner Hebridean island of Skye.

Hamish Henderson (spoken): *Another tune on the pipes now, a*
    Gaelic air, 'Failte Rudha Bhatairnis.'

John Burgess plays.

10. THE BONNY LASS O FYVIE
Sung by John Strachan

John Strachan had voice problems all through the ceilidh. On his *Portrait* album *Songs from Aberdeenshire* he is in much better fettle, and gives seven spirited verses of this martial Aberdeenshire song of death for love, hardly known in 1951, but since massively popular in Scotland in 'sing-along-a-tartan' style. Bob Dylan recorded an American version, 'Pretty Peggy-O.'

Hamish Henderson (spoken): *John Strachan I think has got his turn coming now with a vengeance, because he's going to sing one of the finest eighteenth century folk songs in Scotland I think, 'The Bonny Lass O Fyvie.'*

John Strachan:

> There was a troop o Irish dragoons
> Come marchin doon through Fyvie-oh,
> And the captain's fa'en in love wi a very pretty maid,
> And her name was called pretty Peggy –o.
> *(Spoken):* Noo ah've pitched that too low.

11. MORMOND BRAES
Sung by John Strachan

As the chorus singing of the audience shows, this song was well known in a settled rather bowdlerised text taught in Scottish schools, although appreciative laughter greets John's more earthy verses and vigorous singing style. Collector Gavin Greig called the rich tune "a perfect one-strain melody." John Stachan farmed at Fyvie, and the market town of Strichen is 18 miles away, with Mormond Hill just north east of it.

John Strachan (spoken): *Ah'll try anither een, aye. Ah'll maybe not pitch it right either.*
Member of audience (shouted): *'Weddin O McGinnis Tae His Cross-Eyed Pet.'*
John Strachan (spoken): *Oh, look here, I'll sing 'Mormond Braes,' and the chorus o Mormond, noo the chorus o 'Mormond Braes' is, "Fare ye weel ye Mormond Braes, where aft times ah've been cheery, fare ye weel ye Mormond Braes for there I lost ma dearie." A gey serious business, that.*

(Sings) *'S as I ga'ed doon be Strichen toon*
I met a fair maid mournin,
An she wis makin sair [severe] complaint
For her true love ne'er returnin.
Mormond Braes, where heather grous,
Where afttimes I've been cheery,
Mormond Braes where heather grous,
An there I lost ma dearie

Sae fare ye well ye Mormond Braes,
Where afttimes ah've been cheery,
Fare ye weel ye Mormond Braes
For there I lost my dearie

Young men are fickle, I do see,
Young women should never believe them.
For let the weemen be ever sae true,
The men they aye deceive them.
He promised for tae merry me,
I for a while did think it,
But noo he's got anither sweetheart,
An ye see hoo I've been blinkit [blinkered].

There's mony a horse has snappered and fa'en [stumbled],
An risen an gaen fu rarely.
There's mony a lass has lost her lad
And gotten anither richt early.
Sae I'll ging doon by Strichen toon,
Where I was bred and born,
And there ah'll get anither sweetheart,
An he'll merry me the morn.

There's as good fish intae the sea
As ever yet was taken,
I'll throw my line and try again,
I've been but eence [once] forsaken.
Sae I'll pit on ma goon o green,
It's a forsaken token.
And that will let the young men know
That the bands o love are broken.

12. NOT JUST ELDERLY PEOPLE [Introduction]

Hamish Henderson (spoken): *Now when Jessie came down from the North today, she brought her niece with her, Blanche Wood. And you'll hear now that folk song is not just the preserve of elderly people, though they've got good and full right to it, but also of the younger people, because Blanche Wood is going to sing a song now that she learned from her aunt, 'I'm A Wee Bonny Lassie.'*

13. I'M A YOUNG BONNY LASSIE
Sung by Blanche Wood

Alan Lomax in a 1951 radio programme introduced a recording of Blanche Wood singing this song as follows. "Into the fisherman's villages along the high cliffs of the North-East coast – white houses overhanging a clear green sea – high clear blue skies. I hoped to hear old fishermen with the ballads of the whaling days, and found instead a pretty girl with a love song." This beguiling song is also "absent from the older collections." 'A Peer Rovin Lassie' in *The Scottish Folksinger* has an extra verse. The tune is better known as the Irish 'Brian O'Lynn.' The audience has by now begun to cheer what they are hearing, and applause swamps the recording level.

> *I'm a young bonny lassie, though ma fortune's been bad,*
> *Since I fell in love wi a young sailor lad.*
> *I've been coorted too early, by night and by day,*
> *But the lad I loe dearly has gone far away.*
>
> *My friends and relations have all joined in one.*
> *Tae part me and my love they've done all they can.*
> *Tae part me and my love they've done their own will,*
> *But the more that they hate him I love him the more still.*
>
> *When I look to yon high hills, it maks my hairt sair.*
> *When I look to yon high hills, and my lad isnae there.*
> *When I look to yon high hills, wi a tear in ma ee,*
> *And the lad I loe dearly lies a distance frae me.*

14. THE ALE HOOSE
Sung by Jessie Murray

A small morality lesson on the evils of the Demon Drink, reminding us of the strength and manipulative vehemence of the Temperance Movement in the nineteenth century. The transcript of this song in the School of Scottish Studies archives is annotated, "This hodden-grey tear-jerker is a find – can't trace it in any of the earlier collections." Another such song was addressed to the publican: 'Don't sell daddy any more whisky.'

I'll gyang tae the ale hoose an look for my Jimmy,
The day is far spent an the night's comin on.
Ye're sittin there drinkin an leave me lamentin,
So rise up, my Jimmy, an come awa hame.

Nae mind o the bairnies they're aa at hame greetin,
Nae meal in the barrelie tae ful their wee wames.
Ye're sittin there drinkin and leave me lamentin,
So rise up, ma Jimmy, and come awa hame.

Fa's that at the door that is speakin so kindly,
It's the voice o ma wifie, called Jeannie by name.
Ye're sittin there drinkin an leave me lamentin,
So rise up, my Jimmy, and come awa hame.

Fareweel to the whisky that maks me so briskie,
Fareweel tae the ale hoose I'll visit nae mair.
Since Jeanie is waitin, her peer hert is breakin,
Sae fare thee well, ale hoose, an ah'll awa hame.

15. THE BIG STUFF [Introduction]
Hamish Henderson (spoken): *The collecting of ballads began
following the publication by Bishop Percy of his* Relics Of Ancient
Poetry. *And many of the most famous figures in Scottish literature
have had a part in this collecting, including Sir Walter Scott. Now, in
the areas where Scott was collecting, on the Borders, the great ballads
have nearly died, if not quite died. But up in the North-East of Scotland,
Aberdeenshire, Kincardine and Banff, some of these great ballads are
still sung. And what is happening now, in a moment or two, what's
going to happen now in a moment or two, moment or two, is I think
something quite unique in this festival. You're going to hear one of the
great Border ballads sung by a real folk singer. That's somebody who
hasn't just read it in Scott's Minstrelsy, or in Bishop Percy's book, or in
any other collection, but has heard it from somebody in his or her own
childhood. Now, we're going to hear two or three of them. The first we
are going to hear is by Jessie Murray, who has got a lovely version of
the old ballad 'Barbara Allen.'*

16. BARBARA ALLEN (Child No. 84)[20]
Sung by Jessie Murray

In *Scottish Ballads* Emily Lyle comments, "Reactions to this exceedingly widespread ballad have been varied; while some have been moved to tears, others have been impatient with its hero." She instances the comment of Bertrand Bronson that the song had shown "a stronger will-to-live than its spineless lover." Some versions justify the apparent heartlessness of Barbara by explaining her swain had spoken slightingly of her in the alehouse.

> In Scotland I was born and bred,
> In Scotland I was dwellin.
> I fell in love with a pretty fair maid,
> And her name was Barbara Allen.

> I coorted her for seven long year,
> Till I could coort no longer.
> I fell seek and very seek,
> And ah sent for Barbara Allen.

> Barbara Allen she was sent for,
> To the house where she was dwellin.
> And as she drew the curtain back,
> "Young man, I think you're dyin."

> "Dyin, dear, what do you mean?
> One kiss from you will cure me."
> "One kiss from me you never shall have,
> Though you're dyin, dyin, dyin."

> He turned his face back to the wa,
> And his back tae Barbara Allen.
> "Adieu, adieu, my kind friends aa,
> But be kind to Barbara Allen."
> "Oh, mother dear, you make my bed,
> And make it long and narrow.
> Since my true lover has died for me,
> I will die for him tomorrow."

---

[20] Child numbers are from the identification system of American scholar F. J. Child.

17. JOHNNIE O BRAIDISLIE (Child No. 114)
Sung by John Strachan
John is unprepared to sing this, but makes a fine fist of the exciting saga of Johnnie the noble deer poacher, who fights off the King's Foresters, the gamekeepers. In some versions they kill him, in others he escapes. Here John omits the elegiac final verse sung on his *Songs from Aberdeenshire*, in which Johnnie's bow is broken, his dogs are slain, "His body lies in Monymusk, and his huntin days are deen."

Hamish Henderson (spoken): *Now ah think you'll agree that this is, we're getting on to something of interest now. This is what you would call the big stuff. And the next ballad that we're going to hear is from John Strachan. It's also a wonderful old ballad, and he had it in his own ch-, own childhood from a, a folksinger: 'Johnnie o Braidislie.'*

John Strachan:
Johnnie rose in a Mey mornin,
Called fir water to wash his hands,
And he called for his twa grey hunds
To be bound in iron chains, chains,
To be bound in iron chains.

Noo, Johnnie shot, and the dun deer lap [leapt],
She wis wounded in the side,
And between the water and the wood,
The grey hounds laid her pride, pride [pulled her down],
The gley [sic] *hounds laid her pride.*

Noo Johnnie ate o the venison,
And the dogs drank o the bleed,
And they aa lay doon an fell asleep,
Asleep as tho they'd been deid, deid,
Asleep as tho they'd been deid.
An by there cam a silly auld [mentally deficient] *man,*
An a silly auld man wis he,
An he's awa tae the king's foresters
For to tell on young Johnnie, ee,
For to tell on young Johnnie.

Johnnie shot[21] *at six o them,*
And the seventh he wounded sore,
And he swung his hock [thigh] *owre his horseback,*

---
[21] With bow and arrow.

And he swore that he would hunt more, more,
And he swore that he would hunt more.

18. LORD THOMAS AND FAIR ELLEN (Child No. 73)
Sung by Jessie Murray

Another ballad of love's confusions sung throughout the English-speaking world. Lord Thomas's parents have urged him to marry for money. The ballad story continues with the brown bride taking offence at Lord Thomas's protestation of love for Ellen, and stabbing her to death. Lord Thomas kills his bride, then himself, and all three bodies are laid in one grave. What does brown signify here – an unattractive darkness of hair or of skin?

Hamish Henderson (spoken): *Jessie Murray has got a very fine*
version of the old ballad of 'Fair Ellen.'

Jessie Murray:
    "The brown girl has got houses and lands,
    Fair Ellen she hasn't got none,
    And if you take your mother's advice
    You would bring the brown girl home."

    He dressed himself in scarlet red,
    All mounted ower wi green.
    And every town that he rode through,
    They thought he waur some king.

    When he came to Fair Ellen's gates,
    How loudly he rang the bell.
    There were none so ready as Fair Ellen
    To welcome Lord Thomas in.

    "What news, what news? Lord Thomas," she cried,
    "What news have you brought unto me?"
    "I've come to bid you to my wedding,
    And that's sad news to thee."
    Forbid, forbid, Lord Thomas," she cried,
    "Forbid it not unto me,
    For I thought you the jolly bridegroom,
    And I the bride to be."

    "Come rightle me title me [advise], mother," she cried.
    "Come rightle me all into one.

Will I go to Lord Thomas' weddin
Or will I stay at home?"

"Many one's been your friend, Fair Ellen,
And many one's been your foe.
But if you take your mother's advice
To Lord Thomas's weddin don't go."

When she came tae Lord Thomas' gates,
How loudly she rang the bell.
There were none sae ready as Lord Thomas
To welcome Fair Ellen in.

"Is this your bride, Lord Thomas?" she cried.
"Is this your bride?" cried she.
"For I thought you the jolly bridegroom,
And I the bride to be."

Despise her not, Fair Ellen," he cried,
"Despise her not unto me,
I wouldn't give your little finger
For all her whole body."

19. TEA AND CAKES

Hamish Henderson (spoken): *I think we've arrived at the right minute now after this wonderful ballad singing of Jessie Murray, to have our interval. And so for ten minutes we have the interval – I'm asked to say that there's tea and cakes available at the back there.*

20. TOO GOOD TO STOP AT TEN O'CLOCK

Hamish Henderson (spoken): *Before we continue with this ceilidh, I've got one or two announcements to make. The first one is this. I'm sure you'll all agree that this is too good to stop at ten o'clock. So there'll be a continuation of it, only it won't be in this building, it'll be in a, a building in which a, a little bit more eh of the homely atmosphere can be engendered. And that's up at the St Columba's Church Hall. You can get to it quite easily from here, by just going down to the High Street, and turning left until you get up very near the Esplanade of the Castle, turning left again, and you see the church and you go down into the Church Hall. That's where the social will be. Uh, you'll pay two shillings if you want to come, at, at the door…. Well now, we're going to leave a light on here in the auditorium, because the singers feel, and I don't blame them, that they'd like to see a bit of the audience as well* *as vice versa. Now, uh, the first item in the second half is the piper again playing a selection of jigs, including 'Donald MacLean' and 'The Irish Washerwoman.'*

21. DONALD MACLEAN and THE IRISH WASHERWOMAN
Played by John Burgess
These two jigs are what most people would think of as typical Burgess playing. 'Donald MacLean' was I think **[PROBABLY??]** composed by Peter Macleod, and 'The Irish Washerwoman' is a hallmark of Burgess' playing—he isn't particularly known as a composer, but he has done some stunning arrangements of traditional standards, notably 'The Mason's Apron.' [DP] 'The Irish Washerwoman' is more popular outside Ireland than with Irish musicians. "It has been proposed by some writers to have been an English country dance tune that was published in the seventeenth century and probably known in the late sixteenth century." [Kuntz, *The Fiddler's Companion*]

22. ERIN GO BRAGH
Sung by John Strachan
"Erin go bragh" means "Ireland for ever." Gavin Greig says this song was "an exceedingly popular ditty... with the general crowd" in the North-East, who had a healthy admiration "for pluck and independence." The story reminds us that Scottish support for political rights in Ireland is no new thing. The hero is of a clan identified with Protestant support of the Crown, yet has the look, manner and actions of a Fenian rebel against English rule, and his blackthorn stick identifies him with Ireland.

Hamish Henderson (spoken): *Now for the first song in the second half, we're going to ask John Strachan to sing a very fine old ballad called 'Erin Go Bragh'. It's about a Highland boy from Argyll, who comes to this city, and a policeman stops him in the street and thinks that he's an Irishman. And although he makes plain, this Duncan Campbell, although he makes plain that he doesn't regard that as an insult, he gives the policeman a clout, just to teach him better manners.*

John Strachan (spoken): *Well, really I hope I'll remember't.*

(Sings) *My name is Duncan Campbell from the shire of Argyll,*
I've travelled this country for many's the long mile.
I've travelled O'er England, Ireland and aa,
And the name I go under's bold Erin Go Bragh.
One night in Auld Reekie [Old Edinburgh] as I walked doon the street,

A saucy policeman I chanced for to meet.
He glowered in my face and he gave me some jaw,
Says, "When came ye over from Erin Go Bragh?"

I am not a Paddy, though Ireland I've been,
Nor am I a Paddy though Ireland I've seen.
Although I were a Paddy, that's nothing ava,
There's many's the bold hero from Erin Go Bragh.

Then with a switch of blackthorn I held in my fist,
Around his big body I made it to twist.
The blood from his nappers [head] I quickly did draw.
He paid stock and interest for Erin Go Bragh.

The people came round me like a flock of wild geese,
Says, "Stop that, ye rascal, you'll kill our police."
For every freen I hid I'm sure he hid twa,
It was very tight times for old Erin Go Bragh

Then I came to a wee boatie that sailed on the Forth,
I packed up my alls and I steered for the North.
Farewell tae Auld Reekie, the policeman and aa.
May the devil be with you, bold Erin Go Bragh.

23. PORTKNOCKIE ROAD
Sung by Blanche Wood

A beguilingly simple and open-hearted song that has not been traced in other collections, nor any news of the composer found in the tight little fisher village of Portknockie near Buckie. Lomax wrote of this song in the *World Library of Folk and Primitive Music: Scotland* album [Rounder CD 1743], "The genius loci of the Scottish countryside is song, and there is hardly a rock, glen, clachan, or harbor which has not a song in celebration of its peculiar attractions."

Hamish Henderson (spoken): *As I announced in the first*
half, uh, two of our visitors from the North-East are from Portknockie,
and Blanche Wood is now going to sing a song called "Portknockie."

Portknockie Road I've often trod
When the moon was shining clear,
But another girl has ta'en my part,
And I'm nae mair his dear.

He maybe thinks I loe him yet,
But ah, it canna be,
For I am quite resolved now
To shun his company.

If ever I'm to get a him,
A him to caa my ain,
I'll mak him welcome oot and in
For the days o auld lang syne.

24. THE REID ROAD
Sung by Blanche Wood

An intensely local song with no traced composer or publication. The place-names in the last verse are all shown on an unpublished map of *Portknockie Rock Names* made by Brian Donaldson. The Reid Road is red because of the colour of its earth. It was formerly the main track to the neighbouring village of Cullen, but now is an access path to the links and beach, crossing Portknockie Golf Course beside Hole 9. The language is of the North-East sea coast, and a K-nocker is short for a Portknockie resident.

Hamish Henderson (spoken): *I think you'll agree that song deserves an encore, and it's going to get one: 'The Reid Road.'*

As I cam up the Reid Road, noo this was very droll,
My fit it slippit and doon I dippit intae a sanny [sandy] hole.
I stottit [stumbled] owre a muckle [great] stane, and in
the hole gaed yack,
Thinks I, "My banes are aa smashed up, an this is a job
for Clark."

I thocht my days were ended noo, an I hidnae lang tae live,
But that wis naething tae the time I fell intae the Cliv.
But noo ye see, I'm nae deid yet, or ony signs o deein,
An mony a faa I'll hae again afore I think o leein
[often I'll fall before I decide to die].

O lang may every K-nocker here, an ivery ane abroad,
Live tae see the Sanny Hole and clim the auld Reid Road.
Tae walk aroon the Tronachs, an tae dook in Bogan's Pot,
Tae live an dee amang the braes o Green Castle port.

25. THE MOSS O BURRELDALE
Sung by Jimmy MacBeath

G. S. Morris, composer of this theatrical "cornkister" bothy ballad, was born and educated in the city of Aberdeen, and worked as a blacksmith and a farmer, then ran a motorcycle business and a hotel in Old Meldrum while singing professionally and recording. Jimmy MacBeath tramped the roads, but was not at all of traveller stock. Hamish Henderson's characterisation of the song as a "genuine tinker's song" is therefore well wide of the mark. Jimmy gets one element of the story wrong: Annie runs to get the iron pail and crowns Jock with it. He omits the last verse he sings on his *Tramps and Hawkers* album.

Hamish Henderson (spoken): *We're now going to hear another genuine tinker's song from the North-East, 'The Moss O Burreldales'.*

Jimmy MacBeath:

> Have you ever seen a tinklers' [travellers'] camp upon a
>   summer's nicht,
> A nicht afore a market when aa thing's goin richt,
> When aa the tramps and hawkers they come frae hill and dale
> Tae gaither in the gloamin [twilight, boggy moorland] in the
>   Moss o Burreldale.

Chorus:

> Then the ale was only tippence [two pence] and a tanner bocht a
> gill [sixpence bought a measure of whisky],
> A besom [broom] or a tilley pan [saucepan], a shelt
>   [Shetland pony] we aye could sell,
> En we aa forgot our troubles ower a forty o' sma ale
>   [barrel of weak beer],
> As we gaithered in the gloamin in the Moss o Burreldale.

> Noo, Jock Stewart would hae a fecht and tore his jacket aff,
> But Squeekin Annie settlet him – we aa got sic a lauch,
> He[22] ran ower amon the tilley pans for a wee bit iron pail,
> And they[23] skaipped him [clapped it over him] like a swarm o bees
> in the Moss o Burreldale.

---

[22] Should be "she."
[23] Should be "she."

(Chorus):
Noo little Jimmy Docherty a horseman great was he.
He jumpit on a sheltie's back some tricks tae let us see,
A gallant shoved some prickly whins [twigs of gorse] aneath
   the sheltie's tail,
He cast a shot in a mossy pot [was thrown into a boggy hole]
   in the Moss o Burreldale.

(Chorus)
By this time Stewart got the pail torn aff his achin heid,
And kickit up an awfa soun, enough to waukn the deid,
When Annie said, "Come on, MacDuff, though I should
   get the jail,
Pit them up my mannie, you're nae fit for Annie, the Rose
   of Burreldale."

(Chorus)
But time was nae langer here when muckle Jock MacQueen,
He started tuning up his pipes he bocht in Aiberdeen,
He blew sae hard, the skin was thin, the bag began to swell,
And awa flew Jock wi the sheep skin pyock [pouch] ower the
   Moss o Burreldale.

(Chorus)
For the dogs, they started barkin, and the cuddy [donkey]
   roared hee-haw.
The tramps and hawkers aa turned roon and sic a sicht
   they saw,
It was Docherty [the Devil] as black's Aul Nick, the bairns
   [children] let oot a yell,
We shoodered wur packs, we aa made tracks, fae the
   Moss o Burreldale.

(Chorus)

26. CO SIOD THALL AIR SRAID NA H-EALA (Who Is That Yonder On The Swan's Road?)
Sung by Flora MacNeil

It is no easy task to sing a waulking song on one's own, since one of its characteristics is the division into solo and choral sections. The chorus usually sang vocables, of which those in this song are typical. Waulking songs were used to accompany the work of shrinking cloth by beating it on to a board in a regular rhythm. They are now unique to Gaelic-speaking

Scotland and Cape Breton, Nova Scotia, and although the practice of waulking cloth stopped in the 1950s the songs remain popular. They are almost all of anonymous composition, and the themes vary, sometimes even within one song. They are generally taken up with women's concerns, but again the panegyric element is present, here in praise of the MacNeils.

Flora copes extremely well with the difficulties I mentioned above, keeping the rhythm meticulously on her own. There is nothing predictable about the tune, especially of the refrain, and I think it is a good example of the many particularly attractive melodies belonging to the genre. [MN]

Hamish Henderson (spoken): *Well I think that we are due back in the Western Highlands, for a song from Flora MacNeil – 'The Road Of The Swan.' It means, "I see people on the swan road. They're the MacNeils of Barra. Colonsay will be for their white horses. And the two Uists, North and South, will give them corn and ale."*

Flora MacNeil:
Cò siud thall air stràid na h-eala?

Sèist:
Fàill ill óro faill ù ill o
Faill ù ill ó hó ro éile
Fàill ill óro faill ù ill o

Tha iad ann Clann Nìll à Barraigh
Gu dè ghaoil a th'air ur n-aire?
'G iarraidh gu farsaingeachd fearainn
Rìgh! Nam bith'nn-sa roinn an fhearainn
Bu leibh Rùm is Eige 's Canaigh,
Eilean nam Muc fo'r cuid ghearran,
Colbhasaigh fo'r caoraich gheala.

Translation:
Who is that yonder on the swan's road?
[Vocable refrain follows each line]
It is they, Clan MacNeil of Barra
What, my dear, is on your minds?
Looking for more land
My! If I were dividing the land
Rum, Eigg and Canna would be yours;
Muck for your stallions
Colonsay for your white sheep.

27. MO NIGHEAN DONN BHÒIDHEACH (My Lovely Brown-haired Girl)
Sung by Flora MacNeil
There are very few narrative songs in Gaelic, and those that exist share many characteristics. They are, unlike Scots ballads, in the first person, and they are almost always about a tragic event. Metrically they may be arranged in lines, with end rhyme, but are usually sung with all the lines except the first and last repeated, forming couplets, similar to the formula of 'Another Song to the Prince' above. The theme of this song appears in more than one guise, including one that begins 'It is time for me to rise.'[24] Here Flora illustrates again, as with 'My Fair Young Love,' her ability to move us with the sad story of the man who has lost his one love. There are so many beautiful melodies to Gaelic songs that it is difficult to vary one's comments. One can only wonder at the skills of the original, anonymous, composers and of the singers who passed them on to succeeding generations. [MN]

Hamish Henderson (spoken): *Another song from Flora MacNeil,*
      'Mo Nighean Donn Bhòidheach.'

   Flora MacNeil:
   Nuair a ràinig mi 'm baile
   cha robh aighear no ceòl ann

   Sèist:
   'S na hu a hó hu a hó
   Mo nighean donn bhòidheach
   'S na hu a hó hu a hó

   Bha na mnathan ri fuaghal
   's bha na maighdeannan brònach

   'S bha mo chraobh fhada dhìreach
   na sìneadh san t-seòmar

   'S i na sìneadh fon uinneig
   is cha chluinneadh i mo chòmhradh

   'S truagh nach robh mi san fhiaras
   mun do dh'iarr mi riamh pòg ort.

---

[24] On Greentrax 'Scottish Tradition' CD *Music from the Western Isles*, track 10.

Translation:
When I got to the township there was no merriment or music there.
Refrain: 'S na hu a hó hu a hó, My lovely brown-haired girl, 'S na hu a hó hu a hó.

The women were sewing, and the girls were doleful.
And my tall straight tree was lying in the room.
Lying in the window and she could not hear my speech.
Oh that I was in a fever before I ever asked you for a kiss.

28. FUIRICH AN DIUGH GUS AM MAIREACH (Wait Today Until Tomorrow)
Sung by Calum Johnston
When Mrs Kennedy-Fraser, the great collector of songs whose work is published in three volumes called *Songs of the Hebrides*, went to Barra, she could not have achieved what she did without the help of the local teacher, Annie Johnston. Annie was Calum's sister, and she and Malcolm Johnston were the acknowledged source for the 'Hebridean Weaving Lilt.' Mrs Kennedy-Fraser generally changed rhythms, melodies and texts – indeed the music most often matched the English-language versions – but judging by Calum's singing she seems to have resisted that temptation in this instance. He gives us a hint of his skills in vocal dance music (Puirt à beul)[25] in the subtle rhythms of this song, keeping the tempo going with ease, but introducing variations in the lengths of phrases as required, to accompany the weaving. The refrain lines are a mixture of vocables, weaving terms, and two translatable lines. "A little bird on its nest, it'll sing along with you. Black mountain, sing black, o horo blackbird." [MN]

Hamish Henderson (spoken): *Another song from Calum Johnston, a weaving song this time. The words mean, "Wait till tomorrow and I'll weave a shirt for you," but if you listen to the words of the song and if you've got Gaelic, you'll see that tomorrow is like the Spanish mañana.*

Calum Johnston:
Fuirich an-diugh gus a-màireach
Gràdh air eideagan àrainn ù rù
Gus an snìomh mi lèine 'n t-snàth dhut
Bun a' chib air a' chib
Bun a' bhruid air a' bhruid

---

[25] See *Music from the Western Isles*, CDTRAX 9002 and Calum and Annie Johnston, CTRAX 9013.

Eun beag air a niod, seinnidh e làmh riut,
Beinn dubh seinn dubh o horo lòn dubh
Gràdh air eideagan àrainn ù rù.

Tha bheairt-fhigh' an Coille Phàdraig
Gràdh air eideagan àrainn ù rù
'S tha bhaineach gun bhreith dha màthair
Bun a' chib air a' chib...

Chuireadh an lion 's cha do dh'fhàs e
'S tha 'n dealg-spàil aig rìgh na Frainge

Translation:
Wait today until tomorrow
[refrain line]
until I spin a thread shirt for you.
[refrain lines]
The weaving loom is in Patrick's Wood
And the weaving wife has not been born of her mother yet.

The flax was planted but did not grow
And the king of France has the spool pin.

29. I DON'T THINK WE SHOULD SING ANY MORE (Introduction)
John Strachan (spoken): *I'm not, I don't think we should sing*
any more, but you're the best audience ever ah sang to.

Hamish Henderson (spoken): *Well, time is dictating the fact that*
we're drawing near to the close now. But there are one or two songs
which, there are, which are requested by the audience very strongly.
And the first one is from Jessie Murray: 'Jimmy Raeburn.'

30. JIMMY RAEBURN
Sung by Jessie Murray
Robert Ford, an editor and collector of songs, gave in 1901 a heartrending
account of innocent Raeburn, a Glasgow baker, convicted in the 1840s
of guilt by association – he was drinking with a childhood friend who
had stolen property on him – and transported to the convict cages of
Australia. *The Greig-Duncan Collection* has 17 versions of this song, still
a favourite with singers. Jessie beats out each word with her foot, and
although there is no chorus, the audience is so keen to participate some
begin to hum the tune.

Norman Buchan: *The place was electric, and I was surprised because on the stage was a tiny old lady, less than five feet, dressed in black, fisherwife dressed, and she was chanting out a song called 'Jamie Raeburn.' Now, I'd never heard that song before, but I did know what it was. I knew it was a street ballad from a century and a half or maybe two centuries ago. It was a street ballad that people had sold about a transportation, but I had absolutely no idea that people still sang a song like that. In fact, during the rest of that evening every preconception I had was swept out of existence, and indeed if any man had a Damascus, that was me.* [Radio Scotland, 1994]

My name is Jimmy Raeburn, frae Glasgow toon ah came.
Ma place an habitation ah wis forced tae leave for shame.
Ma place and habitation, noo I maun gyang awa,
Far far fae aa the hills an dales o Caledonia.

It was early in the mornin, before the dawn of day,
Our keeper he came round to us and unto us did say,
"Arise ye hapless convicts, arise ye yin and aa.
This is the day ye huv tae stray fae Caledonia."

We mounted the coach and our hearts wis full of grief.
Our parents, wives and sweethearts could grant us no relief.
Our parents, wives and sweethearts, their hairt wis broke in twa
Tae see us lee the hills an dales o Caledonia.

Farewell my aged father, for you're the best of men.
And likewise to ma sweethairt, for Caitrin is her name.
Nae mair we'll walk by Clyde's clear streams, nor by the Broomielaw,
Fareweel tae aa the hills an dales o Caledonia.

Farewell my aged mother, ah'm grieved for what ah've done.
I hope none will cast up to you the race that I have run.
The Lord he will protec you when I am far awa,
Far far fae aa the hills an dales o Caledonia.

If ne'er we meet on earth again, we'll meet in Heaven above,
Where hallelujahs will be sung to him who reigns in love.
Nae earthly judge to judge us, but him who rules us aa.
Fareweel till aa the hills an dales o Caledonia.

31. A GREAT SONG AT THAT (Introduction)
Hamish Henderson (spoken): *The next song has got to be the last song, though I remind you of the c-, of the social that's going to take place in St. Columba's Church Hall, which is going to start as soon as we can get the singers across there. But I think it's correct that we should turn to the Gaelic language for the last song, and a great song at that. We're going to ask Calum Johnston to give the 'Oran Mhòr Mhic Leoid', which is a song in, it's a, a, it's one of the great songs in the Gaelic tongue, and the poetic concept in it is very great.*

The poet says that he left the castle, and he found on the slopes of the mountains the echo of past mirth, the echo of his own singing. And he then has a conversation with the echo about the fate of the House of MacLeod.

32. ORAN DO MHACLEOID DHUNBHEAGAIN (A Song to Macleod of Dunvegan)
Sung by Calum Johnston
In the heyday of the clan system in Scotland, the clan chief was expected to protect his clansmen and servants. He had a retinue of artists – a piper, harper, bard and chief poet – all of whom were obliged to compose propaganda verse and music for their chief. Roderick Morrison, *An Clarsair Dall* (The Blind Harper; approximate dates 1656-1714)[26], was for a time harper to MacLeod of Dunvegan and when the chief John died, his successor did not fulfil the obligations of his office. Morrison's song remonstrates bitterly with the new chief, who spends his time in London and his money on foppish clothes. In particular he advises him to look to his predecessor, who had "renown in rich measure, and would never leave Dunvegan without music." As Hamish Henderson says, the text is based on an imagined dialogue between Echo and the poet.

The tune of this song is illustrative of the special interests of professional harpers. They tended to be travelling musicians, to the extent of getting their training in other countries; harpers in Scotland and Ireland especially exchanged melodies. This resulted in a corpus of tunes, variants of which may be heard to different songs throughout Western Europe. They tended to be based on repeated melodic phrases in forms such as ABBA. Calum Johnston's tune may be assessed as ABBC.

This would be regarded as a "big" song requiring skills of memory and ways of conveying the text and maintaining interest in the melody

---

[26] See *The Blind Harper* (An Clàrsair Dall), ed. William Matheson, Edinburgh, 1970. A section on Airs and Metres explains the phenomenon of melodies used by harpers. For examples in audio, c.f. *Gaelic Bards and Minstrels*, Greentrax CTRAX 9016D.

through using the variations in the rhythms of the words. [NM]

Chaidh a' chuibhle mun cuairt, gun do thionndaidh gu fuachd am blàths
Nàile! chunna mi uair dùn flathail nan cuach a' bhàigh
Far 'm biodh tathaich nan duan, 's iomadh mathas gun chruas gun chàs
–
Dh'fhalbh na làithean ud bhuainn 's tha na taighean gu fuarraidh fàs.

Dh'fhalbh Mactall' as an Dùn 'n àm sgarachdainn dhuinn r'ar triath;
'S ann a thachair e rium air seachran bheann san t-sliabh;
Labhair esan air thus, "Math mo bharail gur tu, mas fìor
Chunnaic mise fo mhùirn roimh 'n-uiridh an dùn nan cliar."

A Mhictalla nan tùr, se mo bharail gur tusa bha
Ann an teaghlach an Fhiann 's tu 'g aithris air gnìomh mo làmh
"Math mo bharail gur mi, 's cha b'fhurast' dhomh bhith nam thàmh
'G èisteachd broslam gach ceòil ann am fochair MhicLeòid an àigh.

'S mi Mactalla bha uair 'g èisteachd faram nan duan gu tiugh
Far 'm bu mheamhrach am beus 'n àm cromadh don ghrèin san t-sruth
Far am b'fhoirmeil na seòid 's iad gu h-òranach ceòlmhor cluth –
Gad nach fhaicte mo ghnùis, chluinnt' aca san Dùn mo ghuth.

'S an àm èirigh gu moch anns an teaghlach gun sprochd, gun ghruaim,
Chluinnte gleadhraich nan dos 's a cèile na cois on t-suain;
Nuair a ghabhadh i làn, 's i gun cuireadh os n-àird na fhuair
Le meòir fhileanta bhinn 's iad gu ruidhleannach dìonach luath."

Translation:

The wheel (of fortune) has come full circle, warmth has suddenly turned cold. But I once saw here a beautiful castle, well-stocked with drinking-cups that have now gone dry, a song-haunted place abounding in good things, given without stint or question. Those days have left us, and the buildings are chill and desolate.

Echo went away from the castle at the time we separated from our lord; it was as a wanderer on mountain and moorland that he met me. He spoke first, "It is my strong belief that you are he, if I mistake not, whom I saw a year ago and more, being entertained in the Castle which was the resort of poet-bands."

"Echo of the lofty edifices, my belief is that it was you who were in the Fenian clan, telling of my handiworks." "I believe that it was, and how hard for me to be silent as I listened to rousing strains of every kind, played in presence of MacLeod of happy memory.

"I am Echo who once used to listen to the incessant sound of poetry with their enticing skills at time of the setting of the sun in the stream, where the warriors were lively, melodious and musical—although my visage was not seen, my voice was to be heard in the Castle.

"And at time of early rising in a household incapable of gloom or low spirits, the roar of the drones could be heard, and their partner astir from sleep. When it had taken its fill it would not fail to proclaim all it had got, aided by a fluent, sweet finger, dancing, deft and nimble."

33. HAMISH ONCE WROTE A SONG (Introduction)
Mrs Budge (spoken): *Well, to say I feel ashamed to come up and sing on a platform which Flora MacNeil has sung on is just putting it politely. But I feel that everyone here would like to know that Hamish once, em, 1948, on the 25th anniversary of the death of John MacLean, who was one of the great fighters for Scottish republicanism, wrote a song, well, practically I think almost overnight wrote this song, he took it along and set it to an old Scottish pipe tune. Now, Hamish thinks I should sing it, I think Hamish should sing it. Because it really is a man's song, and I haven't a strong enough voice to carry it, and I haven't a trained voice to carry it. And he says he's hoarse, but I'm sure we'll all forgive him, I should think really that Hamish [inaudible].*

34. THE JOHN MACLEAN MARCH
Sung by Hamish Henderson and Mrs Budge
The song was written for and sung at the John MacLean Memorial Meeting in St Andrew's Hall in Glasgow, 1948, and we employ Hamish's own orthography here. The tune is in fact a "piper's version" of an old tune, sung as 'Bonny Glenshee,' that was further adapted for Cliff Hanley's 'Scotland the Brave,' and for Henderson's own alternative Scottish national anthem, 'The Freedom-Come-All-Ye,' written in 1960 for the Scottish CND peace marchers. Both the 'March' and the 'Come-All-Ye' became very popular with Scottish singers in the 1970s. Henderson cuts off to omit his last verse. This song, 'Scots Wha Hae,' 'Erin Go Bragh,' and the Jacobite songs are the only songs with an explicit political dimension sung in the evening. John MacLean was the great hero of Scottish socialism, 'martyred' for his opposition to World War I, a fiery orator, writer and organiser.

Hey Mac did ye see him as ye cam' doon by Gorgie,
Awa ower the Lammerlaw or north o' the Tay?
Yon man is comin' and the haill toon is turnin' oot,
We're a' shair he'll win back to Glasgie the day.
The jiners and hauders-on [shipyard workers] *are marchin' frae*
Clydebank,
Come on noo and hear him, he'll be ower thrang tae bide [busy to
stay].
Turn oot Jock and Jimmie: leave your crans [cranes] *and yer muckle*
[great] *gantries,*
Great John MacLean's comin' back tae the Clyde!
Great John MacLean's comin' back tae the Clyde!

Argyle Street and London Road's the route that we're marchin'
The lads frae the Broomielaw are here—tae a man.
Hey, Neil, whaur's yer haderums [bagpipes]*, ye big Hielan teuchter?*
    [countrified person]
Get yer pipes, mate, an' march at the heid o' the clan.
Hallo Pat Malone, sure I knew you'd be here so:
The red and the green, lad, we'll wear side by side.
Gorbals is his the day, and Glasgie belongs tae him:
Ay, Great John MacLean's comin' back tae the Clyde!
Great John MacLean's comin' hame tae the Clyde!

Forward tae Glasgie Green we'll march in good order:
Will grips his banner weel (that boy isna blate) [bashful].
Ay there, man, that's Johnnie noo—that's him there, the bonnie
fechter,
Lenin's his fiere [comrade]*, lad, an' Liebknecht's* [German communist]
his mate.
Tak' tent [pay attention] *when he's speakin', for they'll mind*
    what he said here
In Glasgie our city—and the haill world beside.
Och hey, lad, the scarlet's bonnie: here's tae ye
    Hielan' Shony *[Highland Johnnie]*
Great John MacLean has come hame tae the Clyde!

(Spoken) *That's enough.*
(Sings)
Great John MacLean has come hame tae the Clyde!

35. SCOTS, WHA HAE
Sung by Hamish Henderson, singers and audience
Generally considered Scotland's own National Anthem. Robert Burns
wrote the lyric as what "one might suppose to be [King Robert The
Bruce's] address to his heroic followers on that eventful morning" of 24
June 1314, when the Scots routed the army of King Edward II of England
and regained their independence. The tune 'Hey Tutti Taiti' is said to
have been played by the Scots as they marched to the battlefield outside
Stirling. We give Burns' own orthography.

Hamish Henderson (spoken): *Scots Wha Hae.*

> *Scots, wha hae wi' Wallace bled,*
> *Scots, wham Bruce has aften led,*
> *Welcome to your gory bed,*
> *Or to Victorie.*
> *Now's the day, and now's the hour;*
> *See the front o' battle lour [frown];*
> *See approach prood EDWARD'S power,*
> *Chains and slaverie!*
>
> *Wha would be a traitor knave?*
> *Wha can fill a coward's grave?*[27]
> *Wha sae base as be a slave?*
> *Let him turn and flee!*
> *Wha for Scotland's King and Law,*
> *Freedom's sword would strongly draw,*
> *FREE-MAN stand, or FREE-MAN fa',*
> *Let him follow me!*
>
> *By Oppression's woes and pains!*
> *By your Sons in servile chains!*
> *We will drain our dearest veins,*
> *But they shall be free!*
>
> *Lay the proud Usurper low!*
> *Tyrants fall in every foe!*
> *Liberty's in every blow!*
> *Let us Do—or Die!*[28]

---

[27] Hamish sings the wrong line.
[28] Sung as "dee."

BIBLIOGRAPHY

1. Buchan, Norman & Peter Hall. *The Scottish Folksinger*. Glasgow: Collins, 1973.
2. *Communist Review*. March, 1952.
3. Croft, Andy, ed. *A Weapon In The Struggle, The Cultural History of the Communist Party in Britain*. London: Pluto Press, 1998.
4. Ford, Robert. *Vagabond Songs and ballads of Scotland*. Paisley, Scotland: Alexander Gardner, 1904.
5. *Frontline* issue five. http://redflag.org.uk/frontline/five/05contents.html
6. Henderson, Hamish. *Alias MacAlias: Writing on Songs, Folk and Literature*. Edinburgh: Polygon, 1992.
7. Henderson, Hamish. *The Armstrong Nose: Selected Letters of Hamish Henderson*. Edinburgh: Polygon, 1996.
8. Kuntz, Andrew. *The Fiddler's Companion: An annotated index of traditional music for the fiddle*. CD ROM. Wappinger Falls, NY, 1996.
9. Littlewood, Joan. *Joan's Book*. London: Methuen, 1994.
10. Lyle, Emily. *Scottish Ballads*. Edinburgh: Canongate, 1994.
11. MacColl, Ewan, *Journeyman*. London: Sidgwick & Jackson, 1990.
12. Robinson, Mairi, editor in chief. *The Concise Scots Dictionary*. Aberdeen: Aberdeen University Press, 1985.
13. *Scotsman* newspaper, August and September 1951.
14. *Scottish Socialist Voice*. Issue 32.
15. Shuldham-Shaw, P and E Lyle et al, *The Greig-Duncan Folk Song Collection*. Edinburgh: Mercat Press, 1980-2002. Eight volumes.
16. *Tocher* (magazine published by The School of Scottish Studies 1971-date.) No. 13 features Calum and Annie Johnston. No. 43 features Hamish Henderson.

RADIO PROGRAMMES

BBC Home Service
Recorded 13th August 1951. "A programme of Scots ballads and folk songs collected in Scotland."
A Ballad-Hunter Looks At Britain, an 8-part series. Programme 5, 'Folksong from the Lowlands,' transmitted 29 November 1957.

BBC RADIO SCOTLAND
Broadcast 5/8/2001. *Unbroken Thread*, Ediburgh People's Festival.
Broadcast 1994. *McGregor's Folk*, The Folk Music Revival. Presenter Jimmy McGregor, producer Anna Magnusson.

RECOMMENDED READING FOR GAELIC SONGS [MN]

1. *Bàrdachd Ghàidhlig*. W.J Watson, Glasgow 1918. (no English translation)
2. *The Blind Harper*. William Matheson, (ed.) SGTS, Edinburgh 1970.
3. *Hebridean Folksongs*. J. L. Campbell and F. Collinson eds. 3 volumes Oxford

1969, 1977, 1981. [Invaluable for information on aspects of waulking and for texts.]

4. *Highland Songs of the Forty-five.* Dr John Lorne Campbell, ed. Scottish Gaelic Texts Society, Edinburgh 1983.

5. *Sàr Obair nam Bàrd Gaelach* –The Beauties of Gaelic Poetry. John MacKenzie. Ed. Glasgow 1841. (no English translation)

6. *Songs of the Hebrides.* London 1909. Boosey & Co, London 1909.

7. Booklets which accompany *Scottish Tradition* series of CDs and Cassettes, Greentrax, Edinburgh. *Music from the Western Isles,* 9002; *Waulking Songs from Barra,* 9003; *Calum and Annie Johnston,* 9013; *Gaelic Bards and Minstrels,* 9016D.

8. Gaelic Song Transcriptions, Translations and Notes by Morag NicLeod.

Special thanks to Janis McNair of Centre for Political Song, and Carole McCallum of University Archives, both at Glasgow Caledonian University, also to Linda McVicar, and Frank Reynolds of Portknockie.

Contributors

Rob Adams is a freelance journalist and music critic who has covered jazz, folk and traditional, world and Americana music for *The Herald* for over two decades.

John Barrow is one of the co-founders of Edinburgh Folk Club and runs Stoneyport Associates, Scotland's premier folk music agency.

Jean Bechhofer, originally from Shetland, is a psychologist and a stalwart of Edinburgh Folk Club.

Margaret Bennett, originally from Skye, is an internationally renowned folklorist, singer and prize-winning author who worked closely with Hamish Henderson in the School of Scottish Studies.

Ivor Birnie of 'Democracy for Scotland' was one of the conveners of the Vigil for a Scottish Parliament at the foot of Calton Hill, which was set up after the UK general election of 1992, and kept their vow to stay until a Scottish Parliament was agreed.

Eberhard 'Paddy' Bort works in the Institute of Governance at the University of Edinburgh; he is chair of Edinburgh Folk Club.

Steve Byrne was involved in the digitising of he School of Scottish Studies' archive; he is also a distinguished singer and songwriter, and the convener of the Hamish Henderson Archive Trust.

Norman Chalmers is a journalist who covers acoustic music for *The List* magazine; as a musician, he has been involved for decades with Jock Tamson's Bairns.

Maurice Fleming from Blairgowrie is a folk collector, writer and journalist and, for 27 years, worked for the *Scots Magazine*, ten as assistant and the rest as editor.

Rob Gibson is an SNP Member of the Scottish Parliament, representing the Highlands, and used to be one of the organisers of the Highland Music Traditional Festivals.

Jim Gilchrist is a features writer for the *Scotsman*; for which he also writes his *must read* Thursday 'Folk, Jazz, etc' column.

Christopher Harvie, a historian by trade, was Professor for British and Irish Studies at Tübingen for 27 years, before he became an SNP Member of the Scottish Parliament (2007-2011).

Hamish Henderson (1919-2002) was Scotland's greatest folklorist, poet and song collector, songwriter, political activist and researcher at the School of Scottish Studies.

Tom Hubbard is a poet and translator, an academic, currently working as a Visiting Professor at the University of Grenoble. His *The Chagall Winnocks wi ither Scots poems and ballants o Europe* (2011) was published by Grace Note Publications.

Rita Hunter is a *Fèis Rois* manager and was one of the organisers of the Highland Traditional Music Festival during its twenty-year lifespan.

Nick Keir was, for a quarter century, a member of Scottish vocal trio The McCalmans; he also worked with 7:84 Theatre Company.

Alastair McDonald, who celebrated his 70th birthday in 2011, is firmly established as Scotland's leading musical minstrel, at home in both the folk and jazz world, with a sprinkling of Music Hall for good measure.

Adam McNaughtan is a former teacher and antiquarian book seller, a singer, songwriter and folklorist who has worked with the School of Scottish Studies.

Ewan McVicar is a singer, songwriter, folk collector and author who has researched the 1951 Edinburgh People's Festival Ceilidh and curated the release of the album based on Alan Lomax's recording of the event.

Tessa Ransford is a poet, translator, literary editor and cultural activist – she was the founding Director of the Scottish Poetry Library in Edinburgh.

David Stenhouse is a journalist and senior radio broadcaster with BBC Scotland.

Peter Urpeth studied literature and philosophy at Middlesex Polytechnic. He worked as a music journalist for *Time Out* and is a former editor of the *Stornoway Gazette*.

Gary West is a renowned piper and the Director of the School of Scottish Studies at the University of Edinburgh.